DATE DUE

4-13-85			
1-17-87			
JAN 0 7 1991			
MAY 1 6 1994			

DEMCO 38-297

PUBLIC HEARINGS PROCEDURES AND STRATEGIES

PUBLIC HEARINGS PROCEDURES AND STRATEGIES

A Guide to Influencing Public Decisions

Dr. Jean Mater

PRENTICE-HALL, INC.
Englewood Cliffs, New Jersey

Library of Congress Cataloging in Publication Data

Mater, Jean.
   Public hearings procedures and strategies.

   Includes index.
   1. Lobbying—United States.   2. Pressure groups—
United States.   3. Legislative hearings—United States.
4. Legislative bodies—United States—Public meetings.
5. United States—Executive departments—Public meetings.
6. Public meetings—United States.   I. Title.
JK1118.M35 1984   328.73'078   84-11539
ISBN 0-13-737610-3

© 1984 by
PRENTICE-HALL, INC.
Englewood Cliffs, N.J.

Printed in the United States of America

ISBN 0-13-737610-3

PRENTICE-HALL INTERNATIONAL, INC., *London*
PRENTICE-HALL OF AUSTRALIA, PTY. LTD., *Sydney*
PRENTICE-HALL CANADA, INC., *Toronto*
PRENTICE-HALL OF INDIA PRIVATE LTD., *New Delhi*
PRENTICE-HALL OF JAPAN, INC., *Tokyo*
PRENTICE-HALL OF SOUTHEAST ASIA PTE. LTD., *Singapore*
WHITEHALL BOOKS, LTD., WELLINGTON, *New Zealand*
EDITORA PRENTICE-HALL DO BRASIL LTDA., *Rio de Janeiro*

To Milton H. Mater,
who provides both information and inspiration

A Guide to
Public Hearings
Involvement

The public hearing has evolved into a unique opportunity to influence public decisions. Businessmen, farmers, neighborhoods, and individual citizens have discovered that public hearings are a legitimate process for shaping government and even business policies. In the past regarded by many citizens as an empty symbolic political exercise, the public hearing now is widely used to activate the basic principle that every major and minor interest should possess a veto power on political decisions. The public hearing provides those who know how to use the process with an opportunity to affect the outcome of public debate.

While acknowledging the influence of public involvement on government decisions, some Americans feel vaguely uneasy with the concept, as if bold discussion of influencing opinions is somewhat indiscreet, like revealing family secrets. Consequently, the only books that tell how to organize campaigns, form coalitions, devise rallying media slogans, and orchestrate a public hearing are guidebooks written for environmental, consumer, social change and other activists. These manuals fail to fill the needs of action-oriented businessmen, professionals, and citizens who are uncomfortable with confrontation tactics, consciousness-raising, and other manipulative techniques, but who still want to share in shaping and implementing public decisions.

Neighborhood leaders, attorneys, scientists, expert witnesses, land planners, corporate government affairs officers, environmental advocates, site location engineers—everyone who attempts to influence a decision at a public hearing—needs more information on the process. So do the officials who conduct the public hearings and weigh the public testimony to reach decisions. This book recognizes the public hearing as part of a process rather than an isolated event. It describes the methods, strategies, and tactics used by those who make public hearings work, drawing on the practices of special interest groups who have successfully captured policy decision-making, and the specific experiences of private and public organizations. The procedures cited apply to a manufacturer struggling to maintain a feasible position in a federal agency hearing, to a Neighborhood Association circling the wagons around a threatened neighborhood in a local hearing, or to an organization trying to obtain recognition at a state hearing. The methods are equally useful for a government attempting to balance constituents' conflicts such as a local conflict between low income renters' needs and environmentalists' wants.

The procedures for presenting or opposing proposals at a public hearing, encouraging fair and accurate media coverage, and coping with difficult public hearing situations, are laid out for both public officials and the public; for proponents and opponents. The information is intended to serve the individual who takes a once-in-a-lifetime stand at a public hearing, the professional whose duties regularly encompass appearances at public hearings, the businessman requesting an air discharge certificate, and the citizen who urges denial of the businessman's request.

Special interest groups attempting to set the agenda for public debate recognize the public hearing process as the poor man's lobby, a lobby available to all groups and, strangely, ineptly utilized by many well-funded interests. A public hearing may be the most egalitarian of citizen participation methods, granting equal standing to all competing interest groups who understand how to use the process. Well-organized interest groups don't always get what they want, but they can expect to effectively make their views felt in decision-making. For better or worse, public hearings provide activists the opportunity to often call the shots in highly technical decisions such as nuclear energy and hazardous waste siting.

Those who previously opted out of the public hearing process, preferring private entertainment to public involvement, now realize that the solution is to level the playing field rather than throw out the game. The birds of a feather who used to flock together for the comfort of associating with others of like values, now organize to fight together to influence public decisions to favor their interest.

Covering all aspects of living—from abortions to funerals, from electric rates to cutting trees, from an emergency 911 number to the impact of population growth in the United States—public hearings call into play organizational, sociological, psychological, behavioral, communicative and technical skills. The application of these to the public hearing process is addressed. The business executive will find a special chapter on business problems. A section on presenting expert testimony is included for the scientist, engineer, or other specialist who is challenged to capsulize years of education and experience into lay language.

This book is a pragmatic approach to what succeeds and doesn't succeed in public hearings. It avoids the continuing debate over the philosophical and political implications of citizen participation, issues of costs and benefits, power and control, economic development, implications in land use and environmental protection, impact on government efficiency, and resolution of social programs.

For easier reference, chapters are arranged in four independent sections. Section One discusses public hearings in perspective. Section Two covers the how-to of strategies, tactics, techniques and methods that are used to influence the outcome of a public hearing. Section Three deals with solving some public hearing problems and Section Four addresses local public officials who manage public hearings.

When words such as "chairman" or "he" are used to spare the occasional awkwardness of "person," the intent is to refer equally to men and women and not to specify either. Any advocacy that has seeped through these pages is inadvertent. The only planned advocacy of this book is urging all citizens to develop skills to assure that the public hearing process fills its legitimate function in participatory democracy.

Jean Mater

Quick Guide to Using This Book

This quick guide is an index to hands-on help in influencing a public decision. Scan the list below for the objective matching or resembling the problem at hand and consult the pages indicated for the subheads. If at all possible, first browse through Chapters 3, 4, 5, and 6 on organization, strategies, tactics, and communication for the basic tools in using public hearings as a political force. Supplement this quick guide with the conventional index at the back of the book.

Objective:
TO WIN PUBLIC SUPPORT FOR A BUSINESS PROJECT
(Site Location, Plant Expansion, Waste Facilities,
Government Agency Decisions)

Objective:

TO INCREASE MEDIA INTEREST IN A DECISION

Objective:

TO DEFUSE A CONTROVERSY

Acknowledgments

To family and friends, who tracked and clipped media reports of public hearings in all sections of the United States, thanks. Directly and indirectly, I am indebted to thousands of persons who have participated in public hearings, the public officials who have listened to public hearings, and the political commentators, researchers, social scientists and others whose work has been incorporated in the methodologies described in this book. Thanks are also due to the companies and organizations who have utilized and learned from the techniques explained in this volume and to Milton H. Mater and others who critiqued the material. I gratefully express my thanks to Philip Lesly, The Philip Lesly Company, Chicago, for his valuable suggestions in defining the scope of this book.

Appreciation is also given to the government agencies whose publications were culled for figures and to the authors and publishers who granted permission to reproduce copyrighted material.

List of Illustrations

xix

Contents

SECTION THREE: SOLVING SOME PUBLIC HEARING PROBLEMS

SECTION FOUR: FOR ELECTED AND APPOINTED LOCAL PUBLIC OFFICIALS

PUBLIC HEARINGS
PROCEDURES
AND STRATEGIES

SECTION ONE

Public Hearings in Perspective

1

Public Hearings Gamesmanship

The proven ability of well-organized single issue groups to affect a wide range of policies in the name of the public interest—but which really confer special favors on small groups—has convinced many less successful participants that the public hearing process is inimical to their welfare. Unorganized groups can't play the game they reason, therefore, the game should not be played. But like it or not, in this era of flourishing participatory democracy, public hearings are assuming an ever more important role in decision-making.

As a mechanism for maintaining a dynamic equilibrium between the government and the governed, the public hearing provides an opportunity for most citizens who get mad about some action at one time or another to tell off the government. Businessmen appeal to decision-makers at public hearings for permits to expand or change their businesses. Community agencies use public hearings as a vehicle to motivate social action and to obtain support for programs. Political entrepreneurs use public hearings to sell their programs and/or themselves.

It has been estimated that an average city holds more than 20 hours of public hearings a week, consuming approximately 20,000 man-hours every year. The United States Forest Service calculated that public hearings on wilderness areas, an issue of major concern to relatively few people in the United States, consumed more than 100,000 man-hours at a cost of approximately $6.6 million dollars.

The law requires public hearings before officials can change land use zones, pass dog licensing ordinances, increase utility rates, declare rare flowers an endangered species, and grant permits for new manufacturing facilities. In addition public hearings are held that affect hundreds of other activities in which citizens and lawmakers engage.

3

Federal grant programs require public hearings before distributing funds including: the special Supplemental Food Program for Women, Infants, Children; Coastal Zone Management; Public Health Services; the Emergency School Aid Act; special programs for the Aging; and the Appalachian Housing Project. All 50 states mandate public hearings on issues ranging from transportation to permits for siting energy facilities.

Governments call public hearings to comply with legal requirements for citizen participation in legislative and administrative processes, for issuing permits, for policy-making and planning. Sometimes governments call public hearings for political purposes. When they need to hear what citizens have to say but a public hearing is not required, officials hold *public meetings, town meetings* or *public workshops*. These meetings and workshops encourage interaction and discussion between the government and the public. A public hearing communicates in only one direction: it lets citizens express their opinions. This formal setting, however, provides no mechanism for dialogue between citizens and government officials, or between citizen groups.

Some observers believe that public hearings function as a panacea for the ills of government by improving public decisions. Others regard them as pacifiers that encourage the public to feel that they have helped make the decision—a form of therapy for those who feel alienated from their government. Sometimes used to delay or avoid making difficult or unpopular political decisions, public hearings are also co-opted as a vehicle for altering political power patterns, reallocating public resources, or protecting the rights of minority and special interest groups.

DEVELOPMENT OF PUBLIC HEARINGS GAMESMANSHIP

Because this process affects so many lives and fortunes, it is little wonder that a type of public hearings gamesmanship has developed which endowes it with a certain legitimacy as a tactic for achieving political ends. Encouraging neighborhood activists, consumer advocates, and public interest groups to emerge as new political forces, public hearings have provided the focus for challenging the prerogatives of the traditional power holders in American society. By providing a window through which citizens and public officials can access the same information, public hearings are a brake on the insensitive, oppressive, or arbitrary government use of power. They are also subject to capricious manipulation by single issue groups and political entrepreneurs.

As a result, public hearings have evolved a high visibility type of theatrical *gamesmanship* for staging dramatic confrontations between special interest groups. Numerous interests play this game. Some of them are listed in Figure 1-1, Who Plays Public Hearings Gamesmanship?

Figure 1-1

Who Plays Public Hearings Gamesmanship?

A broad spectrum of "interests"—individuals or organizations who share a stake in the outcome of a decision—play public hearings gamesmanship.

Vested interests—a group or organization with a fixed, absolute interest (used in law as not contingent upon anything).

Interest groups—organized groups representing narrow and distinct viewpoints, sometimes called special interests such as environmental interests, business interests, consumer interests.

Witnesses—persons who provide evidence at the hearing, particularly in quasi-judicial hearings (hearings subject to additional due process safeguards as if they were held in a court of law).

Citizens—a generic term for an inhabitant or denizen of any place; a member of a state or nation entitled to full civil rights.

Clientele—a bureaucratic designation for a constituency vested with some direct form of authority over program operation, such as public health or community services, usually used for human service programs.

Constituency—a political designation of a group of voters with the potential for being supporters of a program or a project.

Community—unorganized and unrepresented elements of an area affected by a decision.

Figure 1-1 (continued)

> *Community organization*—groups organized to accomplish a
> specific goal; these are usually civic or consumer or-
> ganizations.
> *Neighborhood organization*—an indigenous organization
> based on restricted geographic boundaries.
> *Beneficiaries*—persons who benefit directly from a govern-
> ment or private program, such as migrant workers who bene-
> fit from a health program.
> *Stakeholders*—interests outside a corporation or government
> who have a stake in the decision and actions of the or-
> ganization.
> *Advocates*—persons who consistently support and urge a par-
> ticular view or course of action.
> *Movement*—an association or organization committed to a
> particular social change.
> *Activists*—persons who energetically support a view or course
> of action and are committed to achieve a social change by
> using a variety of strategies and tactics, including those out-
> side the norm of expected behavior.

Three groups make up the audience: (1) the public officials—the
nominal audience who are to be informed and influenced; (2) the public at large whose opinions are susceptible to outside influences; and
(3) the media, who have assumed an oversight function on government activities and who influence opinions by reporting on selected
testimony and by emphasizing and articulating selected ideas. Interest group elites who are schooled in public hearing strategy and tactics orchestrate prepared, persuasive testimony to reach these three
audiences, influence the outcome, and win the coveted two minutes
on the evening TV news or the front page photo space in the newspapers.

Participation in public hearings is a learned and cumulative activity. As participants develop skills (and win some political victories)
they acquire self-confidence and demand larger roles in government
decisions. And as more citizens decide to participate, it is to be expected that they will also sharpen their ability to manipulate public
hearings.

DEFICIENCIES OF THE PUBLIC HEARING PROCESS

A consequence of public hearings gamesmanship is that many observers have become disillusioned about the value of public hearings. Although the public hearing provides government officials with a relatively inexpensive, flexible, quick and easy-to-administer way to meet citizen participation requirements as well as accommodate just a few people or very large crowds, its deficiencies sometimes mask its advantages.

Public Hearings Are a Poor Setting for Disseminating Information

Because it provides no procedure for rebuttal or organized presentation of factual information, the public hearing easily slips into a venting of emotions rather than disseminating facts. There is little opportunity to correct distorted information. Testimony is frequently irrelevant to the issues on the agenda. Without a mechanism for interaction between groups or individuals, the public hearing limits reaching consensus, setting priorities, clarifying issues, reflecting diverse policies, or utilizing other citizen participation techniques. Nor has a scheme been devised to ensure that officials will weigh citizen views in reaching a decision. The presentation of testimony is usually the citizen's only input because with little opportunity to follow through, citizens tend to view an appearance at a public hearing as an end in itself.

Public Hearings Breed Confrontations

The public hearing format has been criticized as a breeding ground for confrontation, negative responses, and manipulation. An action is announced—for example, a zone change. Those who disagree with the change are more likely to appear at the hearing than those who support it. The American Society of Planning Officials summarizes the public hearing quandary: "On most major issues . . . there will be substantial public attendance . . . opponents will appear without special prompting. They will feel that their interests are adversely affected . . . and they will be strongly inclined to express themselves against the measure . . . Usually proponents are less strongly motivated . . . unless there is effective organization they may stay at home, leaving . . . the governing body feeling that the down-turned thumbs they see represent the public as a whole."[1] When both parties play fairly at public hearings gamesmanship, proponents express themselves at the hearing, at the least neutralizing "the down-turned thumbs" impression on public officials and thereby leveling the playing field.

The standard seating arrangement of the hearing breeds an atmosphere of court room confrontation. Officials are seated in a row, frequently on an elevated platform with an identifying nameplate in front of each official indicating his or her importance. The citizen who is being heard faces the board, his back to the audience. In controversial issues, proponents and opponents tend to line up on opposite sides of the aisle. Occasional applause or boos add to the confrontational atmosphere.

When public officials use hearings to generate public support for specific recommendations or plans, they emphasize the positive attributes and omit negative aspects. The public hearing is part of the plan to sell the public on a project or principle. Public officials also use hearings to set the stage for legislation which constituents may otherwise not accept. Some public officials attend training seminars to learn how to win public approval for projects. The Institute for Participatory Planning offers seminars to public officials and professionals serving the public which include such salient topics as: "Programs for Developing Necessary Public Acceptance" and "How to Get Your Most Difficult and Controversial Projects and Programs Implemented."[2] Sometimes, however, a government delays action on a controversial issue by calling for additional public hearings until the conflict becomes less strident. That this action may cause extensive, expensive delays on important projects exacerbates the problem.

Public Hearings Do Not Represent
the General Public

An orchestrated public hearing may provide a lively evening's entertainment. But this entertainment can be hazardous to the health of democracy. Dr. O. M. Solandt, a noted Canadian scientist, wrote in his 1975 "Report of the Solandt Commission" that vested inter-

---

[1]Reprinted with permission from *Public Hearings, Controversy, and the Written Response* by Frederick H. Bair, Jr., PAS Report Number 240, 1968, p. 5. Copyright © 1968 by the American Society of Planning Officials (now the American Planning Association), 1313 E. 60th St., Chicago, IL 60637.

[2]The Institute for Participatory Planning, Laramie, Wyoming

ests within the public are a source of manipulation of public hearings. "As a result of my experience," he writes, "I feel that . . . the public hearing mechanism may be evolving into an institutional structure by means of which a minority can short-circuit the established mechanisms of democracy and achieve its own ends without the opposition ever being mobilized or heard."[3]

Because the testimony may not represent the view of the general public, public officials can never be sure how representative the presentations are. In 1978, the Advisory Committee on Intergovernmental Relations (using the International City Management Association survey facilities) surveyed governments on their experience with citizen participation. Most local officials responded that public hearings are a device used primarily by special interests. An Alabama city reported ". . . citizen participation could be a useful guide for formulating programs, however . . . it usually is the case that only special interest groups attend hearings." This conclusion was shared by a southern California city which noted ". . . citizen participation appears to be generally in the form of special interest groups . . . Rarely do 'public hearings involve the general public.' " A letter to the editor of the *Toronto Star* (April 13, 1974) by a sociology professor described a public hearing as: "an exercise in futility and likely to give rise to quite misleading conclusions . . . (They) elicit the views of entirely unrepresentative sections of the population, particularly extremists representing minority positions."

Sewell and Burton[4] have found that public hearings do not attract a representative cross-section of people and are not an impartial or unbiased means of assessing public preferences. However, some other researchers maintain that the input received at the hearings is corroborative of the views of the general public.[5]

Studies conducted in the 1970's confirm the generalization that participation in public hearings is a luxury of the educated and afflu-

---

[3]O. M. Solandt, "Report of the Solandt Commission," *A Public Inquiry into the Transmission of Power Between Lennox and Oshawa* (Toronto, Ontario, 1975). As quoted in *Public Participation in Planning,* edited by W. R. D. Sewall and J. T. Cooppock, p. 108.

[4]W. R. D. Sewell and I. Burton, *Perceptions and Attitudes in Resources Management,* Ministry of Energy, Mines and Resources (Ottawa, Canada, 1971).

[5](Canadian) Environment Conservation Authority, 1971. Public hearings on a proposal to restore water levels in Cooking and Hastings Lakes, Edmonton.

ent.[6] The lower economic and educational spectrum of the public is generally underrepresented in many environmental public hearings.

An agency conducting a public hearing must constantly remind itself that it is appointed or elected to represent the thousands of citizens in a community who do not express themselves publicly, not only the 50 to 70 people speaking at the hearing. Underrepresentation of the poor and powerless in the public hearing process prompted the New Frontier and Great Society administrations of the 1960's to require participation by "target" populations in official decision-making. The Community Action Program (CAP) viewed active participation by constituents as a means to reform unresponsive institutions. The Model Cities effort depended on citizen participation to legitimize its programs. But, despite prodigious efforts by program operators, those at the bottom or periphery of society remained chronic non-participants. As Kasperson concluded, "The intended recipients were sold out."[7]

WHO IS WINNING THE GAME?

In the early 1970's, public hearing gamesmanship victories went to the advocates for social equality, environmental purity and consumer protection, supported by networks and grass-roots groups and guided by a spate of activist books on how to influence public decision-makers.[8] Regulations, policies, and decisions made during that period testify that throughout most of the 1970's these groups outperformed others in public hearing gamesmanship.

---

[6]A. Sharaf 1977, "Local Citizen Opposition to Nuclear Power Plants and Oil Refineries," unpublished Ph.D. dissertation, Clark University, 1977. R. F. Goodman and B. B. Clary, "Mass Community Attitudes and Action Response to Airport Noise." *Environment and Behavior* (1976), 8441-470.

[7]Roger E. Kasperson, "Participation Through Centrally Planned Social Change: Lessons from the American Experience on the Urban Scene," *Public Participation in Planning,* ed. W. R. D. Sewell and J. T. Coppock (New York: John Wiley & Sons, 1977), p. 186.

[8]Saul D. Alinsky, *Rules for Radicals* (New York: Vintage Books, 1972).

Ecotactics (New York: Pocket Books, 1970).

Donald K. Ross, *A Public Citizen's Action Manual* with an introduction by Ralph Nader (New York: Grossman, 1973).

The rise of environmental monitors—professionals in environmental organizations who monitored the making and execution of policies affecting environmental quality—developed a network of sophisticated individuals and organizations who were quickly available for public hearings. As organized environmental special interest growth exploded, these monitors developed into powerful public hearing participants. (Membership in the influential Sierra Club grew from less than 10,000 in 1950 to almost 170,000 in 1980. Similar growth was also enjoyed by the National Wildlife Federation, National Audubon Society, Izaak Walton League, Friends of the Earth and other environmental groups.)

Other public interest groups entered and won games: Consumer advocate Ralph Nader raised $2 million annually to support a talented staff in Washington, D.C. Common Cause developed into a model for citizen action. The national campaign against nuclear energy was supported by at least 140 anti-nuclear groups. As Professor Roger Kasperson, political geographer and observer of environmental politics, noted: ". . . studies of localized nuclear opposition . . . public participation in water quality and highway planning . . . and community action to reduce airport noise . . . confirm a well-established generalization—that public participation in the United States remains a prisoner of social class; it is a luxury of the educated and affluent."[9]

Through it all, the ubiquitous silent majority remained silent. Frustrated with the time and energy demands of public hearings, the small business owners, the small homeowners, the "mind-our-own business" middle class ignored public hearings. As late as 1980 *Nation's Business,* the business magazine published by the United States Chamber of Commerce, emphasized businesses' remoteness from the public hearing process by titling an article on public hearings "Public Hearings—New Turf for the Executive Crusader" (underline added for emphasis).[10]

Not till the waning years of the 1970's and the early 1980's, did average citizens recognize that they, too, could play public hearings

---

[9]Roger Kasperson, "Citizen Participation in Environmental Policy-Making, the U.S.A. Experience," *Involvement and Environment,* Vol 1, ed. Barry Sadler (Edmonton, Alberta: Environmental Council of Alberta, 1978), p. 134.

[10]Jean Mater, "Public Hearings—New Turf for the Executive Crusader," *Nation's Business* (March, 1980), pp. 16 b-d.

gamesmanship. They organized counter single issue groups: Citizens for Food and Fiber to counter Citizens Against Toxic Sprays (CATS); Women in Timber to counter Wilderness Coalitions; Facts About Tomorrow's Energy (FATE) battled the anti-nuclear Clamshells. Counter groups developed new networks, organized seminars to train members in strategies and tactics, and showed up at public hearings. Influential books were countered by other influential advocacy books; for example, *The Pendulum and the Toxic Cloud: The Course of Dioxin Contamination*[11] met its match in *Are Pesticides Really Necessary?*[12]

Special interest groups and counter groups are now removing or at least diminishing the one-sidedness of public hearings: all parties are learning to play by the same rules, increasing diversity of views and concerns and lessening the probability of any one special interest group capturing policy-making.

---

[11]Thomas Whiteside, *The Pendulum and the Toxic Cloud: The Course of Dioxin Contamination* (New Haven: Yale (University Press, 1979).

[12]Keith Barrons, *Are Pesticides Really Necessary?* (Chicago: Regnery Gateway, 1981).

2

Types Of Public Hearings

Public hearings permeate almost every aspect of American life and are intimately involved in everyday activities to a greater extent than most citizens realize. The impressive diversity of public hearings is illustrated by the following brief list of decisions on which public hearings were held: a city hearing on implementing an emergency 911 number; a health planning agency hearing on metropolitan cardiac care services; a planning commission hearing on using a basement for grocery delivery; a county hearing on a permit to construct a hotel; a budget hearing on service for the aging. Whatever their purpose, wherever they are held, advertisements and reports identify such hearings simply as "public hearings." This is as if all public hearings were identical and do not vary significantly in purpose, format, testimony, procedure, and outcome. Also, many procedures that are not identified as public hearings are really quasi-public hearings and merit the same preparation as a hearing. The type and purpose of each hearing affect preparation, strategy and tactics selection, as well as the time and energy committed to influencing the outcome.

THE LANGUAGE OF PUBLIC HEARINGS

Public hearings have developed their own vocabulary. Unfamiliar legal terms compound the public hearing mystique. These words have specific meanings, as described in Figure 2-1, A Glossary of Public Hearing Terms.

Figure 2–1

A Glossary of Public Hearing Terms

Appeal

A request to a higher authority or a higher court to review the actions of the official board to determine if the board acted improperly or without sufficient legal or factual basis.

Contested Case

A proceeding before an agency: a. in which the individual legal rights, duties or privileges of specific parties are required by statute or constitution to be determined only after an agency hearing at which those parties are entitled to participate. b. for the suspension, revocation or refusal to renew or issue a license where the licensee or applicant for a license demand a hearing. c. where the agency by rule or order provides for hearings.

Default

An omission, neglect, or failure of any party to take a step required in the progress of a proceeding such as a contested case.

Default Order

An order issued by an agency in a contested case after a party fails to appear for a hearing.

Deliberations

The process of considering the evidence and arguments presented in a hearing before making a decision.

Evidence

Anything presented to prove or disprove a matter in a hearing.

Ex Parte

Done for, in behalf of, or at the request of one party only.

Final Order

Final official action expressed in writing.

Findings

Determinations made in a judicial or administrative proceeding concerning the existence of some fact.

Figure 2-1 (continued)

Hearsay	Evidence from a source other than the personal knowledge of the witness, such as repetition of what others have said.
Intervention	A request by a third party to be received as a party in a proceeding involving other persons.
Order	Any official action expressed orally or in writing directed to a named person or persons outside the official agency.
Party	Each person or agency entitled as of right to a hearing before an agency; each person or agency named by the official board to be a party; or, any person requesting to participate as a party or in a limited party status who has an interest in the outcome of the proceeding or represents a public interest in such result.
Person	Any individual or public or private organization.
Prima Facie	Sufficient facts to prove a case; adequate to establish a fact.
Proponent	A party who is the offeror or primary supporter of something.
Rebut	To defeat or take away the effect of something; to offer argument or evidence against something.
Record	A written or recorded account of a proceeding or hearing.
Statute	A law enacted by a legislative body which declares, commands or prohibits something.
Tribunal	A person or group of persons with the authority to make a decision resolving a dispute after hearing arguments and considering evidence offered.
Verbatim	Word-for-word.

TEN PURPOSES FOR CALLING A PUBLIC HEARING

Public officials schedule public hearings to accomplish one or more of ten specific objectives:

• *1. To comply with the law:* Local, state and federal laws mandate that public officials call public hearings prior to arriving at certain decisions such as: permits for changes in land use as in rezoning or resource utilization; and power plant changes or any actions that might alter the quality of air, water, or noise level. Public hearings are often required for grievances on procedure, civil rights infringement, allocation of community resources, policy-making and administrative rule-making. Procedure is often as important as substance in mandated hearings.

• *2. To obtain information from or about citizens:* Officials call public hearings to hear citizens' views on issues, goals, alternative policies and actions. For example, a city government uses a public hearing to hear citizen reaction to compulsory weatherization of owner-occupied homes; a county Public Utility District schedules hearings to obtain information on how a proposed rate change will affect ratepayers.

• *3. To give information to citizens:* Some hearings aim to inform the public about a program or project. Informational hearings do not preclude citizen comment, but citizen input is not the primary purpose. Examples include a federal subcommittee calling a hearing to inform the public on Northwest water and power resources; a state holding a hearing to announce redefinition of Congressional boundaries; county supervisors calling a hearing to announce that the County Clerk's office will be open only in the mornings due to the budget defeat.

• *4. To improve public decisions or programs:* Public officials may attempt to improve public decisions or programs by obtaining ideas from the public, especially on difficult, unpopular programs. For example, a Senate Appropriations Committee asks for comment on decreasing federal aid to education; a City Council slates a meeting on reducing Fire Bureau and Police Department budgets; the local Health Department asks the community what to do about its failing septic tanks.

• *5. To enhance acceptance of public decisions on programs:* Officials call some hearings to sell citizens on programs, projects, services, and decisions—a Mass Transit Department calls a public hearing to seek citizen endorsement of a proposed change in the bus route; the United States House of Representatives' Committee on Aging holds a hearing to sell the Administration's proposed budget to the senior citizen constituency.

• *6. To alter political power patterns and resource allocations:* Public hearings may focus on plans to centralize or decentralize programs, oppose "The Establishment," or change the government through the political process. Examples are: hearings on altering the local patterns of human services; United States Fish and Wildlife hearings on the closure of a mountain refuge to campers; state environmental quality hearings on allowing an environmental coalition to review conditions of permits.

• *7. To respond to citizen concerns:* As a mechanism for social action, public hearings help emphasize the power of constituent activists. Special interests use the hearings to dramatize and focus on preferred policies and their implementation. The four million handicapped children in the nation used public hearings to win regulations to implement the 1975 Federal Education for the All Handicapped Children Act. The Fair Share groups used hearings to generate rules prohibiting utilities from shutting off service during the winter, if such action endangered the health of an individual.

• *8. To delay or avoid difficult public decisions:* Sometimes public officials call a public hearing to delay or avoid making an untimely or unpopular decision. Faced with a no-win controversy on a zone change, a City Council calls for further studies to be presented at a later public meeting; reluctant to announce an unpopular decision on a hazardous waste facility, County Commissioners delay with another public hearing.

• *9. To gain political advantage:* As an opportunity for immediate and extended media coverage, public hearings provide a showcase for political entrepreneurs. An official or committee calls the hearing with public comment orchestrated for dramatic interest to capture media attention. Showcase hearings target controversial or human issues affecting a broad constituency.

• *10. To seek collaborative solutions to problems:* When officials sense that the parties in a conflict are not far apart, collaborative solutions are politically attractive. A public meeting is called "to see if we can't work things out." Collaborative solutions make the responsible officials look politically effective without incurring costs in community conflict, and help officials avoid hazardous choices between political values and symbols.

QUASI PUBLIC HEARINGS

Quasi public hearings take on the form and procedure of public hearings although they are not designated as official hearings. The following are examples of quasi public hearings.

• *Private sector stockholder meetings* may be transformed into public hearings by activist minority shareholders. The stockholder meetings of some companies with investments in South Africa or companies who supply military equipment have experienced open policy debate similar to a public hearing. Students protesting an action by university officials, tenants demanding action from landlords, and stakeholders confronting decision-makers at any time are staging a quasi public hearing.

• *Litigation* or courtroom proceedings constitute a public hearing with formalized procedures and prescribed outcomes. A forum or conference is another form of public hearing in which statements, disclosures of information, and discussion influence public opinion and eventually affect public decisions.

• *A formal invitation to comment* on proposed changes in legislation such as the Environmental Impact Statements required by the National Environmental Policy Act (NEPA), functions as a "silent public hearing." A public agency invites comment for a period of time. Proponents and opponents submit written comments or informally contact the agency. In this way, the agency hears the public.

• *Citizens can initiate public hearings.* Citizens have the right to demand a public hearing; they do not have to wait for officials to act. A civic group protesting funding by the city of an anti-nuclear conference demands that the city hold a public hearing. A neighborhood disagrees with the decision of a state agency and demands that the agency schedule a public hearing. Few official boards will turn down such a demand.

• *Citizens sometimes hold their own public hearings.* Employees laid off by the closure of a factory call a "People's Public Hearing" to focus attention on the factory's management policies; stockholders hold a hearing to discuss a Board of Director's decision; members of an electric Co-op hold a public hearing to discuss policy on closed meetings. Although these hearings have no legal status, they serve the same function as a required public hearing—citizens voice their concerns; the media report the concerns; officials hear the concerns.

HOW TO DETERMINE THE PURPOSE OF THE HEARING

Public hearings announce stated agendas: to consider actions; to gather public reaction, to discuss; and, to hear from citizens. The hearing held to comply with the law usually carries the title "Official Notice of Public Hearing" or "Notice of Public Hearing" which refers to the specific provisions in the ordinance or legislation requiring the hearing.

Citizens' views are specifically requested in announcing hearings for the purpose of obtaining information about citizens' needs. Hearings to give information to citizens frequently present the results of a study or a report of a commission or panel. At these hearings, the audience can expect more opportunity to listen than to speak.

Hearings held to improve public decisions provide specific questions on which public views are solicited. A typical announcement of this type of hearing is one from the U.S. Small Business Administration which begins: "The Office of Advocacy has been holding hearings on the Federal Paperwork Reduction Act. The goal of the hearings is to assess the impact of the Paperwork Reduction Act. . .on the small business community and to explore ways to provide greater relief from paperwork burdens." Next, seven questions are suggested for comment. The hearings are used as the basis for testimony to Congress.

Rarely does a public hearing announcement state that its purpose is either to lure the public into accepting a program or to delay a decision until conflict reduces from boil to simmer. It is necessary to read between the lines to discover these purposes. When a state Elections Committee proposes to encourage balloting by mail and then holds public hearings around the state, it is probably selling its proposal. When the City Council schedules "a fresh airing" on an old controversy, delay is likely the objective.

One can expect hearings whose purpose is the alteration of political power patterns or a response to citizen concerns to be preceded by considerable media attention and to be orchestrated by the special interest groups promoting the action. These hearings tend to be emotion-packed and well-attended.

Hearings whose primary objective is gaining political advantage focus on the political entrepreneur who seeks the advantage. No matter whether the entrepreneur is a United States Senator, a state Senator or an ambitious County Commissioner, he or she occupies center stage and pre-hearing discussion features his or her opinions.

The hearing aimed at finding a collaborative solution also focuses on the official who calls for "working this out." Announcements of the hearing reflect the political symbolism identified with the problem. If the collaboration works, the official emerges as the hero or heroine. If it doesn't, the parties are said to display intransigence.

A CLASSIFICATION OF PUBLIC HEARINGS

In addition to diversity of purpose, public hearings are classifiable by the *type of activity,* the *level of government,* and *procedural requirements.*

Type of Activity

Three types of activity involving citizen/government interfaces use or require public hearings:

1. General government.
2. Physical developments.
3. Human services.

General Government

General government hearings are called for decisions involving: a.) *Budget and finance*—federal allocations for programs, state legislative hearings on allocations of financial resources, and local preparation of budgets prior to public vote. b.) *Comprehensive planning*—land use planning and goals, adopting a growth management plan, construction of a resort complex on an estuary. c.) *Legislation*—legislation on placing regulatory powers over a scenic area, regulations on oil and natural gas drilling, international trade commission legislation on taxing Canadian lumber, local ordinances on burning leaves in back yards. d.) *Administrative rule-making*—federal rules on the education of handicapped children, state rules on limiting the words or abbreviations on custom automobile license plates, local adoption of a student conduct code by the school board.

Physical Development

Physical development hearings include deliberations on: a.) Community and/or economic development—federal urban renewal projects, state tax incentives for industrial location, a city's conditional use permit for a gravel dredging operation. b.) Transportation—a federally funded freeway project, widening a state road, putting a bicycle path through a community park, abandonment of a bus route. c.) Environmental protection—an Environmental Impact Statement (EIS) on a development in a coastal zone, state policy on permitting burning of grass fields, aerial spraying for a gypsy moth infestation of local trees. The public provides input in at least three points in the development of an EIS: 1) the public scoping process that precedes the EIS; 2) the completion of the draft EIS; and, 3) the issuance of the final EIS. d.) Energy—the Nuclear Regulatory Commission decision on reactivation of the Three Mile Island Nuclear Reactor, State Public Utility increases in consumer costs for electric power, local mandatory energy conservation measures. e.) Natural resources (and agriculture)—federal listing of endangered species, allocation of water rights, local permits to cut street trees.

Human Services

Officials hold hearings on human services including: a.) Aging—programs to aid older persons, funding Senior Citizens' Centers, property tax relief, policies on guidelines for local government agencies on aging. b.) Housing—housing and community development grants for housing rehabilitation, designation of a historical landmark, permission to demolish a building. c.) Criminal justice—centers for juvenile offenders, expansion of detention facilities, exemption of public records from disclosure. d.) Health and safety—metropolitan cardiac care services, expansion of a hospital (using federal funds), management of commercial radioactive waste, installation of a warning siren in a populated area near a nuclear plant. e.) Leisure time—expansion of a ski lodge in a state park, federal setting aside of areas for wilderness. f.) Education—changes in requirements for teaching certificates, disputes on tenure of professors, increase in the price of school lunches.

Level of Government

Public hearings may be classified according to the level of the government involved.

Federal government

The federal government holds public hearings to receive comment: on proposed legislation; in the development of policies; and, for administrative rule-making and program operation—such as amendments to the Clean Air Act, restriction of public access to private companies' pesticide safety and health data, and cost-benefit analysis of new rules.

The United States Senate and House of Representatives operate under a committee system, for example, the House Judiciary Committee. Most of the committees have standing subcommittees and frequently appoint ad hoc subcommittees, as the Senate Committee to Investigate Organized Crime in Interstate Commerce. These committees or subcommittees hold hearings on all major and controversial legislation before drafting a proposal in its final form. The hearings vary both in length and number of witnesses who testify. Federal agencies (executive department and independent agencies such as the Federal Communications Commission) provide for public hearings in most rule-making.

Executive Order 12044 (1978) provides for citizen participation in federal rule-making: "It establishes a system for executive agencies to manage their regulatory responsibilities and included provisions for expanding public participation in the development of significant agency regulations." Some federal grant programs with public hearing requirements are: Health and Human Services (HSS); Department of Labor; Water Resources Council. Senate and House committees involve citizens by holding hearings outside the capitol. For example, the United States Senate Committee on Small Business hearings on the impact of paperwork on small business were held in several cities around the country.

The compensation of participants in federal hearings remains a controversial practice. Some federal agencies compensate interested persons who participate in rule-making. According to the Federal Trade Commission, under the FTC Improvement Act of 1975 preparation, hearing participation and post-hearing participation are reimbursable. The preparation of a petition or participation in judicial review of a Trade Regulation Rule are not reimbursable.

The National Research Council, reviewing decision-making in the Environmental Protection Agency, notes:

> Good decision-making. . .requires assurance that all aspects of the public interest are articulated. . .Yet, interests often go unrepresented, in part because the costs or benefits of a decision to segments of the public are not clear and in part because funds to enable meaningful participation are not available. . . .citizen organizations—primarily national nonprofit membership organizations, such as the Environmental Defense Fund, the Natural Resources Defense Council, the League of Women Voters, and the Sierra Club—have had a significant impact on EPA's development and implementation of environmental policy. . .Congress provided under Section 101e of the Federal Water Pollution Control Act Amendments of 1972 that public participation should be "provided for, encouraged, and assisted" by EPA. . .In addition, Congress clearly contemplated an active "watchdog" role of this kind for the public because it provided explicitly for citizen suits in most of the statutes administered by EPA. . .
>
> EPA has, in the past, provided funds to such organizations as the Conservation Foundation, the League of Women Voters, the American Lung Association, the National Wildlife Federation, the Sierra Club, and others to. . .encourage or facilitate public participation in environmental planning and decision-making.[1]

The National Research Council included in its conclusions the specific recommendation that the Environmental Protection Agency financially support groups or individuals who can contribute to decision-making.

State Government

State governments hold hearings in conjunction with policy development and proposed legislation, administrative rule-making, and program operations. All states issue a calendar for both house and committee consideration. Floor action agendas are usually available daily; committee schedules are published weekly. Upon request, most states make available a list of bills under consideration and a schedule for floor and committee meetings. The District of Columbia and 42 states provide citizens the opportunity to present their comments. State agencies issue public hearing procedures in accordance with their state Administrative Procedure Act.

---

[1] *Decision-Making in the Environmental Protection Agency,* National Research Council, Vol. II (Washington, D.C.: National Academy of Sciences, 1977), pp. 96–103.

Local Governments

Local governments (cities, counties, townships) call public hearings for policy development, legislation, administrative rule-making, and program operations. Implementation in a Housing and Community Development Block Grant, proposed television cable service, a garbage franchise are examples. Regional governmental organizations sometimes use public hearings in policy development and program operations.

The outcomes of local hearings personally and visibly affect citizens, who also recognize these hearings as a greater opportunity for personal contacts with decision-makers. The businessman who petitions a local Port District for State Revenue Bonds to expand his business may be appealing to associates or even competitors. The parent requesting a traffic light at a dangerous school crossing faces City Council members who are also parents thus sharing the same concern. As a result, citizens find local governments increasingly approachable. Power in American decision-making is changing from "top-down" to "bottom-up" as local public hearings consider significant issues, and officials deliberate publicly in an environment of high visibility.

Procedural Requirements

Procedure in public hearings may affect the outcome more than substance does. Although regulations and ordinances prescribe public hearings, in recent years court decisions have significantly influenced the conduct of public hearings. Judicial opinions often conflict on the procedural due process requirements to be imposed and when they should be required. The trend is to increased accountability and more stringent rules.

Quasi-judicial Proceedings

Quasi-judicial proceedings require public officials to act in a judicial capacity—fair, unbiased, with careful consideration of the facts and arguments in the written record as the basis of a reasoned decision. Quasi-judicial proceedings resemble a court case with due process safeguards: all the testimony and evidence is entered in the record; the parties, under oath, are treated as witnesses, with an opportunity for cross examination. Filing of notices follows a rigid schedule using interrogatories, depositions, subpoenas. Motions are made and ruled on. Ex-parte contact—private communication between the decision-makers and any party to the decision—is prohibited. Individuals and organizations are allowed to petition to intervene as parties in the hearing.

The formal procedure, reminiscent of the court room, intimidates citizens and further polarizes adversaries. Some contested case hearings provide for *limited appearances*—an opportunity for the public to address the decision-makers, avoiding the bother of petitioning, intervening, cross examining, filing evidence, and other legal gymnastics. Limited appearance statements are recorded but the decision-makers are instructed not to consider them as evidence. Although limited appearances express only public sentiment and are not part of the evidence, an examination of hotly contested conflicts indicates that public sentiment, while not providing the rationale for a decision, undoubtedly influences that decision.

Hearing Officer Proceedings

A Hearing Officer, sometimes called a Hearing Official, conducts some public hearings. The Hearing Official approach was initiated in the late 1960's in Maryland and in the Pacific Northwest but is still considered somewhat innovative. The Hearing Official process may require state enabling legislation.

A Hearing Officer is an appointed officer—usually a full-time, paid, trained official, who conducts quasi-judicial hearings. He enters written findings based on the record established at the hearing. He sometimes is authorized to make a final decision; or he forwards a recommendation to a legislative or administrative body for the final decision.

Some municipalities use Hearing Officers to make initial land use decisions—conditional use applications, zone changes, landfill projects, or decisions on erection of radio transmission towers. The public hearing conducted by the Hearing Officer may replace a public hearing before the lay review body empowered to grant the permit or settle a grievance. The Hearing Officer follows procedural due process, using staff input, preliminary studies, or written recommendations.

The once-only applicant seeking a variance to construct a garage often appreciates the more relaxed and informal appeal to a Hearing Official because the single official tends to be less threatening and often reacts on a one-on-one basis. Developers and repeat applicants find that a Hearing Officer shortens the waiting time for a decision and more readily complies with strict procedural due process, insuring the validity of the decision.

Hearing Officers also relieve elected and appointed officials from the burden of conducting many public hearings and wrestling with strict procedural requirements. Public administrators find that the Hearing Official process improves the staff's input to the decision.

The Hearing Officer concept is not universally popular. Some lay bodies are concerned that the cost and possible delays as a result of adding another step to the process negate the advantages. Others believe that the Hearing Official may have too much authority and enjoy too much opportunity to play politics. A Hearing Officer could usurp the responsibility of authorities by selective handling of testimony. He may impair the credibility of the decision-making process by capturing media attention, especially in the simultaneous release of recommendations to the media and to the authorities. For instance: The Hearing Officer released a copy of his recommendation to the media based on the evidence of over 40 hours of public hearings. The recommendation included four options, all supportable by the evidence. One option was recommended as best. The media picked up the best option, reporting it as the official recommendation. This forced the board to be defensive in considering the other options. The Hearing Officer's action had virtually precluded the alternative options.

Mediation Proceedings

When public officials recognize that the issues have become uncomfortably polarized, they occasionally turn to mediation—a voluntary process in which those involved in a dispute jointly explore and reconcile their differences. For mediation to reconcile differences, both parties in a dispute must share:

— The sense of urgency: something must be settled because the parties agree that adverse consequences are imminent.
— The willingness to participate voluntarily.
— The recognition that mediation offers a quicker, surer solution than the courts or a public vote.

The party confident that a public hearing will result in a favorable decision rarely agrees to risk compromise in mediation. The party initiating the request for mediation signals a feeling of a political disadvantage.

The mediator has no authority to impose a settlement; he assists the parties in resolving their differences, persisting until they reach a workable solution. Mediation has been more effective in state and federal issues than in local conflicts. Large projects—power plants, dams, or highways—appear to be more susceptible to mediation than local zoning controversies. A quarterly entitled *Environmental Consensus,* published by RESOLVE—a non-profit organization made up of a cross-section of environmental, business and labor leaders—provides information on developments in mediation and disputes settled by mediation.[2]

Another method of *alternative dispute resolution* used by businesses to avoid litigation is the mini-trial. The Center for Public Resources, Inc., a leading proponent of the alternative resolution technique, offers a judicial panel with private judges who handle disputes more quickly, and often less expensively, than the traditional system of justice.

---

[2]*RESOLVE,* 360 Bryant St., Palo Alto, California 94301.

SECTION TWO

Influencing Public Hearing Decisions

3

The Public Hearing Process: Organization and Preparation

Recognition of the difference between the *public hearing process* and the *public hearing event* differentiates advocates who successfully influence public decisions from those citizens who merely dabble at hearings. Effective advocates have learned that the public hearing itself is the climax of a carefully organized strategy. Most of the process takes place before the hearing event: setting the stage; creating perceptions; studying how to influence decision-makers and the media; evaluating opposition actions. The hearing event is but one link in carefully crafted organization and preparation, planned to the last detail with one objective: to influence the decision.

The procedures used by groups who have developed what political analysts call an "agenda-setting capacity,"—the ability to shape the government's policy priorities by leading the public to view certain values as more important than others—are time-tested: identify the problem; organize campaigns; form coalitions; use the media; select and implement strategies; and use those tactics that guarantee a sparkling performance at the hearing. The public hearing process is as productive in protesting rezoning in a neighborhood or persuading the state legislature to adopt a new housing policy as it is in influencing Congress to pass new safety legislation. The process is appropriate for proposing or opposing projects, policies or regulations. This chapter describes the public hearings process. Succeeding chapters tell how to apply the process to influencing public decisions.

31

PUBLIC HEARINGS AS A ZERO-SUM GAME

The public hearing process acknowledges that public decision-making is a zero-sum game. When citizens, either as individuals or in groups, request permission to undertake many activities, decision-makers assume the role of referee between competing interest groups to grant or deny the petition. When some citizens urge that the petition be granted and others urge denial, the public hearing becomes a zero-sum game: someone wins and someone loses. Two parties advocating diametrically opposite outcomes (as so frequently happens) create a controversy; each constituency attempts to influence the decision-makers to favor its special interest. In large urban centers, multiple players complicate the decision process with block associations, organizations of welfare recipients, citizen street politicians, ethnic groups, taxpayer groups, and protest groups of all persuasions promoting conflicting outcomes.

The public hearing process airs the conflict. The strong possibility that a well-organized effort will persuade decision-makers to favor a particular outcome lures individuals to devote time and energy to the contest. Influential interest group elites (who, according to many observers, have captured policy-making in modern democracies) have mastered the art of using the public hearing process.

The public hearing process that successfully influences a decision is founded on organization and preparation. Organization increases the probability of success; delaying planning until the week or day before the hearing jeopardizes success. The process is based on the political truism that, although government by faction is universally decried, unorganized groups can't play the game. The art of organizing and the skill of the resulting organization transforms mere process into a game of wits. While the annals of activism extol individuals who almost single-handedly have influenced public policy, the heroic David who slays the Goliath of organized groups is the exception. In reality the hero is a one-man play, carrying out single-handedly all of the group roles.

ORGANIZATION FOR THE PUBLIC
HEARING PROCESS

An organized interest group is characterized by possessing an objective, structure, identity, commitment to action, and members to execute the commitment. As the first step in the process of influencing public decisions, organization implies a long-term effort. Preparation refers to the short-term activities directed to resolving a specific controversy at a designated public hearing. The word "advocacy" has been selected to describe the outcome promoted, rather than "cause" or "movement," because it covers a broad spectrum of global significance or insignificance. To term an organized effort to protest a utility rate increase a "cause" or a "movement" seems pompous, but advocacy includes any effort from a local utility rate protest to supporting national social change activities.

Both organization and preparation focus on winning support from the three groups of players in the public hearing process and their supporting casts:

— *The decision-makers* and their advisors—staff, specialists, task forces, commissions, experts, and counsel (sometimes called government elites).
— The *public* and its opinion leaders—movie and TV celebrities, elected officials, educators, writers, public figures and special interest elites.
— The *media* and their sources of information—press releases, speeches, news services, authorities, related news events.

The public hearing process targets all these players.

Advocacy Group Objectives

Organization for public hearings establishes and maintains an advocacy group whose objective is to increase public awareness of the problems and solutions, enhance media awareness of the problems and solutions, and to help decision-makers understand the problems and persuade them to accept the advocacy group's proposed solutions. The formation of an advocacy group adds credibility to the advocacy by providing a vehicle to let the public and media know what the advocacy group is, what it stands for, what it does, why it does it.

The advocacy must be some compelling concern—civil rights, saving the environment, preserving the integrity of the neighborhood, or protecting children from a school closure—that rouses otherwise disconnected persons to act in concert. The group stands for something; it urgently presses an advocacy "do" or "don't" message: "Save the wilderness," "Prevent a garbage burning plant," "Protect our homes," "Enact an anti-abortion law."

Advocacy Group Structure

The advocacy group is an organizational umbrella, an immediate identification, and so endows its membership with a certain legitimacy. Some advocacy groups sponsor continuing organized activity to promote a range of ideas on a broad concept. For example, the Sierra Club, one of the most influential advocacy groups in the United States, centers on the ecology of the Earth's life support systems; Zero Population Growth concentrates on population stability; the National Urban Coalition focuses on urban problems.

Other advocacy groups promote, or oppose, a single project or a single issue. The single-issue advocacy group organizes, acts, accomplishes its mission (or fails) and eventually dissolves: The Citizens League Against the Sonic Boom (CLASB) was the single-issue advocacy group that prevailed on Congress not to fund the supersonic transport (SST); The Knoxville, Kentucky single-issue group, Citizens for Home Rule (CHR), fought Knoxville's annexation of a new area; Neighbors Opposed to Port Expansion (NOPE) single-issue group delayed an airport expansion for many years. Many homeowners' groups, parents' organizations, taxpayers' alliances and similar ad hoc groups organize to promote only one issue.

The environmental movement of the 1970's and the nuclear freeze movement of the 1980's created advocacy groups to further their objectives. The nuclear freeze movement merits study by any person or group advocating a position. Figure 3–1 lists a few of the advocacy groups created for the nuclear freeze movement. Note the credible professionals (lawyers, physicians, planners, engineers, scientists) and the respectable church, civic, and student groups who have joined to further this cause.

Ongoing advocacy groups and single-issue advocacy groups organize as chartered, funded groups with paid staffs or, more often, as informal, volunteer groups. Either involves a substantial commitment of time, energy, patience and diplomacy. Indispensible to an effective advocacy group are a cause, a message, a leader, members and action-orientation.

Instant identification is a product of organizing an advocacy group. The group gains instant identification by selecting a name, preferably one that creates a meaningful, positive acronym: Preserve Our Park (POP); Public Land Use Council (PLUC); Proponents for a Responsible Economic Future (PREF); Association of Community Organizations for Reform Now (ACORN); Neighbors Opposed to the

Figure 3-1

Advocacy Groups to Promote the Nuclear Freeze Movement

CALS (Citizen Action for Lasting Security)
CALC (Clergy and Laity Concerned)
Church Women United
City Draft Counselors
Fellowship of Reconciliation
Lawyers Alliance for Nuclear Arms Control
Physicians for Social Responsibility
Planners, Engineers, and Architects for Social Responsibility
SCOPE (Student Committee on Peace Education)
Survival Action Committee
Union of Concerned Scientists

    This list, adopted from one distributed to the media, through the school system, churches and public library, included names and telephone numbers of contact persons. A supplement listed additional supporters and contacts—the League of Women Voters, the United Nation's Association Chapter and most of the local religious organizations.

Garbage Operation (NOGO). Negative or silly acronyms are unproductive: Committee Against Downtown (CAD); Neighbors Against Garbage (NAG). Time Magazine's amusing piece on advocacy groups in Memphis, Tennessee (Fig. 3-2) shows the usefulness of names and acronyms in providing instant identification.

    Visibility of a group is heightened by a slogan, designing a logo, selecting one color for all printed material, or any means that instantly telegraph the advocacy group's identity. Instant visibility need cost no more than a sheet of colored art paper. At a crowded public hearing in Montana the opponents of a controversial bill pinned green paper circles to their jackets. At a fraction of a penny each, those green circles

Figure 3-2

The War of Advocacy Names and Acronyms

BOFFO IN THE BUFF
Some kind of night at the opera

It is not an everyday event for a woman to rise topless from a large cauldron in Memphis. But when Cheryllynn Ross did so last week as Hecate during the New York-based Metropolitan Opera touring performance of *Macbeth*, she was risking more than a chill: the city's tough new antinudity ordinance, aimed chiefly at topless dancers, could have brought quick arrest. Two division commanders of the local police were on the scene. Would they rush the cauldron and haul its contents off to the slammer?

Well, no. But as the curtain went up a stir in the back of the first balcony proved almost as dramatic. At a cry of "Bravo!"—"Brava!" would have been more correct—20 men and women bared their chests and held up candles, lighters and flashlights so that their fellow opera lovers in the audience of 2,360 could catch their act. All were members of an antiordinance group called MASH (Memphians Against Social Harassment), formed last month by Memphis Restaurateur Paul Savarin to combat MAD (Memphians Against Degeneracy), the pro-ordinance lobby. Rudi E. Scheidt, president of the Memphis group that sponsors the Met visit each year, called the protest "a hell of an embarrassment to Memphis." But most citizens took the incident in stride. Carey Wong, of Opera Memphis, was rhapsodic: "It was a lovely gesture, a captivating moment." David Reuben, spokesman for the Met tour, suggested that if the Met could survive the 1906 earthquake in San Francisco, where it performed *Carmen* with Caruso, it would probably survive the topless tremors in Tennessee too.

To many Memphis residents, upset by the proliferation of adult bookstores and topless nightclubs, MAD is not out of its mind. But even though Police Director John Holt insisted after the protest that the ordinance would still be enforced, he announced his own surprise: three high-ranking police officers on duty that night were put on suspension, without pay, two of them

Figure 3-2 (continued)

for being in the vicinity of the opera hall against orders. MASH jumped back into the fray with a declaration that policemen, like all other citizens, are entitled to go to the opera. As for MAD, perhaps it could expand to meet the new crisis, possibly forming new groups called Memphians Against Damsels Doing Ecdysiast Routines (MADDER), Memphians Against Chest Hair at Operas (MACHO) or, to honor the Met, Memphians Against Culture Buffs Exposing Themselves Heedlesssly (MACBETH).

TIME, MAY 23, 1983

identified the opponents as the TV camera panned the room. An identifying sticker also provides a quick method of counting supporters at a public hearing. One group at a public hearing held to air pros and cons for a new factory planning to locate in a small community printed orange stickers bearing the message "we want IT" (the initials of the company). As participants streamed into the school cafeteria, the Support IT (SIT) advocates provided stickers for supporters. Decision-makers and the media did not miss the overwhelming support as the orange stickers popped up on most jackets.

Commitment to Action

Organization follows basic procedures: elect officers, meet, raise funds, act. The advocacy group depends on finding at least one committed person with energy and enthusiasm to lead, who will encourage members to attend meetings, write letters to the editor, distribute handbills, man telephones, testify at public hearings, carry petitions and perform all those other activities necessary to deliver the advocacy message. The desire to "do something," to change or prevent change, an orientation to action takes precedence over social club activities.

Under the leadership of the committed person the advocacy group devises an action plan, usually consisting of eight steps:

1.) Elect officers—a President or Chairman to preside at meetings and oversee the activities of the group; a Vice President or Vice Chairman; a Treasurer to keep financial records; a Secretary to keep records. 2.) Locate a meeting place—the public library, a member's office conference room, or living room.   3.) Designate responsibilities—select an individual with some knowledge of or access to the media to handle publicity; a person with access to an attorney to handle legal aspects; other individuals with talent and interest to work on appropriate tasks. 4.) Raise basic funds—for postage, attorneys' fees, special studies or experts. (If an ad hoc group develops into an ongoing advocacy group, paid staff may be necessary.)   5.) Agree on policies, procedures and goals—this may be the most difficult task in organizing an advocacy group. The task can be simplified by recognizing the concerns that inspired initial formation of the group. 6.) Determine the general strategy to accomplish the goals. (Suggested strategies are detailed in Chapter 4, "Public Hearing Techniques and Strategies.")   7.) Devise an action plan to implement the strategy, with all actions leading toward the anticipated public hearing as the strategic climax.   8.) Implement the basic steps in preparing for a public hearing.

Advocacy Group Membership

An advocacy group searches for and uses its members. Organization styles vary, but all interest groups who make an impact scour their membership for talent—the persuasive speakers, the experts, the articulate advocates, the persons familiar with the problems that prompted the advocacy. Advocacy groups are skilled at developing teams who are willing to work—to man the telephone tree; distribute pamphlets; stuff envelopes; appear at the public hearing; testify at the hearing; circulate petitions; and, carry through the myriad tasks necessary for the public hearing process to influence opinions. Characteristically, these groups do not wait for persons to request membership but vigorously pursue prospects, obtaining names from sign-up sheets at meetings, postage-paid cards left at the library, clip-and-send-in advertisements, radio call-in shows, and their file of newspaper clippings.

Information Gathering

Advocacy groups are vigorous information gatherers. They expend considerable effort on assembling the voting records of decision-makers. They analyze the thinking styles of decision-makers, the predilections of opinion leaders, and the beliefs of reporters, broadcasters and other media personnel. They maintain lists of the credible, knowledgeable experts. They maintain lists, prepare profiles of decision-makers and media, and assemble files. They clip newspapers and magazines, monitor the media and know where to book their Speaker's Bureau. By making data collection an ongoing function, they have the information where and when they need it, permitting them to work effectively on weekends and evenings.

The information gathered by some advocacy groups is impressive: The Connecticut Citizen Action Group (CCAG) compiled 1500 pages of the records of all Connecticut legislators. They analyzed all debates on the floor of the House and the Senate and prepared a 10 to 15-page profile on each legislator. A similar project by the New York Public Interest Research Group (NYPIRG)—one of the nationwide student activist Public Interest Research Groups initiated by Ralph Nader—prepared profiles on New York legislators.

Sources of information for advocacy groups are as near as the public library, newspapers, government offices, and the telephone. The public library carries volumes that list organizations such as Gale's *Encyclopedia of Organizations* and *Business Organizations and Agencies Directory*. Organized groups use newspapers as a basic research tool, clipping and filing stories related to their advocacy, stories about decision-makers, and stories about adversary groups. Government offices have available summaries of meetings, minutes of previous public hearings, ordinances, regulations, and other information that provides valuable insight on what goes on behind the scenes. Such information is usually available through Freedom of Information provisions of federal, state, and local jurisdictions. The Federal Administrative Procedures Act provides that, except for national defense and other specific exemptions, each agency must make available information on agency rules, records, and opinions. In most states Open Records Laws give citizens access to state and local government records. Usually, all one needs to do is write a letter similar to the sample Freedom of Information Request Letter as shown in Figure 3–3. The media are sensitive to hesitation by officials in releasing information. If requested records are not made available, it is good practice to notify the media and co-opt their interest in publicizing the advocacy.

PREPARING FOR THE PUBLIC HEARING

The public hearing process consumes time and energy, but the process pays off: by the time the public hearing is held the organized advocacy group has equipped itself with manpower, identity, an

Figure 3–3

A Sample Freedom of Information Request Letter*

Tele. No. (business hours)
Return Address
Date

Name of Public Body
Address

To the FOI Officer:

This request is made under the federal Freedom of Information Act, 5 U.S.C. 552.

Please send me copies of (*Here, clearly describe what you want. Include identifying material, such as names, places, and the period of time about which you are inquiring. If you wish, attach news clips, reports, and other documents describing the subject of your research.*).

As you know, the FOI Act provides that if portions of a document are exempt from release, the remainder must be segregated and disclosed. Therefore, I will expect you to send me all nonexempt portions of the records which I have requested, and ask that you justify any deletions by reference to specific exemptions of the FOI Act. I reserve the right to appeal your decision to withhold any materials.

I promise to pay reasonable search and duplication fees in connection with this request. However, if you estimate that the total fees will exceed $____, please notify me so that I may authorize expenditure of a greater amount.

(*Optional*) I am prepared to pay reasonable search and duplication fees in connection with this request. However, the FOI Act provides for waiver or reduction of fees if disclosure could be considered as "primarily benefiting the general public." I am a journalist (*researcher, or scholar*) employed by (*name of news organization, book publishers, etc.*), and intend to use the information I am requesting as the basis for a planned article (*broadcast, or book*). (*Add arguments here in support of fee waiver*). Therefore, I ask that you waive all search and duplication fees. If you deny

Figure 3-3 (continued)

this request, however, and the fees will exceed $____, please notify me of the charges before you fill my request so that I may decide whether to pay the fees or appeal your denial of my request for a waiver.

As I am making this request in the capacity of a journalist (*author, or scholar*) and this information is of timely value, I will appreciate your communicating with me by telephone, rather than by mail, if you have any questions regarding this request. Thank you for your assistance, and I will look forward to receiving your reply within 10 business days, as required by law.

Very truly yours,

(Signature)

-----

*FOI Service Center, Reporters Committee for Freedom of the Press, 800 18th St., N.W., Washington, D.C. 20006

information system and is ready to take steps to influence the decision. The public hearing process has set the stage, rehearsed the players, and laid the foundation for selecting strategies to achieve the planned outcome. Groups who have not invested the time and effort in organizing find themselves outclassed and outmaneuvered at the public hearing.

The public hearing event climaxes the process. Interest groups who have succeeded in affecting public policies prepare for a public hearing as if producing a play: they develop a plot, write the script, cast the actors, select a manager, and plan every detail to achieve a unified, persuasive impression. As in a play production, preparation is the key to a successful outcome. Preparation for a public hearing includes ten principles—principles so basic that they apply to any type of hearing at any level of government. Time pressures may sometimes force a group to skimp in carrying out these actions, but groups determined to affect the outcome of the hearing rarely risk skipping any of these steps. These are the ten ground rules of preparing for a public hearing, call them the Ten Commandments of a Successful Public Hearing:

Study the Problem

Study all facets of the problem—the facts, principles, data, history, public perceptions, decision-maker's views, media biases and other factors that may affect the outcome. Control the information and do not depend solely on the data presented by officials or the opposition. Knowing more about the problem than any other person has often provided the winning leverage in the public hearing battle.

Define the Problem

Define or describe the policy, issue or project to be discussed at the hearing. A well-worn saying maintains that when people with opposing views agree on the definition the controversy disappears. It is common to hear after hours of heated discussion, "Oh, I thought the road was going down here, past the duck pond. The North end isn't so bad." Or, "I thought that 30 people would lose their jobs if we denied this application. You say that no jobs are in jeopardy?" In most controversies the substantive issues quickly become muddied with peripheral interrelations and consequences and tangential arguments. Assumptions are treated as facts, hidden agendas remain hidden, the background and history unexplored. Defining and describing the problem in the simplest of terms clarifies the controversy and helps focus on solutions.

Determine the Applicable Regulations, Ordinances, and Procedures

If all other strategies fail to achieve the desired outcome, finding a breach of regulations, ordinances or procedures may produce results. When the project or action is subject to an Environmental Impact Statement, procedure is often the hook on which to base strategy. Historic instances of failure to follow procedures prescribed in the regulations testify to the importance of this step. The Citizens to Preserve Overton Park (Memphis, Tennessee) invoked Section 4(f) of the Department of Transportation Act of 1966 in their classic opposition to construction of a highway through Overton Park. The Environmental Defense Fund—an environmental monitoring group—frequently bases strategy on non-compliance with the requirements of the Environmental Impact Statement (EIS) under the legal umbrella of Section 102 of the National Environmental Policy Act.

Select Strategies to Influence the Decision

Selecting strategy is the heart of preparation. Strategy determines the basis of the appeal to decision-makers (and to the media and public): Shall it be the public interest? What the public wants? Fairness? Legality? Strategy selection synthesizes the information, definition, procedures and data gathered about the problem with both estimates of opposition action and analysis of the decision-makers thinking styles. Strategy considers what the planners think opponents will do and how decision-makers will react. A strategy planning session of a successful interest group resembles a military exercise. "Our side" is posed against "their side"; what "they" will do is weighed against how "we" will counteract it. Possible courses of action are compared. The strategy that will maneuver "our forces" into the most advantageous position to influence the decision is finally selected.

Prepare a FACT SHEET

All the information gathered is culled for a FACT SHEET, focusing on the heart of the problem. The Fact Sheet sifts and condenses essential information, simplifies complex data, provides definitive answers to public concerns and relays the advocacy message to supporters, the public, media, and decision-makers. Fact sheets provide a method for collecting and disseminating information and creating the desired perception. Ranging from one-page summaries to persuasive calls-to-action, the many types of fact sheets are among the most useful tools in preparing for public hearings. (Nine types of fact sheets are described in the chapter on Techniques and Strategies.) Despite the obvious value of fact sheets, major projects involving millions of dollars have bogged down without fact sheets to communicate the meaning of voluminous technical reports. When a fact sheet is provided, decision-makers and media almost invariably read it first.

Plan Tactics to Implement
the Strategy Selected

If strategy is the heart of planning, tactics are its arms and legs propelling the advocacy to the planned outcome. Without tactics to carry out the strategy, little happens. The organized advocacy group provides the troops to carry out the tactics; otherwise planning becomes an ego trip for the leaders rather than an effort for social change. Ex-

perienced groups select tactics that are compatible with the character
and lifestyle of their members.

Manage Media Coverage

Groups that influence public decisions understand how to reach
the public through the media. Effective communication is their most
powerful single weapon. They recognize the role of the media in decision-making and know how to use the media. A skillfully executed
media program arouses public opinion and creates a grass-roots demand for the government action promoted by the advocacy.

Assemble and Train the Hearing Team

There is little happenstance in a carefully orchestrated public hearing: the supporters who present testimony are selected and rehearsed
like the cast in a play. The most articulate experts are recruited and
coached to make readily understandable presentations. Planners assist
supporters in preparing testimony, to assure that all the elements necessary to make the hearing record are included. Allies are located; coalitions formed. The number of speakers necessary to carry out the tactics
is predetermined and the organization network used to procure the
speakers.

Select a Floor Manager for the Hearing

"If you can't locate or cajole someone to be the hearing floor
manager, think twice about using the public hearing to influence the
decision." This is a piece of advice given hearing planners. The hearing floor manager is the conductor of the orchestra, the producer of
the play, the person who puts the act together. Without a director the
act tends to lose its focus, wandering aimlessly. Lacking cohesion, each
participant makes his own statements without regard for other statements made or to come. The outcome of the unorchestrated hearing
then depends on luck rather than planning.

Implement the Plans

The plans are only as good as implementation. The public hearing is the hour of truth. If Sally's little girl comes down with the mumps
and she cannot bring the identifying buttons to the hearing; if the
sparkling testimony is not delivered because the star performer must
work that evening to complete a rush brief; if the weather is too good

or too bad and supporters don't show up; if any contingency intervenes, the planning effort is wasted. Effective advocacy groups implement the plans despite emergencies.

THE SOLITARY ADVOCATE

Some individuals, because they are by nature loners or have difficulty working with others, avoid groups. But by understanding how to work the political system and persisting in their quest they have none the less changed the course of local, state or national history. These solitary folk heroes succeed because they are willing and able to play all the interest group roles themselves, from writing publicity releases, acting as a one-man speaker's bureau, doing the research, evaluating public opinion, selecting strategies and contacting decision-makers. The one-man campaign waged by John Banzhaf III to ban cigarette commercials from broadcasting illustrates how one person can be the equivalent of an entire interest group.

The Challenge: In 1954 the American Cancer Society published a study showing a relationship between cigarette smoking and health. Some time thereafter John F. Banzhaf III, a citizen without political pull or access to the government, decided that broadcasters should not be permitted to run TV and radio commercials advertising cigarettes. He started a one-man campaign to ban cigarette commercials from the air. Using the laws on the books and the media and backed by research and monitoring radio and TV stations, Banzhaf's campaign resulted in the passage of the Public Health Cigarette-Smoking Act. This is how Banzhaf accomplished his mission:

1. He was determined. John Banzhaf did not like cigarette smoking and was willing to fight on his own time and with his own limited funds to point out the dangers as he saw them.

2. He knew how to use the media. When Banzhaf decided to invoke the FCC's "fairness doctrine" to obtain free air time for anti-smoking messages in order to balance the cigarette commercials, he requested equal time from station WCBS-TV, New York. He sent mimeographed releases of his request to newspapers, magazines and the news desks of broadcasters.

3. He contacted decision-makers. Banzhaf petitioned the FCC to intervene and enforce the availability of time for anti-smoking messages. By this time Banzhaf's name was a media word and the FCC paid attention.

4. He was articulate. Persuasive letters, news releases that the media used, reports, and testimony were the foot soldiers in this fight. Banzhaf knew how to put his message across.

5. He was willing to work. Banzhaf, working alone, accomplished the tasks usually undertaken by organized special interest groups: letter writing, telephoning, preparing news stories, contacting the media, appearing at public hearings, speaking to service clubs.

6. He was willing to risk ridicule. Banzhaf expected the airways to deny his anti-smoking time request. He was willing to risk the expected ridicule in order to accomplish his objective.

7. He understood and used regulations. Banzhaf familiarized himself with the "fairness doctrine," station licensing procedures, and other regulations to further his cause. He left nothing to chance.

8. He adopted a strategy. He adopted a Public Interest Strategy, supported by Legal Strategy tactics. Using scientific studies and reports on the hazards of smoking, he devised a convincing case that the public interest demanded anti-cigarette information to be disseminated through anti-smoking commercials.

9. He identified the advocacy. Banzhaf created Action on Smoking and Health (ASH) to legitimize the anti-smoking campaign, gaining credibility and instant identification.

10. He created his own celebrity status. Unknown when he began his crusade, Banzhaf's aggressive media actions quickly made him newsworthy. Banzhaf's persistence and innovativeness intrigued the press and they eagerly reported his activities. By maintaining close contact with the print media he co-opted them as collaborators in his campaign. By the time he finished his crusade, when Banzhaf spoke everybody listened. He served as a one-man public consensus.

Banzhaf was a one-man special interest group who astutely used interest group techniques to successfully promote his views.

4

Public Hearing Techniques and Strategies

As the climax of the process of influencing a public decision, the public hearing is the *coup de grâce,* the finishing stroke that accomplishes the advocacy group's objective. Interest groups with a record of successes in influencing the outcome of public hearings study and define the problem, determine the applicable regulations, devise strategies and tactics, prepare fact sheets, manage media coverage, and orchestrate the hearing. This chapter describes how to plan a public hearing, including those steps listed above. Subsequent chapters describe how to select tactics and manage communications.

STUDYING AND DEFINING THE PROBLEM

Studying and defining the problem involves learning as much about the problem as possible; in other words, doing one's homework.

Why Study and Define the Problem

The more information a group has about a problem, the more power it has in influencing the solution. One cannot but be impressed with the information-gathering efforts of successful advocacy groups. Many conduct their own studies, do their own research, consult their own experts and reach independent conclusions. They use this information to challenge government officials and industry and, having immersed themselves in the problem, advocates get to its heart. The information-gathering includes peripheral data which sometimes is as important in influencing the outcome as the heart of the matter.

Studying the problem helps accomplish these objectives:

— Define the problem in the simplest of terms.
— Identify the best strategy and tactics for the mission.
— Clarify concepts and resolve ambiguities.
— Minimize confusion.
— Put the problem in perspective.
— Discover useful peripheral information.

An example of the value of arming oneself with information is the effort of a group of citizens who wanted to prevent the railroad from abandoning train service to Harlem Valley, New York. Leading the fight was the Harlem Valley Transportation Association (HVTA) which tried to force the railroad to maintain the service. Distributing a monthly newsletter, printing posters and bumper stickers, writing press releases, inducing a well-known writer to publish an article, and appearing at six public hearings helped bring public pressure on the railroad. But what helped resolve the conflict was a piece of obscure information dug out by HVTA: They discovered that the National Environmental Policy Act (NEPA) required an environmental impact statement. Arguing that cessation of railroad service would increase air pollution and create other environmental damage, HVTA obtained a ruling that the Interstate Commerce Commission could not approve abandonment of any rail service unless it proved that this action did not significantly affect the quality of the human environment. HVTA, using peripheral information overlooked by others, successfully challenged government and industry.

Using Information

The information gathered is used to define the problem and set its parameters:

1. *Determining whether the problem is an issue, policy or project:* An *issue* is a point, matter or question to be disputed or decided: Equal rights for women; a code of student conduct; the relationship between the federal government and the states on nuclear energy.

A *policy* is any governing principle, plan or course of action: The United States Department of Justice proposes "Regulations Prohibiting Discrimination on the Basis of Sex" as the *policy* that implements an *issue* which was ruled upon by the United States Supreme Court on the equity of women contributing more to a pension plan than men in equivalent jobs.

A *project* is a proposal of something to be done: a drainage project; construction of a manufacturing facility or condominium; low income housing. Projects subject to public hearings usually involve permits from some governing body.

2. *Defining the problem.* If the problem is an issue or policy, it should be defined in one or two sentences. For example, the policy of "Prohibiting Discrimination on the Basis of Sex" might be summarized as: "The policy prohibiting the use of fringe benefit plans which discriminate in benefits or in employee contributions on the basis of sex."

If the problem is a proposed project, *all* the information about the physical parameters of the project should be recorded including land use, ecosystems, community and regional impacts, socioeconomic impacts. Notations should be made on whether the proposed project affects each impact positively or negatively and verification should be done on all assumptions, maps, drawings and statistics. This mini-Environmental Impact Statement insures against adversaries springing surprises at a public hearing.

3. *Determining the heart of the problem.* The heart of the problem is determined by separating the basic principle of the debate from tangential arguments. When Michigan residents debated whether the University of Michigan should sell its stock in American companies doing business in South Africa, the discussion focused on the morality of apartheid, although the parties agreed that apartheid should be protested. The basic problem of the debate was really how to most effectively protest apartheid.

The campaign in the mid-1960's to preserve the Right to Work Law—the right of an individual to work at a job of his/her choice without being forced to join a union or organization—demonstrates the value of focusing on the heart of the problem. The campaign was waged on the principle of the right to work; pros and cons of labor unions, union leaders, and other organizations were avoided. By focusing on the heart of the problem, the campaign was kept clean and credible.

Hidden agendas often obscure the real issues. Hidden agenda statements mask biases such as benefits for a few versus benefits for many, beauty versus progress, maintaining the exclusivity of an area, or preserving vested interests.

4. *Obtaining as much information on the problem as possible.* Investigating the background and history of the problem discloses

whether the proposition has been discussed previously. Was it turned down? Why? Have conditions changed? Have attitudes changed? Learning as much as possible about the problem provides the data to document a strong case. Digging for information pays: opponents of a proposed road in an old section of a town attempted to delay construction by invoking Section 4 (f) of the Department of Transportation Act, which called for additional public hearings before cutting a road through a park. Proponents of the road did their homework also, discovering that the wooded area the opponents called a park was never designated as one. It was a publicly owned timbered area that had been used for recreation so long residents of that end of town assumed it was a park. Section 4 (f) was not applicable and the construction proceeded on schedule.

5. *Defining the advocacy position.* Stating precisely what position the group advocates prevents misunderstandings. Using the Department of Justice proposed Regulations as an example, the advocacy position might be stated as: "We advocate the policy of prohibiting the use of fringe benefit plans which discriminate on the basis of sex." Or, "We oppose the policy of prohibiting the use of fringe benefit plans on the basis of sex."

Finding the Information

Every citizen has access to information about problems subject to the public hearing process. Mostly, the information is available for the asking:

1. If the public hearing is on proposed legislation, the bill is the best source.

a. A copy is available from the appropriate elected official (United States Representative or Senator, state legislator, local representative). Congressmen and Senators maintain state offices for liaison with constituents.

b. The *Congressional Record* covers floor actions and Extensions of Remarks and lists all actions and remarks both by the name of the member of Congress and by subject. Most reference libraries carry the *Congressional Record*. The *Congressional Quarterly, Inc.* provides summaries of actions.

c. The *Calendar of Federal Regulations* (available from the Superintendent of Documents) includes background on the bill. The *Calendar* contains detailed information on proposed regulations and rules, including the Legal Authority for the rule, Reasons for Including the Entry, Statement of the Problem, Alternatives Under Consideration, Summary of Benefits, Summary of Costs, Related Regulations and Actions, Active Government Collaboration, Timetable for meetings and public hearings, Available Documents, and Agency Contact.

d. Trade, professional or other groups with an interest in the bill willingly provide information. For example, a proposed bill on "Safety and Health Regulations for Work in Confined Spaces in Construction" will be closely followed and commented on by the construction industry, labor unions and many special interest groups.

2. The Environmental Impact Statement contains most of the essential information on the utilization of a natural resource.

a. On a natural resource utilization or any project requiring an Environmental Impact Statement every citizen may request the responsible agency to add his or her name to the list of recipients for comment. The U.S. Department of Interior, the U.S. Department of Agriculture, the Corps of Engineers, the Department of Energy, the Department of Transportation, Housing and Urban Development and other departments concerned with projects that impact the environment prepare Environmental Impact Statements.

b. Documents relating to a specific bill or area of interest are also available from state counterparts of these agencies. For example, an energy conservation advocacy may ask to be included in the state agency list for comment on energy problems.

3. The permit application contains information on a project.

a. On request, copies of the permit application, minutes of meetings, public hearings, and official actions of city or county authorities can be consulted.

b. On projects requiring rezoning or zoning variances the zoning ordinances, comprehensive plans, the site, and neighbors should be consulted.

4. For any public hearing, media reports provide valuable clues.

a. Newspaper stories on the problem are published in the papers that cover the debate. Only local newspapers usually cover local problems, but the radius of media interest depends on which levels of government have designated accountability on the problem. Housing projects, timber cutting, kindergartens, and the construction of beach homes would appear to be strictly local concerns. But if these projects involve federal aid they are subject to federal guidelines. Beach home construction may be regulated by the Coastal Zone Management Act of 1972; federally funded low income housing is subject to the Housing and Community Development Act rules; local timber cutting may be affected by the Resource Conservation and Recovery Act

(RCRA). The dividing line between local, state and federal issues has blurred in recent years. An example is the nuclear-freeze movement—Congress is accountable to the people for national defense, but many cities decided that they too had a role in national defense, generating spirited debate and local resolutions to Congress. On the other hand, many cities assume accountability for constitutional and moral issues, including ordinances on gay rights, repeal of a blue law to permit Sunday sales, permitting topless bars, and legalizing card parlors.

b. Monitoring broadcasts relating to the debate reveals media biases. Videotapes and cassettes provide easy monitoring methods and may be used when convenient.

c. The media version of the problem usually determines the public perception.

APPLICABLE REGULATIONS AND PROCEDURES

Public hearings required by law are subject to regulations and procedures that govern when they are held, the level of government authority involved, how they are conducted, and the type of decision to be reached. Some procedures are flexible; others include minute details.

Why Regulations and Procedures Are Important

Regulations and procedures affect the selection of strategies for the hearing process. An intimate knowledge of the regulations helps the advocacy group control the number, type and outcome of the hearings. Some regulations have broad impact on many activities: The Department of Transportation Act of 1966; The National Environmental Policy Act (NEPA); and the Uniform Public Assembly Act of 1972 belong in the library of every advocacy group. State and local Administrative Procedures Acts determine the ground rules of public hearings. The laws are so complex, and the turnover in decision-makers and staff so frequent that no advocacy group can safely assume that the government automatically follows the correct procedures. Doing one's homework on regulations pays.

The question of whether public hearings are required is often a pivotal decision in a controversy. The "don't rock the boat" policy of some governments and organizations leads to attempts to skip holding public hearings, in the hope that a low profile will enable a proposal to slip through without arousing public interest. The long fight to prevent Interstate Highway 40 from going through Overton Park in Memphis, Tennessee is an example of citizen vigilance on regulations that forced the government to hold public hearings. The advocacy group, Citizens to Preserve Overton Park, Inc., used the provisions in Section 4 (f) of the Transportation Act to obtain reconsideration of the planned Highway.

> Section 4 (f) states, in part: "It is hereby declared to be the National policy that special effort should be made to preserve the natural beauty of the countryside and public park and recreation lands. . . The Secretary (of Transportation) shall not approve any program or project which requires the use of any publicly owned land from a public park. . .unless (1) there is no feasible and prudent alternative to the use of such land and (2) such program includes all possible planning to minimize harm to such park. . . ."

Regulations of the Department of Transportation Act require a highway "corridor" hearing and a highway "decision" hearing. The Citizens to Preserve Overton Park, Inc. argued that the Tennessee Highway Department had not complied with the public hearing regulations of Section 4 (f). The long struggle to preserve Overton Park was possible only because the group investigated and used the regulations.

Using Regulations and Procedures in the Public Hearing Process

Familiarity with regulations and procedures is useful in selecting strategies and in protecting a decision if it favors the advocacy, or in upsetting a decision, if the decision is not in the advocacy's interest.

Selecting Strategies

a. When the strategy is based on non-compliance with regulations: As noted in the fight to preserve Overton Park, federally-funded road projects demonstrate how regulations affect strategy selection. Subject to regulations of the Department of Transportation Act of 1966 (the Federal Aid Highway Act of 1956), roads come under the jurisdiction of the Federal Highway Administrator, the State Department of Transportation, the State Highway Department, and the local Public Works or Roads Departments. The Bureau of Outdoor Recreation of the Department of the Interior, the State Tourist Bureau and other regulatory agencies may also be involved. Regulations on federally funded road-through-park decisions require two public hearings. If any of the hearing steps are skipped or any of the accountable agencies do not participate, non-compliance with regulatory provisions may be charged. Non-compliance provides the basis for selecting a strategy termed the Legal Theory Strategy (one of the six strategies described later in this chapter).

Non-compliance with the provisions of the National Environmental Policy Act (NEPA), requiring federal agencies and industries to prepare Environmental Impact Statements (EIS) before undertaking any action significantly affecting the quality of the human environment, is a frequently used basis for the Legal Theory Strategy. Environmental Impact Statements must be opened for public comments. When an agency decides an EIS is not needed, the review of a decision not to prepare an EIS also requires public hearings. The conduct of the EIS and the adequacy of the EIS constitute the basis for opposition to projects, and utlimately, for litigation.

The Environmental Defense Fund uses the Environmental Impact Statement requirement that federal agencies must prove that any planned action is ecologically sound as the basis for numerous landmark Environmental Defense Fund cases. These include action to require environmental impact statements prior to constructing a highway (Century Freeway in L.A.) and intervention in strip mining because no impact statement was prepared (Kasanke Sand Corp.).

Non-compliance may also include regulations indirectly related to the problem. *The Calendar of Federal Regulations* includes related regulations: a proposed bill on "Safety and Health Regulations for Work in Confined Spaces" cites pertinent paragraph numbers of regulations related to the proposed bill.

b. When the strategy is based on non-compliance with procedures: Federal and state executive orders, the Freedom of Information Act, the government in the Sunshine Act, anti-secrecy laws, conflict-of-interest policies, and open-meeting laws specify notice, times and locations of public hearings. Non-compliance with the provisions of these regulations indicates selection of the Legal Theory Strategy.

Hearing procedures are often specified in considerable detail, as shown in Figure 4–1. A useful procedure is to outline the provisions of the act that applies to the specific public hearing. Using the outline as a checklist, compliance with each requirement is marked off. Im-

Figure 4-1

**The Coastal Zone Management Program
An Example of Detailed Federal Procedures
on Public Hearings**

The nature of the Coastal Zone Management Program involves the resolution of conflicting interests. Public hearings are designated to disclose public needs and aspirations. Preparation for and conduct of public hearings are specified as follows:

1. Hearings must provide at least 30 days of public notice.
2. Notice must be of a "press release" type as well as meeting legal notice requirments.
3. The agenda, data, and other documents must be available for public review in the locale of the hearing.
4. The Secretary (of Commerce) will not approve any plan unless he has determined that sufficient hearings are held with a full and effective opportunity for public involvement in every portion of the plan.
5. Hearings must be held in the geographic areas affected.
6. Hearings must be held at times convenient for affected parties (i.e. summers for tourists using beach areas).
7. Summaries of the hearings must be prepared and made available to the public within 30 days of their conclusion.

proper adherence to procedures may be due to the level of government. At times several regulations and procedures may apply to a hearing.

Federal grant programs require public hearings to be conducted on a state or local level. For example, the Appalachian Health Program is required to assure participation in the state and regional planning process by the affected public. In addition to the hearings, the state must assure early public notice and availability of draft plans and programs. All of this is provided for by several different regulations.

Cities and counties use public hearings in applying for and administering federal grants. More than 90 percent of cities and almost 90 percent of counties have used public hearings in Community Development Block Grants. Over half of the cities and counties use public hearings in water and sewer, housing. transportation, 701 planning, and health grants. Some federal grants require that certain interests— parents, the poor, racial and ethnic minorities, local governments, economic interests, community-based organizations, consumers or other stakeholders—participate in grant decisions. If the legislation designates that certain "interests" participate in the planning or administration of a grant and these interests are notably absent from public hearings, the validity of the decision may be questioned.

State and local budgets are usually subject to public hearings, although the laws vary significantly from state to state. At least 15 states require both publication of the budget and public hearings. About a dozen states require municipalities or counties to publish the budgets and hold hearings. (State requirements on public hearings are contained in the "Memorandum to House Intergovernmental Relations Subcommittee," by Congressional Research Service, Library of Congress, Washington, D.C., December 30, 1975, pp.1–2.)

Forty-eight of the states and the District of Columbia have Administrative Procedures Acts. Of these, 42 states and the District of Columbia provide an opportunity to present their comments in written or oral form. Twenty-six states codify their administrative rules and regulations.

Each federal agency publishes its own administrative procedure rules. The *Code of Federal Regulations* from the Superintendent of Documents in Washington, D.C. contains a codification of official documents. The Superintendent also publishes a two-volume research guide titled *List of CFR Sections Affected*. The Code of Federal Regulations divides into Titles: for instance, Title 43 of the Office of the Secretary of Interior pertains to Regulations Relating to Public Lands. A section of Title 43 details Department of Interior Hearings and Appeals Procedures.

The Advisory Commission on Intergovernmental Affairs 1979 publication, "Citizen Participation in the American Federal System" (for sale by the Superintendent of Documents) includes tables, charts, lists and information on regulations and procedures of states, localities and the federal government.

Permit Regulations

Public hearings must be held before granting permits in many physical developments. As environmental regulations in federal, state and local governments multiplied in the 1970's and 80's, industrial developers faced the increasing burdens of confusing, duplicative requirements and delays in obtaining permit approvals. A few states have initiated changes to streamline, simplify and coordinate state and federal environmental programs by holding joint hearings in which one or more permitting authorities participate. Several states, including Washington and Maryland, allow applicants to request joint hearings. Further information on regulations and administrative procedures that may affect public hearing strategy in environmental matters is available from the U.S. Environmental Protection Agency, Office of Policy and Resource Management. Some insight into the comment procedures and statutes of the Environmental Protection Agency permitting process are included in Figure 4–2.

Figure 4–2

Environmental Protection Agency Public Hearings

The Environmental Protection Agency (EPA), perhaps more than any other agency, touches every facet of life. Most manufacturers of chemicals, foods, or other products go through EPA administrative rule making or permitting hearings.

The statutes that grant most of the EPA decision-making authority are:

- The Clean Air Amendments of 1970 and subsequent amendments.
- The Water Pollution Control Act Amendments of 1972, and subsequent amendments.

Figure 4-2 (continued)

- The Federal Environmental Pesticide Control act of 1972 and subsequent amendments.
- Resource Conservation and Recovery Act of 1976 and subsequent amendments.
- Safe Drinking Water Act of 1974.
- Toxic Substances Control Act of 1976 and subsequent amendments

Under the federal Administrative Procedures Act (APA), the EPA has five comment procedures roughly catalogued as:

1. Informal Notice-and-Comment Rule Making.
2. Notice-and-Comment Rule Making with a public hearing (but not with cross-examination).
3. Rule Making on a Trial-Type Hearing Record.
4. Procedures classified as "an opportunity for written and oral presentations of data, views, and arguments."
5. Adjudication on a Trial-Type Hearing Record.

The EPA is also a party in hearings in the administration of acts such as the Federal Insecticide, Fungicide and Rodenticide Act (FIFRA), which provides that all pesticides used in the United States be registered with the EPA. If the EPA finds that, for instance, a pesticide presents the possibility of unreasonable risk to man or the environment it invokes the Rebuttable Presumption Against Registration (RPAR), now known as Special Review. In any controverted registration, formal administrative hearings are conducted by an Administrative Law Judge (ALJ). These hearings are adversary proceedings, very much like a trial before a court of law. Opposing attorneys cross examine and a record is compiled on which the ALJ must rely in preparing his decision. Despite the formality and technical nature of these hearings, FIFRA hearings are often media events.

Information on public hearing requirements of the permitting process in individual states may be obtained from the department responsible for environmental conservation, natural resources, environmental protection, energy, or other resource. Several states have permit coordinators.

Most states publish administrative rules including sections on

General Rules of Practice, Rules of Procedure Governing "On the Record" Rulemaking Hearings, Specific Procedures, information to be furnished in Applications for Permits, and Specific Standards for permits under the jurisdiction of the agency. Local jurisdictions prepare written procedures on permit requirements, ordinances, appeals, and other requests subject to public hearings. Some planning commissions provide citizen guidance for zone changes.

Hearing Conduct

A regulation occasionally applied to determining public hearing strategy is the Uniform Public Assembly Act of 1972. This Act "facilitates and protects the holding of public assemblies . . . subject only to restrictions . . . as are appropriate to safeguard the civil liberties of nonparticipants." The Act "attempts to maximize the possibilities that discussions and negotiations will occur between sponsors and governmental authorities with successful results." The Uniform Public Assembly Act provides the leverage for groups to claim that they were denied the opportunity to testify at a public hearing.

THE PUBLIC HEARING STRATEGY

The strategy is the road map for the public hearing, bringing together the information gathered about the problem and the pertinent regulations and procedures to craft a plan for accomplishing the advocacy objective. Success in influencing a public decision depends on selecting the strategy responsive to the problem, the decision-makers, the public perception of the problem, and the character of both supporters and opponents.

Why Determine Strategy?

Determining strategy imposes a discipline on the planners. Strategy planning forces advocates to take the time to think through how to influence the outcome. Otherwise, an advocacy group plunges into the fray without asking why its advocacy should be supported by decision-makers and what values are at the heart of the problem.

Participating in a controversy without a basic strategy decision is a common failing of inexperienced advocacy groups, accounting perhaps for industry's dismal record in using the public hearing process. The following two examples are illustrative:

For many years, farmers who grow grass seed have been burning the field stubble after harvesting, blanketing the skies with dense smoke. Although nearby residents grumbled at the field burning, it was not until the environmental movement encouraged citizens to act rather than complain that the grass seed growers found themselves facing proposed legislation on field burning. The proposed regulations threatened to reduce the growers' profit margins, driving some out of business. The campaign to stop field burning was based on residents being unfairly burdened with respiratory problems. Grass growers, however, focused on high costs of alternative field treatments, failing to devise a strategy responsive to the community health problems. The grass growers learned, to their dismay, that business profits are no match for allegations of unfair treatment of the public.

A similar example of failure to select a responsive strategy was an industry group faced with an RPAR of a chemical used in processing. An RPAR is the Rebuttable Presumption Against Registration of a substance, issued by the United States Environmental Protection Agency (EPA) when it determines that sufficient risk exists to warrant a review of the risks versus benefits. The EPA evaluation proposed changes in the use of the chemical. The changes, if effected, would have eliminated over half the market for the end product and abolished almost 20,000 jobs throughout the country. The industry group undertook a campaign of lobbying, preparing rebuttals, organizing a grass-roots effort, and counter proposals. But the campaign concentrated on the tactics without selecting a basic strategy failing, therefore, to respond to the health factors that prompted the decision. Again, industry profit dollars lost to a public health problem.

How to Select the Public Hearing Strategy

Selection of a strategy is a *responsive* and *directive* action. *Responsive action* is selection of a strategy that responds to the influences on the outcome, namely:

1. The nature of the problem
2. The decision-makers—their authority, thinking styles and voting records
3. The public perception of the problem
4. The opponents and supporters of the proposed solution
5. The media perception of the problem

Each of these factors affects strategy selection:

The Nature of the Problem

The problems discussed in increasing telephone rates differ from the problems discussed in a public hearing on closing a school for the blind; a public hearing on timber harvesting in wilderness areas of national forests differs from a request to change a local zone. Most public hearing discussions fall into one of six types of problems:

a. What the public wants
b. The public interest
c. Proper procedure
d. Equitable treatment for all citizens
e. Making wise decisions
f. Finding a compromise solution

Each problem suggests a strategy. The six strategies identified for these problems are:

a. The Public Consensus Strategy
b. The Public Interest Strategy
c. The Legal Theory Strategy
d. The Fairness Strategy
e. The Mistake Strategy
f. The Mitigation Strategy

How these strategies are used and the advantages and disadvantages of each are discussed later in this chapter.

The Decision-makers

The authority of the decision-makers to solve the problem affects strategy selection. A hearing on constructing a local road is not the appropriate forum for discussing the legality of the state highway tax. The state tax is outside the authority of local officials. Nor does the State Highway Department have jurisdiction over the city income tax. If the strategy selected is not appropriate for the authority the five minutes allotted for testimony is wasted.

Local, state or federal officials can be consulted for the scope of the authority holding the hearing, although political entrepreneurs without authority to make a decision may schedule public hearings as an opportunity for a media statement. The Town Hall hearings on the Nuclear Freeze conducted by local authorities in the 1980's were outside the scope of local government but did make a media statement.

The "thinking styles" of decision-makers also affects strategy selection. Behavior experts have identified five thinking styles: Analyst, Realist, Idealist, Pragmatist, and Synthesist.

Analysts are usually straight-line thinkers interested in the best way to solve the problem; *Realists* are fact-oriented; *Idealists* value sincerity and are less inclined to cost/benefit considerations; and *Pragmatists* prefer to get on with the job. If the majority of decision-makers have been identified as Idealists, the Mistake Strategy may be less effective than the Public Interest Strategy. A Pragmatist majority might be open to the Mitigation Strategy. It should be emphasized that the thinking styles of decision-makers is only one of the considerations in strategy selection. It is difficult to assess thinking styles and different situations do push individuals into different styles of thinking. Consider a public hearing on a local problem. When the hearing opens at 7:00 P.M. the Idealist may respond in his habitual idealistic pattern. By 9:00 P.M., his thinking process may alter to a realist's interest in the facts. When the hour of 11:00 P.M. approaches he may be thinking like an impatient pragmatist, "Let's get on with it." The five Thinking Styles are described further in Figure 4–3.

The voting record of decision-makers also affects strategy selection. The voting record of many decision-makers may predict future votes. For this reason, many organizations "rate" the votes of Congress and legislatures, scoring each congressman and legislator. Decision-makers are considered liberal or conservative, friendly or unfriendly by the rating organization. Many political observers are convinced that decision-makers vote in a fixed pattern. Based on this conviction, Political Action Committees (PACS) expend their energy and money attempting to elect the "right" persons—that is, persons who are likely to favor a particular outcome. PACS such as Americans for Constitutional Action (ACA), Americans for Democratic Action (ADA), AFL-CIO Committee of Political Education (COPE), American Conservative Union (ACU), U.S. Chamber of Commerce, Trade and Professional Associations, and special interest groups, all publish vote ratings of public officials.

Public Perception of the Problem

How the public perceives the problem—a reflection of the media perception—affects strategy selection. If the public has become convinced that its health and safety are at risk, as in nuclear energy and hazardous waste disposal, a strategy that evokes considerations of equal emotional value (i.e. the Fairness Strategy) is called for. The public

Figure 4–3

Thinking Styles

Robert Bramson and his associates have identified five major styles of thinking:[1]

1. The Synthesist approach
2. The Idealist approach
3. The Pragmatic approach
4. The Analytical approach
5. The Realist approach

To influence decision-makers keep in mind these characteristics:

1. *The Synthesist:* For a synthesist to agree on any subject he must first find the basic value or essence of the issues. He makes inferences from the data presented. Synthesists are debators, who enjoy the fun of arguing. They try to understand different perspectives, sometimes becoming argumentative and disruptive, curious and restless. They appear devious but are anxious to be thought competent and to be admired. The Synthesist may ask abrasive questions at a public hearing. "Let me play the Devil's Advocate," he challenges. Or, "what you really mean is. . . ."

2. *The Idealist:* Idealists gravitate to commissions and unpaid political appointed or elected positions. Idealists believe in goals and higher values; they insist on high standards. They demand much of themselves and others. They search for the agreement that will bring together differing views and win universal support.

Idealists genuinely want to be helpful to others, but need to be appreciated and trusted. They respond to emotional appeals. They are concerned about how people feel. The Idealist may believe that to consider sources of funding in a decision is hard-hearted; that human needs are most important. Though receptive to differing views, idealists resist compromising their high standards.

3. *The Pragmatist:* The Pragmatist impatiently drums his fingers on the table, or fidgets when someone presents a com-

Figure 4-3 (continued)

plex analysis or theorizes on the consequences of the decision. He prefers to skip the details, to get something done, to get on with the job. Pragmatists are not method-oriented or bound by theories but are optimistic about being innovative and willing to compromise if "we can just get on with it." The Pragmatist may irritably state "get to the point" at a hearing. He has little tolerance for the long-winded.

4. *The Analyst:* Analysts are logical, analytical, and look for the best way to solve a problem. They relish detail and orderly, rational thinking. They place their confidence in careful, methodical presentations. Analysts frequently find other people illogical or, at least, not as logical as they are. They have difficulty understanding Idealists, Synthesists, and Pragmatists. The Analyst may interrupt impatiently when an end-run is attempted with "What's that got to do with the issue?"

5. *The Realist:* Realists are result-oriented. Skip the compromise, analysis, idealism, and far-out ideas of the Synthesists. Consider only the facts. Realists have little patience for the 50 page report. Give them a concise summary. Because they are forceful and hard-driving, Realists sometimes intimidate other decision-makers. Therefore, if a presentation convinces the Realist, he may help persuade others. "A fact is a fact," the Realist states authoritatively, "any intelligent person can see that."

---

[1]Robert M. Bramson, *Coping With Difficult People* (Garden City, New York: Anchor Press/Doubleday, 1981), pp. 185–191.

perception based on misinformation demands a strategy that corrects the misinformation (i.e. the Mistake Strategy).

One of the methods for determining public perception is the *Public Acceptance Assessment*—a ten-step process for identifying public perceptions that may influence groups or individuals to aggressively attempt to affect the decision on a project or program. The Public Acceptance Assessment identifies not only the perceptions but the actions that respond to the perceptions. The Public Acceptance Assessment also predicts the probability of public reaction to the proposal. The first seven steps identify the perceptions and the interested publics; the eighth step examines the causes of these perceptions and evaluates which perceived impacts can be altered or mitigated before public concern polarizes. The ninth step predicts the probability of public action on the project with and without mitigation efforts. The tenth step concludes with recommendations for proposal alterations including financial and time trade-offs. Figure 4–4 summarizes the ten steps in conducting a Public Acceptance Assessment.

Figure 4-4

Ten Steps in Conducting a Public Acceptance Assessment*

The Mater Public Acceptance Assessment evaluates the probability of public acceptance of a project or program. It is based on how the public perceives the facts, discerning areas of potential public controversy before the public is aware of specific concerns. Used in the planning phase, it is a tool to minimize conflicts, assist in timely implementation, decrease the cost of implementation of projects, and earn public acceptance.

Step 1. Describe the project or program. Use the Environmental Impact Statement or a description checklist.

Step 2. Determine the impacts of the project on the public. Use the Environmental Impact Statement or Checklist in Step 1.

Step 3. Determine which publics care about the impacts. Which segments of the public believe they will be affected by the project?

Step 4. Find out how the public perceives these impacts. What do they think will happen?

Step 5. Find out why they care. Do they hold certain values, beliefs and attitudes?

Step 6. Evaluate how much they care. Do they care enough to take some action?

Step 7. Analyze whether those who care have sufficient influence to affect the outcome. Are they leaders or are they persons with little credibility?

Figure 4-4 (continued)

> *Step 8.* Decide which impacts can be altered. Can the perceived negative impacts be mitigated to accommodate public concerns?
>
> *Step 9.* Predict the probability of public action on the project. Using the checklists, obtain a quantitative estimate of the probability.
>
> *Step 10.* Draw conclusions and make decisions on proceeding with the project. Compare the costs of mitigating adverse perceptions to the cost of handling public opposition.
>
> Each step involves using pre-printed checklists. The checklists quantify the evaluations.
>
> _____
>
> *Jean Mater, *Citizens Involved: Handle With Care!* (Timber Press, P.O. Box 92, Forest Grove, Oregon 97116.) Pre-printed checklists available.

When conducted in the early planning stage of any proposal, the Public Acceptance Assessment reveals obstacles to approval and indicates the strategy that might overcome those obstacles.

The Character of Supporters and Opponents

The six strategies may be executed in a variety of styles ranging from low-key to aggressive, imaginative actions. For example, the Fairness Strategy may be demonstrated by communication techniques and testifying at the hearing, or by using vigorous activist styles that demand considerable energy and risk from supporters. An advocacy group consisting of businessmen and professionals is usually more comfortable with the Public Consensus Strategy or the Legal Strategy than with the Fairness Strategy. However, these strategies may be less effective if opponents use the Activist Styles as described at the end of this chapter. (How to handle activist tactics used by opponents is covered in the chapter on Tactics.)

The Media Perception of the Problem

The media's perception of the problem markedly influences strategy selection. If the press or a broadcaster becomes an advocate, however subtly, of one side or another, the strategy selected must consider the media position.

The public perception created by the media weighs heavily in strategy selection. Local media can define the scope of the strategy by the issues featured and by selecting the headline to reinforce the perception. Typical of media influence is the case history of prolonged neighborhood opposition to permitting a concrete plant to locate in its environs. Although the noise level, aesthetic considerations, traffic hazards, and economic viability were the major issues brought up in the first public hearing, the local media selected the question of how much water the plant would require as its feature. The city, county, concrete manufacturer, and a reputable engineering firm presented documentation that 5000 gallons of water would be required each day from a holding pond. One neighbor, however, claimed that on the basis of his twenty-year experience in the area, the plant would use 50,000 gallons every day. As a result the wells in the area would be depleted, and the drinking water would become salty.

Although he used no statistics, engineering studies, or other data to corroborate his contention, the next afternoon the local newspaper headlined the report of the hearing: *Concrete Plant to Make Water Salty.* The lead paragraph began: "Do you want your water to taste salty? That's what John Smith warned the County Supervisors would happen if they issued a permit to the proposed XYZ plant." (Names changed) As a result of the local press selection, salty water became the focus for the Mistake Strategy used by the opposition.

SIX BASIC STRATEGIES

Each of the six basic strategies—The Public Consensus Strategy, The Public Interest Strategy, The Legal Theory Strategy, The Fairness Strategy, The Mistake Strategy, and the Mitigation Strategy—has advantages and disadvantages and a menu of tactics for implementation. The strategies are described in this chapter and the tactics for each strategy are discussed in the next chapter.

The Public Consensus Strategy

This strategy is based on the premise that public officials prefer to act in concert with their constituents. Essentially a political strategy, the Public Consensus Strategy demonstrates which action constituents strongly urge and is a key element in public hearings gamesmanship.

Used when no clear "right" or "wrong" action has emerged, the Public Consensus Strategy defines the correct decision in terms of numbers. Phrases that characterize this strategy are: "The citizens demand," "The public believes," and "The voters urge." Large numbers of persons testifying, petitions, marches and other evidence of mass support demonstrate the demands, beliefs, and urgings. The Public Consensus Strategy has been utilized to introduce and obtain passage of innovative regulations, to site (or prevent the siting of) manufacturing facilities, and to introduce new policies.

The ordinance passed in 1971 by the city of Bowie, Maryland (one of the largest cities in Maryland) to ban throwaway cans and bottles illustrates the power of the Public Consensus Strategy. Bowie teacher Ellis L. Yochelson believed that throwaway cans and bottles were degrading the landscape and abetting a throwaway economy. Utilizing Public Consensus Strategy tactics—a communications campaign, petitions, forming a network, massing supporters at the public hearings—Yochelson orchestrated so impressive a demonstration of public consensus that he succeeded in getting the ordinance passed despite well-funded opposition.

The disadvantage of the Public Consensus Strategy is the need for superior leadership and organization to marshal a large number of volunteers. The advantage of this strategy is that it usually accomplishes what it sets out to do. So effective is the Public Consensus Strategy that it is frequently used in combination with other strategies.

The Public Interest Strategy

This strategy is based on establishing that the outcome advocated is in the public interest (which is considered good), as distinguished from private interests (which are considered bad). The Public Interest is often defined by narrow special interests who successfully assert that they are acting for the public good: Ralph Nader's political cadres are the self-proclaimed definers of consumer public interests. The Environmental Movement declared that protection of endangered species was in the public interest although most Americans had never heard of the various species in question.

The Public Interest Strategy is used for environmental, health, safety and natural resources. Phrases common in the Public Interest Strategy are "Pitting short-term profits against long-term preservation," "Economic versus ecological values," and "Exploitation versus Conservation."

The landmark legislation of the 1960's, 70's and 80's broadened the concept of the public interest. It is now in the public interest to protect wilderness (The Endangered American Wilderness Act of 1978), Endangered Species (The Endangered Species Act of 1973), Hearing (The Noise Control Act of 1974), Rivers (The Wild and Scenic Rivers Act of 1968), Artifacts (The Archaeological and Historic Data Conservation Act of 1974), and other facets of health, safety, scenery and history.

An example of the Public Interest Strategy is the fight to preserve the wilderness area of Big Thicket, Texas—300,000 acres called the "biological crossroads of North America" because of its diversity of climatic zones, plants, birds, alligators and rare species. In the 1960's, Conservationists decided that the lumber companies were exploiting—an operational word in the Public Interest Strategy—a unique and irreplaceable resource. On the premise that the area represented a public good that belonged to the people and that its environmental qualities were "public goods," the Big Thicket Coordinating Committee, the Big Thicket Association, and more than forty citizens' groups formed a coalition to preserve the Big Thicket from economic development. Utilizing Public Interest tactics to persuade officials to subordinate the economics of local employment to the new economics of the public interest, the citizens' groups promoted legislative action to transform the area into a national park.

The disadvantage of the Public Interest Strategy is the difficulty of identifying the public interest of a proposal. The concept of public interest and public good is tentative and often tenuous, changing from era to era. The advantage of the Public Interest Strategy is its attraction for public officials, the media, and the public. The Public Interest Strategy works well in combination with the Public Consensus Strategy, the Legal Theory Strategy and often with the Fairness Strategy.

How the Public Consensus Strategy has been used to oppose the Public Interest Strategy is shown in Anatomy of an Environmental vs. Business Conflict, Figure 4-5.

The Legal Theory Strategy

This probes for non-compliance of regulations or procedures. It requires familiarity with regulations and frequently demands the services of a qualified attorney. The implied threat of litigation underlines the Legal Theory Strategy. Claims of improper notice, inade-

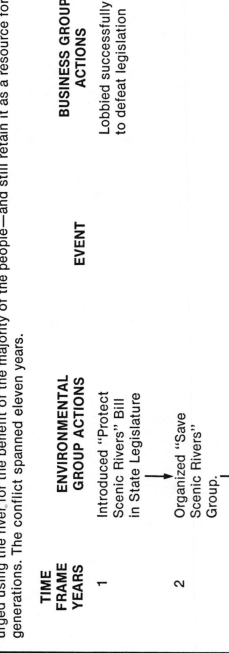

Figure 4-5

Anatomy of an Environmental vs. Business Conflict

This anatomy is based on a conflict about a Scenic River Basin in a southeastern state. The local environmental groups fought to preserve the river solely for the enjoyment of its natural beauty. Local businessmen urged using the river for the benefit of the majority of the people—and still retain it as a resource for future generations. The conflict spanned eleven years.

TIME FRAME YEARS	ENVIRONMENTAL GROUP ACTIONS	EVENT	BUSINESS GROUP ACTIONS
1	Introduced "Protect Scenic Rivers" Bill in State Legislature		Lobbied successfully to defeat legislation
2	Organized "Save Scenic Rivers" Group.		

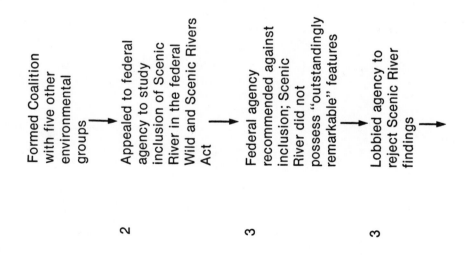

Formed Coalition with five other environmental groups

2

Appealed to federal agency to study inclusion of Scenic River in the federal Wild and Scenic Rivers Act

3

Federal agency recommended against inclusion; Scenic River did not possess "outstandingly remarkable" features

3

Lobbied agency to reject Scenic River findings

Figure 4-5 (continued)

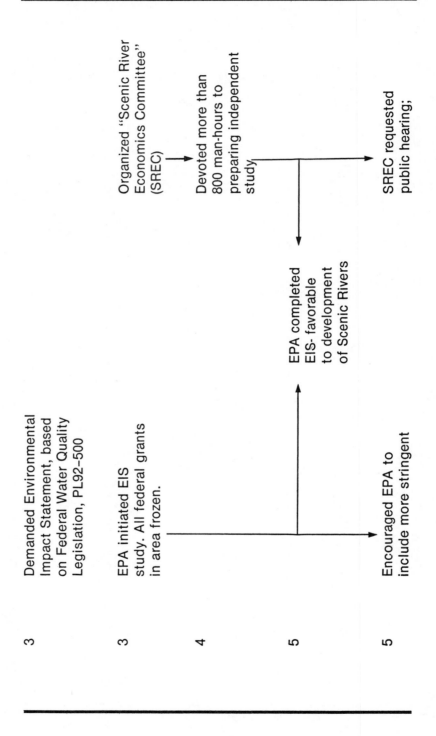

3   Demanded Environmental Impact Statement, based on Federal Water Quality Legislation, PL92–500

3   EPA initiated EIS study. All federal grants in area frozen.

        Organized "Scenic River Economics Committee" (SREC)

        Devoted more than 800 man-hours to preparing independent study

4   EPA completed EIS- favorable to development of Scenic Rivers

5   Encouraged EPA to include more stringent

5   SREC requested public hearing;

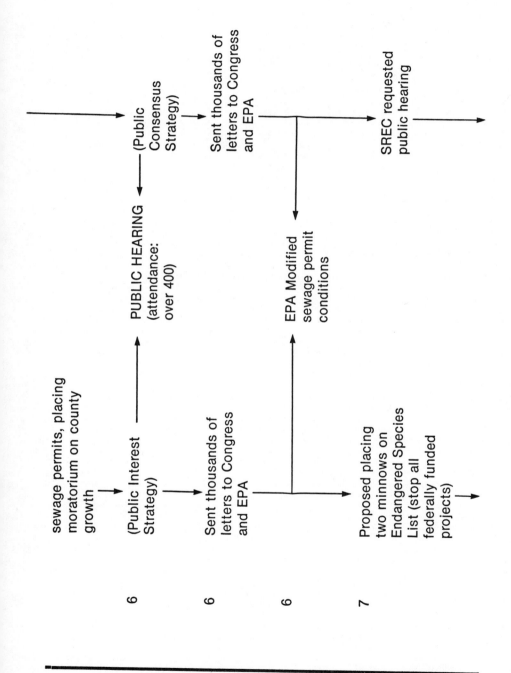

6　sewage permits, placing moratorium on county growth

6　(Public Interest Strategy) → PUBLIC HEARING (attendance: over 400) → (Public Consensus Strategy)

6　Sent thousands of letters to Congress and EPA → Sent thousands of letters to Congress and EPA

6　EPA Modified sewage permit conditions

7　Proposed placing two minnows on Endangered Species List (stop all federally funded projects)

SREC requested public hearing

Figure 4-5 (continued)

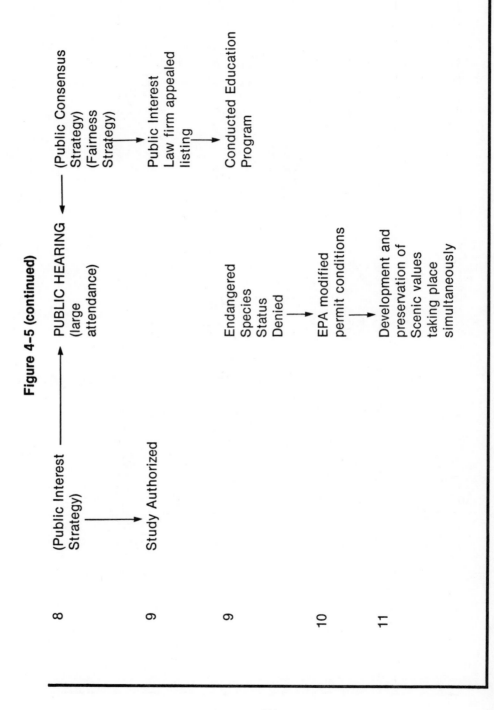

8   (Public Interest Strategy) ⟶ PUBLIC HEARING (large attendance) ⟶ (Public Consensus Strategy) (Fairness Strategy)

9   Study Authorized

9   Endangered Species Status Denied

10   EPA modified permit conditions

11   Development and preservation of Scenic values taking place simultaneously

Public Interest Law firm appealed listing ⟶ Conducted Education Program quate opportunity to be heard, lack of a quorum, inappropriate action of a chairman are typical of those that serve the Legal Theory Strategy.

The Legal Theory Strategy is effective in land use conflicts, in controversies where the Public Consensus, the Public Interest and the Fairness Strategies do not appear to have sufficient clout, and in the permit process. When the Legal Theory Strategy is utilized references to "Section 5, part 1" or "Section 4 (f)," or "Inadequate EIS" or similar code phrases signal the specific basis for questioning the legality of an action or policy.

Anti-nuclear activists have used the Legal Theory Strategy as a fall back strategy to oppose construction of new nuclear energy plants. Residents of the state of Washington paid for both a legal challenge and the defense of a voter-approved measure aimed at controlling nuclear plant spending. Expenses for the lawsuit challenging the measure, known as Initiative 394, were passed on to utilities and ratepayers. Expenses for defending the initiative were assumed by the state and also passed on to state taxpayers.

The Harrisburg (Pennsylvania) citizens' group, People Against Nuclear Energy (PANE) which opposed future operation of the Three-Mile Island nuclear reactor, used the Legal Theory Strategy in its attempt to force the Nuclear Regulatory Commission to consider the impact on the mental health of nearby residents before permitting the Three-Mile Island reactor to resume operation.

The advantage of the Legal Theory Strategy is its relative independence from public consensus, depending instead on narrowing the window through which the fate of the issue, policy, or project is determined. Disadvantages of the Legal Theory Strategy are cost, which may run into hundreds of thousands of dollars, and the need for making the record during the public hearing. In many tightly orchestrated "showcase" hearings, the written and oral testimony are entered into the record with the expectation that the final decision will be made by the Courts and not by the hearing officials.

The Fairness Strategy

This strategy plays upon the basic human desire of public officials to make a fair decision, or at least one that is perceived as fair. The Fairness Strategy aims to persuade decision-makers that the only fair outcome is the one that favors a particular group. The Fairness Strategy often is a win/lose game. Words common in the Fairness Strategy are "equity," "discrimination," "abuse," "elitism," "egalitarian," "powerless" and other connotations of adversarial rela-tionships.

Fair share groups, community organizers, poor people's move-ments, "rights" groups (women's rights, rights of the handicapped, the elderly, the disadvantaged), student groups, collaborative action groups, and neighborhoods all use the Fairness Strategy. Based on political equity, the Fairness Strategy is widely used in public hear-ings for federal grant programs, e.g. the Community Health Center Programs, Title XX of the Social Security Act, the Community De-velopment Block Grants. Utility rate hearings, special tax hearings, and any legislation affecting a particular segment of the population are major subjects for the Fairness Strategy.

The Fairness Strategy was used in a well-organized campaign to develop support for rent control at the neighborhood level in a Cali-fornia city. To bolster their contention that large corporations and private enterprise had failed to serve the public fairly and that govern-ment should intervene to achieve a more equitable solution, a coali-tion of renters and senior citizens fought the environmental groups whose previous slow-growth policies had prevented apartment con-struction. The public hearings, punctured with cries of "unfair," re-sulted in restrictive rent control legislation.

Disadvantages of the Fairness Strategy are the community polarization often resulting from this strategy and the subjectivity of the meaning of fair. Advantages of the Fairness Strategy are the im-plications that the decision-makers are playing according to the rules and will make a just, honest, impartial, and unprejudiced decision. Fairness is an attribute to which everyone aspires.

The Mistake Strategy

This depends on prophesizing dire results as a consequence of the decision. It warns public officials that they are making an unfor-givable error if they favor or deny a particular outcome. The Mistake Strategy often is called upon when Public Consensus, Public Inter-est, and Fairness do not appear to be working. The mistake may be overt or covert. Opponents of changing a zone from residential to light industrial, after failing to establish that the zone change is against the public interest, is unpopular, or unfair, may—as a last resort—main-tain that officials are making an error if they interpret the definition of a light industrial zone to include a specific manufacturing plant.

The Mistake Strategy attempts to persuade public officials that a particular decision will be a gross mistake. Conflicts in the Mistake Strategy are sharply defined. Decision-makers are urged to sacrifice one perceived need for another. The Mistake Strategy can be identified by phrases such as "conventional assumptions," "cost/benefits," "scenarios," "zero-risk," "worst case assumptions," and "psychological reaction."

An example of the Mistake Strategy was the successful campaign of 1968 to 1971 against federal support of the supersonic transport program (SST). Following a ten-year period of substantial federal funding of the SST, popular views about the benefits and costs to society of the SST underwent a change so dramatic that Congress reversed its commitment. The change was skillfully orchestrated by the Citizens' League Against the Sonic Boom (CLASB), organized by William A. Shurcliff in 1967. Aided by the Sierra Club and the Coalition Against the SST, CLASB encouraged citizens to question the conventional assumptions regarding economic growth and progress. Using estimates of massive prospective population disturbance and enormous potential damage to buildings should the SST be deployed, CLASB funded an extensive media campaign to persuade the public and its officials that the SST would be a colossal mistake. Although a team of scientists appointed by then Secretary of Interior Stewart Udall reported that many contentions about the SST sonic boom were based on emotion, prejudice, and scanty evidence, CLASB convinced public officials that the SST would nevertheless be a mistake because of its psychological, and sociological effect on the American people. As a result of the persistent and effective economic and ecological arguments of the citizens' groups, the House of Representatives in March 1971 reversed its support for the SST by a 215 to 204 vote.

The Mistake Strategy enjoys the advantage of playing upon the normal and widespread human fear of the unknown. It also puts decision-makers at a greater political risk than other strategies. Disadvantages of this strategy are its requirements for research and for a skillful conductor to orchestrate the outrage.

The Mitigation Strategy

This strategy depends for its effectiveness on the preference of public officials to please as many constituents as possible, and on the desire of the public to get something done. When issues have become so polarized and the confrontations so strident that they stand in the way of achieving a reasonable consensus, mitigation—making the decision less painful—offers hope for an acceptable decision. Mediation is a tactic effectively used in the mitigation strategy. Infrequently utilized in the 1970 environmental decade, mitigation is expected by many political and business leaders to be the strategy of succeeding decades in order to reconcile the nation's economic, energy and environmental goals.

Mitigation is a reconciling, conciliatory strategy. Mitigation Strategy key words are: "balance," "coalition building," "cooperation," "working together," "avoiding high-blown rhetoric," "willingness," "don't turn back the clock," "conflict resolution," "reasonable levels," "solutions," "continuing dialogue," and "compromise."

The Mitigation Strategy is most effective when initiated early in the public participation process. Politicians and the public need to be mentally prepared for mitigation. One of the principal benefits of conducting a Public Acceptance Assessment is the early disclosure of possible mitigation.

The National Coal Policy Project exemplifies the Mitigation Strategy. Mitigation can be equally effective in enhancing the acceptability of a policy decision or a project location. Mitigation is the ultimate achievement of a public hearing: Officials hear the public and then attempt to reach a decision that mitigates public concerns.

Disadvantages of the Mitigation Strategy are the necessity for all parties to share a sense of urgency for resolution of a conflict and willingness of all parties to reconcile differences. If one party feels confident that he will win a total decision, he has little incentive to compromise. The advantage of the Mitigation Strategy is an outcome acceptable to a larger number of constituents.

ADJUSTING STRATEGIES TO THE LEVEL OF GOVERNMENT

The six public hearing strategies have been used with all levels of government and for elected and appointed officials. They are adjusted to accommodate the sophistication of each level.

At the *federal* level, officials and the media are most sophisticated; they've seen it all and are accustomed to receiving thousands of letters or messages on a controversial issue. To influence the decision of federal elected officials, demonstrations of public consensus must be massive, backed by an impressive media campaign and wide distribution of data. In the SST controversy, the Citizens' League Against the Sonic Boom (CLASB) distributed reports, articles and news releases to 200 leading newspapers, 50 columnists, 50 TV and radio stations, Congressmen and government agencies. Over 100,000 copies of the documented, persuasive 153-page, *SST and Sonic Boom Handbook,* written by Dr. William A. Shurcliff, were sold or distributed free throughout the country. The back cover of the influential *Handbook* stated: "This book demonstrates that the SST is an incredible, unnecessary insult to the living environment, and an albatross around the neck of whatever nations seek to promote it. It tells what you can do to stop it in time and shows why the supersonic transport must be stopped—now!"

Federal Agencies conducting regulatory public hearings need the services of the best and brightest technical experts to establish the public interest, the services of a specialist attorney qualified to practice law in Washington, and experienced public relations consultants.

Federal Commissions, for example, the President's Commission on Population, often bring the issue to the people in field hearings, usually stacked with local officials, local agencies, educators and others with a stake in the decision. To obtain a slot in the hearing schedule sometimes requires a media campaign prior to the hearing.

State Governments whose decisions more visibly impact citizens are receptive to the Public Consensus Strategy and the Fairness Strategy. A state representative or state senator is closer to his constituency than a Congressman or United States Senator, and is more accountable and more sensitive to their concerns. It is easier for citizens to attend a public hearing in the State Capitol than in Washington, D.C.

State Agencies are concerned on a day-to-day basis with the permitting process. All strategies are applicable, although the Mitigation Strategy has not found extensive application in individual states. The Legal Theory Strategy is extensively applied in state regulatory hearings.

Local Governments with their more personal relationship to constituents are most readily appealed to with the Public Consensus Strategy or the Fairness Strategy. The concerns of local voters influence city and county officials. Overburdened district attorneys or county counsels have scant opportunity to familiarize themselves with the constantly increasing number of regulations and become ready prey for the Legal Theory Strategy.

Appointed Commissions are not constrained by accountability to an electorate and are less influenced by the Public Consensus Strategy than by the public interest as defined in their scope of authority. Appointed planning commissions, for example, are more apt to be influenced by a demonstration of the Public Interest Strategy or the Mistake Strategy. The recommendations of most Commissions are advisory to elected officials, making the Public Consensus Strategy appropriate when appealing a Commission recommendation.

STRATEGY STYLES

Strategies may be further diversified by the style with which they are executed. Strategy styles are classified as: *collaborative* (based on the assumption that a resolution can be arrived at that accommodates the common values and interests of all parties); *campaign* (focusing on communication); or *confrontation* (disrupting normal activities to force organizations or communities to accept a proposed outcome).

Collaborative styles are tried when there is no major difference in values between adversaries. Collaborative strategies seek to clear up misunderstandings and find the common ground for agreement. Fact-finding, meetings, newsletters, fact sheets, educational workshops and forming coalitions are the major tactics of this style. When collaborative styles are used, the public hearing ratifies the collaboration.

Campaign styles aim to persuade decision-makers that a proposal conforms to their values and is in their interest. The persuasion takes place through the media, testimonials, endorsements and other Public Consensus tactics. The full force of the persuasion is marshalled for the public hearing.

Confrontation styles are a last resort when the difference in values between adversaries is irreconcilable. The decision is awarded to the contestant who demonstrates the most power. Confrontation is a risk-taking style, involving disruption of normal activities to force political decisions. Disruptions occur through strikes, pickets, boycotting, harassment, sit-ins, shop-ins, sleep-ins and camp-ins. When confrontation styles are used, the public hearing becomes a volatile battlefield.

Confrontation styles include *civil disobedience*—protest, dissent or assembly that violates the rights of others such as engaging in marching or picketing which blocks traffic. Civil disobedience takes the form of refusal to obey a law because of disapproval of that particular law, for instance, avoiding the military draft. Civil disobedience is also used as a means of protest in order to bring pressure on the public or government to accomplish some purpose. When a deliberate attempt is made to harm someone, the motive for civil disobedience including motives stemming from the highest moral principles, does not confer immunity for violation of the law.

Non-violent non-participation is confrontation by refusal to engage in routine or other activities: refusing to purchase goods; refusing to vote; refusing to salute the flag; refusing to leave a library or public building—all usually legal activities within the right guaranteed citizens by the constitution. By eroding the orderly transactions of life and disrupting normal activities or inconveniencing others, non-participation results in coercing decision-makers. Sit-ins, freedom walks, boycotts, picketing, and mass demonstrations are weapons of protest, dissent and criticism.

ACTIVISTS' STYLES

Many persons associate the public hearing process with fringe groups or extremists, called activists. The common dictionary definition of an activist as "an especially active vigorous advocate of a political cause" inadequately describes the activists of the latter half of the twentieth century. Activists who use the public hearing process share the characteristic of commitment. They band together into special interest groups which are usually privately funded (or sometimes by the federal government), frequently non-profit, tax-exempt, to aggressively attempt to influence public decisions.

Activists use the same strategies and strategy styles as other groups, but they display more daring and assume greater risks because they champion causes, rather than mere proposals. The causes of the Sixties—civil rights, anti-poverty and peace—attracted young and old activists who learned how to use the peaceful exercise of the First Amendment rights as an instrument for change. They learned that civil disobedience attracts media attention. The environmental decade of the Seventies spawned a new breed of activist who, drawing on the activists' successful experience of the Sixties, used similar strategies to advocate protection of the environment and ecology.

Planning public hearing strategy includes determining whether the adversaries play gamesmanship according to accepted rules of decorum. Agency staffs and public officials quickly learn the groups and persons who appear at every public hearing. There are: energy activists; land-use activists; environmental activists; social activists; welfare activists; and, innumerable other special interest, highly visible activists.

An instructive exercise in Figure 4–6 allows advocacy groups to rate the tactics they are willing to use compared to their adversaries' tactics. Numerous establishment-type grass-roots groups who have calculated the Activist Index rate themselves a low 6 to 12 on the Activist Index. In calculating their adversaries' Activist Index, the same groups rate activist adversaries a high 15 to 25!

Certain characteristics are the critical success factors that account for activists' records in accomplishing social change:

1. A high degree of *Organization* that not only promotes the cause but also supports the activities of its members. The Clamshell Alliance's supporting structural organization encouraged members to

---

Figure 4–6

Calculate Your Activist Index*

For an advocacy you believe in, would you be willing to:

		Yes	No
1.	Testify at public hearings	___	___
2.	Write letters to the Editor	___	___
3.	Get 10 other people to write letters to the Editor	___	___
4.	Knock on doors to explain your position	___	___
5.	Work at a booth at a fair	___	___
6.	Engage in a debate at a public meeting	___	___
7.	Arrange a demonstration, field trip or tour	___	___
8.	Obtain signatures on petitions	___	___
9.	Arrange to stack a public hearing	___	___
10.	Lobby your congressman	___	___
11.	Contribute to a litigation fund	___	___
12.	Hold a media briefing	___	___
13.	Hold a Bike-A-Thon	___	___
14.	Initiate a recall of a public official	___	___
15.	Blockade a railroad crossing	___	___

Figure 4-6 (continued)

16. Bring goats to a public meeting   ___ ___
17. Occupy public lavatories until officials agree to a proposed action   ___ ___
18. Boycott an activity   ___ ___
19. Hold a demonstration   ___ ___
20. Deliberately disrupt a public meeting   ___ ___
21. Throw a cream pie at a public official   ___ ___
22. Hold a sit-in   ___ ___
23. Heave horse manure at public officials   ___ ___
24. Participate in a truck blockade   ___ ___
25. Deliberately break a minor law and go to jail   ___ ___

Scoring: Give yourself 1 point for yes answers to questions 1–10. Give yourself 3 points for yes answers to questions 11–14. Give yourself 6 points for yes answers to questions 15–24. Give yourself 8 points for a yes answer to question 25.

---

* ©Copyright: Dr. Jean Mater, 1979

take personal risks. Organized in 1976 to stop a proposed nuclear power plant from being built in Seabrook, New Hampshire, the Clamshell Alliance adopted a strategy of massive non-violence. The "Clam" marshalled its supporters to occupy the Seabrook site three times within ten months. The third occupation involved over 2,000 trained, committed objectors. The 1,414 members who were arrested in May 1977 vowed to stay in jail to prove their determination to stop the nuclear plant. Through "affinity groups" of 10 to 15 people who were trained as a unit in non-violence, the Clam developed a strong sense of community among its members. An "Occupiers' Handbook" containing legal information, suggestions on what to pack, and rules for all occupiers—such as no alcohol or drugs, no running, no fires after dark—supplemented the affinity group's training.

The New Hampshire Clam set the pattern for similar Alliances throughout the United States, The Abalone Alliance which protested the Diablo Canyon nuclear plant near San Luis Obispo, California is a typical Clam.

2. A practice of forming *Coalitions* based on the recognition that a single group working alone may not have the clout to effect change. Activists tend to collaborate or network with other organizations and groups. Working usually within the existing political system but not limited by the conventional instruments of power, they can put together an impressive demonstration for the Public Consensus Strategy. Activist coalitions have been a powerful force in battling racism and sexism, reducing hours in the work week, legitimizing gay rights and obtaining public funding for many causes.

3. Holding others' actions *Accountable* to the public. The Consumer movement's significant impact on policy-making in the United States is based on accountability. Ralph Nader's University Public Interest Research Groups (PIRG)s hold corporations, elected officials, the government agencies (whom they term "bureaucracies"), and regulatory agencies accountable, demanding increased responsiveness to their definition of "the public interest."

PREPARING A FACT SHEET

The FACT SHEET distills the information about the proposal to a concise message that advances the strategy. Fact Sheets serve proposals of any magnitude and can be inexpensively put together and copied.

Why Prepare a FACT SHEET?

Fact Sheets perform many tasks including:
a. Summarizing and organizing pertinent information
b. Defining the problem in the simplest terms
c. Explaining concisely the predicted consequences
d. Summarizing complex environmental impacts
e. Publishing evidence to support predictions
f. Providing directions for supporters
g. Notifying supporters of the date, time, location, and procedure of the public hearing(s)
h. Publicizing names, addresses and telephone numbers of key resource persons
i. Suggesting alternatives, mitigation and trade-offs
j. Rebutting claims of opponents
k. Evaluating relevance of data.

How to Use a FACT SHEET

The FACT SHEET is an indispensable tool in the public hearing process. It is used as:

a. A policy paper
b. An information source for preparing public hearing testimony
c. Background information for the media
d. The basis for a press conference
e. A flyer to distribute to the public
f. The front sheet of the packet distributed to decision-makers (The Fact Sheet may be the only page in the packet a hurried, harried official may read.)
g. The information presented to legislators and other potential supporters
h. A vehicle to establish credibility and legitimacy
i. A proposal for alternative solutions, mitigations of adverse environmental impacts, and trade-offs
j. The master list of information to be presented at public hearings especially in quasi-judicial hearings where decisions are based on "findings" in the record.

Types of FACT SHEETS

FACT SHEETS are written in many formats, from brief, one-page summaries to longer "white papers." Content and focus of fact sheets are tailored to the level of government and the intellectual level of the advocacy group involved, and to be responsive to the issues.

The *ONE-PAGE SUMMARY* presents information in bite-size pieces. Because it is the one page that all parties will most certainly read it justifies the effort required to condense a complex debate into one page. Figure 4–7 illustrates A One-Page Summary Fact Sheet for a technical project.

The *ENVIRONMENTAL IMPACT STATEMENT SUMMARY FACT SHEET* summarizes environmental impacts whose details are probably too long and too complex for most persons. This type of Fact Sheet is valuable when the environmental impact is an essential element of the debate. For example, Figure 4–8, is an excerpt from the first page of a twelve-page summary of a three-volume Environmental Impact Statement on a Highway By-pass.

The *QUESTION AND ANSWER FACT SHEET* lists the important questions raised about the problem and answers with the ad-

Figure 4-7

One-Page Summary FACT SHEET

These are the FACTS about the Lincoln Wind Energy Generating Plant

— The Lincoln Wind Energy Plant will offset the need for oil, coal, gas and other non-renewable energy resources by using wind, a permanent and constantly renewable source of energy, and protect the State's environmental quality.

— More than 815 wind generators on 650 acres of land will produce 40 megawatts of electricity. The generators will be sited in rows, set back from the property line. Each wind generator will consist of a steel tower, a housing for a transmission generator and controls, and a rotor with two or three spruce laminated blades.

— The transmission line will be built in the existing transmission line corridor. The wind turbine blades are designed not to interfere with radio, television or microwave signals; the company has agreed to take action to remedy any interference that may occur at its own expense.

— The Wind Energy Plant conforms to the comprehensive land use plan and the County Commissioners have approved the plant. There will be no adverse environmental impacts on wildlife, plants, or recreation uses.

— The Wind Energy Plant will be designed to make no noise. Noise will be monitored by the Department of Environmental Quality. Safety precautions require an extensive fence to protect the public from any contact with the blades or electrical equipment.

— The Wind Energy Company is experienced in constructing wind energy parks and has the personnel, organization, managerial and technical expertise to build and operate the Wind Energy Plant.

Figure 4-8

**Environmental Impact Statement
Summary FACT SHEET**

These are the facts about the Circle Boulevard/Walnut
Boulevard Extensions

The Federal Highway Administration and the State Department
of Transportation have just issued a three-volume Draft Environmental Impact Statement, totalling 525 pages, on the Circle
Boulevard/Walnut Boulevard Extensions which together form a
traffic network to accommodate the growth of the Northwest
area. This Fact Sheet puts the findings of these volumes plus
some additional information in a convenient form to answer
questions you may have on this network.

Question 1.   Where will Circle Boulevard and Walnut Boulevard
be extended?

Answer: To handle the increasing volume of Northwest
traffic, we will have to extend Circle Boulevard
1850 feet west to Witham Hill Drive (Section A on
enclosed map) and extend Walnut Boulevard 3900
feet from Kings Boulevard to Highland Boulevard
(Section C on map). These extensions will form the
traffic network long planned for the Northwest.

Compiled by Community Club and *Complete the Circle* Committee

vocacy group's position. A sample from a Question and Answer Fact
Sheet such as in Figure 4-9, shows that this is a convenient method
for assigning testimony on "findings of fact" to be entered into the
public hearing record.

An *INFORMATION ONLY FACT SHEET* which is restricted
to presenting statistics, facts and figures, with no or low-key comment, is useful when stating an advocacy position might impair cred-

---

Figure 4-9

Question and Answer FACT SHEET

These are the facts about X Y Z products company's proposed
Glass Wool Manufacturing Facility

Q.1.   What will the proposed glass wool plant do?
        A. The X Y Z Products Glass Wool Plant will produce an
            exceptionally high quality glass wool in a grade not
            available from other sources. Glass wool manu-
            facture is a part of the ceramics industry, utilizing on-
            ly inert, inorganic, non-metallic materials in a high
            technology, very specialized manufacturing process.
            The X Y Z Glass Wool Facility is scheduled to pro-
            duce 1000 lbs. of glass wool per hour on a 24-hour
            basis. Most of the glass wool manufactured will be
            in the 4-5.5 micron average diameter range.
            X Y Z has invested 2 million dollars in research to de-
            velop its ability to produce this grade of glass wool,
            employing engineers and scientists trained at Uni-
            versities such as Capitol State University.

---

ibility. An example is Figure 4–10 which lays out, without comment,
the facts on a budget proposal.

An *INFORMATION AND DIRECTIONS FOR ACTION FACT
SHEET* summarizes the essence of the problem and tells supporters
what they can do to influence the outcome—write letters, assist in the
campaign, attend the pubic hearing. By publishing the names and addresses for letter writing and the time, date and place of the public
hearing, this type of Fact Sheet facilitates action on the part of supporters. An example of what might be included is shown in Figure 4–11.

The *INFORMATION AND CONCLUSIONS FACT SHEET*
summarizes the information and establishes conclusions from this in-

Figure 4–10

Information Only FACT SHEET

The Facts about Foster Community College Budget Proposal

1. The operating levy is $1,500,623. This is $42,345 less than last year's levy.
2. Instructional programs have been cut by $30,201. The programs cut are community education classes, industrial apprenticeship programs, and farm management programs.
3. Full-time faculty has been cut by 25 full-time and 48 part-time positions.
4. Library book purchases have been reduced 32% from last year.
5. 91% of the college's last graduating class found jobs within two months of graduation.
6. 23,487 people took classes last year at the college, including about 1,400 senior citizens.
7. The college is enrolling 320 fewer students than last year.
8. The tax rate for this budget would be the same as last year.
9. The County taxpayers pay 7% of the total college budget.
10. The college has not increased its budget proposal for three years, despite inflation.

formation. By leading the reader to a conclusion, this type of Fact Sheet invites but does not urge agreement. The Information and Conclusions Fact Sheet in Figure 4–12 illustrates how credibility is established, the facts summarized, the problem stated and the conclusions of the advocacy group drawn. This Fact Sheet is especially appropriate for quoting credible leaders.

The *INFORMATION AND ADVOCACY FACT SHEET* presents information and urges decision-makers and the public to adopt the advocacy position. Figure 4–13, a Fact Sheet on a National Park

Figure 4-11

Pages from an Information and Directions for Action FACT SHEET

The records show that the Planning Commission supports the extension, all State Agencies support the extension, and every engineering study made supports the extension. A handful of people who want to keep the area exclusively for themselves are the only opposition.

What can you do to help obtain approval from the City Council?

1. Write letters expressing your support:
   — to the Editor: City Gazette
   415 SW Stone,
   Noname, State 97338

   — to the Council Members: see attached list for names and addresses

   — to the Land Planning Division:
   Mr. Richard Manson
   Chairman, Land Planning Division
   672 State Street
   Capitol, State 97332

2. Come to the public hearings on:
   May 30 — 7:30 P.M.   Cafeteria/Auditorium, City High School
   May 31 — 7:30 P.M.   Library, City
   July 12 —10:00 A.M.   State Land Use Building, Capitol

3. Plan to testify: For further information or help in planning testimony contact Larry Handel of Complete the Circle Committee, 1850 N.W. Sell Place, Phone: 853-6560.

4. Offer to help man the booths at the Fair, distribute handbills, make telephone calls and do the work necessary to keep a handful of people from having their way at your expense. Fill out the information on this page NOW, tear

Figure 4–11 (continued)

off on the perforated line and send to Larry Handel, 1850 N.W. Sell Place, Noname, State 97338.

Count me in. I want to help Complete the Circle. I'm available to:

testify____telephone____man the Fair booth____distribute handbills____

help at the hearing____serve coffee and cookies____

stuff envelopes____address envelopes____speak to service clubs____

I can work evenings only____daytime only____after school only____week-ends only____any time you need me____

Name _____

Address_____

Telephone (Home)_____

(Business)_____

Service proposal to limit snowmobiling, asserts the advocacy view using "unfair," "discriminate," "safety" and other emotive words to arouse the public.

The *NEWSLETTER FACT SHEET* presents a continuum of information, conclusions, urgings and briefings in a controversy that spans a long time period. Figure 4–14, is a small section of a newsletter published to keep the public in touch with developments in an airport controversy, Newsletter Fact Sheets include announcements, alternatives, explanations, and facts that concern citizens.

A *WHITE PAPER* is a special type of Fact Sheet that covers the history of the problem, with supporting data, advantages and disadvantages of various positions, chronology, expert opinion—an "ev-

Figure 4-12

Information and Conclusions FACT SHEET

WHY WE ARE WORKING TO REOPEN THE JOHNSON SCHOOL

Who we are: We are the Johnson Education Coalition, a group of parents and citizens like you, who have worked with the School Board to keep Johnson School open. After two years of public hearings, the Board reversed its earlier decision and ordered Johnson school closed. We don't think this is the way to make public policy.

The Facts: The Johnson school was built on Bush Street in 1935; it has 600 students, 1st to 6th grades, serving the 200 families in the Johnson neighborhood. The Johnson school is the only school in the neighborhood. If it is closed the 600 children will be distributed to three other schools in different neighborhoods. The School Board claims the closure is necessary to balance the budget. We don't think you can put a price tag on our children's education. We believe closing the Johnson school will seriously harm our children's education.

The Problem: We have found that the only way to reopen Johnson school now is to split away from City School District and form our own District. The new District can then order the Johnson school reopened. We have found that secession from a school district is not easy. We have prepared 20 pounds of reports, testimony, and documentation to convince the State Legislature that they should agree to our secession. The testimony at the public hearings filled seven volumes of transcripts.

The Conclusion: The Johnson Education Coalition has studied the School Board figures and the transcripts of the hearings. All the information points to keeping the Johnson school open. We intend to continue this effort for the sake of our children, and to establish the principle for all the children in the State that they are more important than dollars. Please help.

Figure 4-13

Information and Advocacy FACT SHEET

WHY THE NATIONAL PARK SERVICE PROPOSED POLICY
IS UNFAIR TO SNOWMOBILERS

— The Park Service is proposing to reduce by half the Sunshine Park area available to snowmobilers. The eight-mile stretch in which snowmobiles can now run has already been reduced from last year. The new proposal leaves too little area for the number of snowmobilers who enjoy the sport.

— The State Snowmobile Association believes the new policy is unfair to the people of the State. It discriminates against the 1200 snowmobilers who use the Sunshine Park area in favor of the 800 downhill and cross-country skiers who ski in the area. We don't want to deprive skiers of their right to ski, but we don't want them to deprive us either.

— We share with the Park Service the desire to protect the Park's aesthetic values and wildlife resources. The code of conduct of our members calls for policing ourselves in these areas. After all, a snowmobile costs from $2000 to $6000. We're a responsible family sport and we enjoy the scenic beauty as much as anyone.

— If the area we can use is further restricted in order that cross-country skiers can enjoy more silence, we feel that the safety of our members will be jeopardized. Crowding so many snowmobilers into a smaller area is not a safe practice.

— Skiers and hikers have a right to enjoy skiing. We have a right to enjoy snowmobiling. We feel that it is unfair to increase the enjoyment of the few skiers at the expense of the many snowmobilers.

— In the interest of fairness and equity we are appealing to the Park Service not to restrict us further. Please join us at the Public Hearing at the school house on Monday night.

erything you want to know about the problem." An expensive, time-consuming venture, the White Paper is usually reserved for important, complex issues when printing funds are available.

How to Use the FACT SHEET to Implement the Public Hearing Strategy

Use the FACT SHEET format that best serves the strategy. The One-Page Summary is appropriate for all strategies, but the Environmental Impact Statement Summary is best suited to the Public Interest Strategy. The Question and Answer format lends itself to any strategy, as does the Information and Conclusions format. However, the Information and Advocacy format is not as effective for the Legal Theory Strategy or the Mitigation Strategy as the others. It is often desirable to prepare several Fact Sheet formats, a different one for each audience

---

·Figure 4–14

Newsletter FACT SHEET

SAFE PASSAGE NEWSLETTER

Published by CARR (Citizens Against Restricted Runways) to keep you posted on the Arundel Airport Expansion Plan.

Number 8   April issue
Bob Haddock and Jane Nye, Co-editors

AIRPORT LAYOUT ALTERNATIVES TO BE STUDIED

For the past five months CARR has been urging the Board of Governors of the Arundel Airport to reveal the alternatives the planners have come up with and to hold public hearings on these alternatives. The Board has finally agreed to hold a hearing and to present the alternatives. MAY WILL BE A BUSY MONTH FOR ARUNDEL AIRPORT NEIGHBORS WHO CARE ABOUT THE SAFETY OF ARUNDEL AIRPORT.

Figure 4-14 (continued)

Four alternatives, including three different layout plans and the alternative of doing nothing, will be presented by the planners at an informal information session, with a public meeting the following week.

— Information session—Arundel District High School, 5 to 8 p.m., May 12
— Public hearing—Arundel public library, back room, beginning at 7:30 p.m., May 17

The three different layout plans were designed to answer CARR's concerns with the safety of planes and residents, landscaping and buffering, preservation of agricultural land, and traffic.

Alternative No. 1 would include a total of about 320 acres during Phase I development. Development cost would be about $8 million.

Alternative No. 2 would move the runway 650 feet east of the present runway and use about 400 acres. This alternative would cost about $7.5 million.

Alternative No. 3 would move the runway about 1200 feet east and include about 450 acres. This alternative would cost about $7.6 million.

Alternative No. 4 is a do nothing alternative.

How to Prepare a Persuasive FACT SHEET

A FACT SHEET works only if the readers respond to the message—if the communication is relevant to the reader. Persuasive fact sheets demand careful writing and rewriting.

Persuasion vs the Facts

Public officials exhort the public to present factual testimony and to avoid emotion in public hearings. The American Society of Planning Officials states "A prime hope of the planner and other officials involved is that commentary from those attending hearings will be carefully prepared and well reasoned."[1] However, while decision-makers may attempt to reach conclusions on a conscious, rational level, they are human beings and these conclusions are tempered by prejudices, assumptions, fears, emotional responses and the desire to please constituencies. Officials, as are most persons, are influenced by appeals to both reason and emotion, by words and concepts that trigger subconscious responses based on beliefs, attitudes, opinions and values. The difference between beliefs, attitudes, opinions and values is crucial to persuasion:

—A "belief" implies the acceptance of something as the truth, whether based on reasoning, prejudice or authority.

—An "attitude" is a habit of acting, feeling or thinking that indicates a disposition or mood.

—An "opinion" is a conclusion or judgment which a person deems true or probable.

—A "value" is something a person desires or thinks is desirable.

Consider this example: A person believes in God. Based on this belief is the attitude that churches are healthy for society. His opinion of a particular church is high. He values religious beliefs.

Apply these concepts to a typical public hearing debate about allowing snowmobiling in a state park. The swing vote is an official who believes that people should enjoy nature. His attitude is that man's activities disturb nature. His opinion is that snowmobiling disturbs nature and therefore is not a good activity. He values what's best for nature. His belief, values and attitude are probably fixed. But the snowmobiling advocate may find evidence to change his opinion of snowmobiling to that of an activity that is compatible with nature in this instance. The anti-snowmobile advocate has the easier task of reinforcing the official's opinion.

Although some psychologists maintain that it is futile to attempt to change attitudes, recognizing and appealing to a person's values is the path to persuasion. As the British social scientist Oppenheim notes ". . . attempts at changing opinions are often misdirected unless they take into account the underlying attitudes."[2] Speakers with sensitivity to the values of others deliver the inspiring, motivating and

---

[1] "Reprinted with permission from *Public Hearings, Controversy, and the Written Response* by Frederick H. Bair, Jr., PAS Report Number 240, 1968, p. 5. Copyright © 1968 by the American Society of Planning Officials (now the American Planning Association), 1313 E. 60th St., Chicago, IL 60637.

[2] A. N. Oppenheim, "Opinion," *A Dictionary of the Social Sciences*, ed. Julius Gould and William L. Kolb (New York, N. Y.: The Free Press, 1964), p. 477.

challenging speeches audiences admire and applaud.

Beliefs and values are not merely products of the intellect; they are confirmed by the heart, by feelings. Persuasive testimony aims to provide information to appeal to the decision-maker's emotionally based evaluation mechanisms.

Cognitive Meaning vs Emotive Meaning

When trying to make a point, a person who relies only on cognitive meaning (that is, informing or stating facts) is less persuasive than the person who also involves emotive meaning (words with positive or negative overtones). For instance, "bureaucrat" is perceived negatively; "public servant" may be positive; and "government official" neutral.

Emotive phrases reflect the strategy of the advocacy. Consider an Information and Advocacy Fact Sheet in the snowmobile controversy: The emotive phrase "Give the bureaucrats a stranglehold on how Americans relax" reflects the Fairness Strategy. Rewriting it as "Give public servants an opportunity to protect the interests of all Americans" adapts it for the Public Interest Strategy. If a Fact Sheet were written for the Mistake Strategy it might suggest "Give government officials some guidelines."

When the American Society of Planning Officials hopes that commentary at public hearings will be "well reasoned," it indicates a preference for testimony couched in cognitive words that do not get in the way of rational objective thought. However, effective advocates typically employ emotive language, as in this statement by the President of the 170,000-member Sierra Club: ". . . the practices being developed . . . are shoring operations for industry profits . . . with the result so much at variance with the ecological ethic that its accomplishment will be a disaster." The statement contains four strong emotive words: "shoring," "profits," "variance," "disaster." Note how the statement implies the conflict and adversarial stance that attracts the media. Contrast the impact of the Sierra Club statement with a similar statement in cognitive language: ". . . the practices being developed . . . tend to improve bottom line performance with the results deviating from those desired by ecologists."

Testing the FACT SHEET for Clarity

If fact sheets fail at instant comprehension, they defeat their purpose. A comprehensible Fact Sheet uses simple language and avoids flossy, pompous, jargonistic writing. Translating complex ideas into simple language challenges the most capable writer. Clarity tests such as Rudolf Flesch's "Reading Ease" formula (explained in Figure 4–15) and the "Fog Index" (described in the Chapter on Communication) send the Fact Sheet through a filtering mechanism to ensure clarity.

Preparing FACT SHEETS for Diverse Audiences

Fact sheets that influence decisions grab the reader's attention. For general public distribution it is safer to assume that the reader has minimum understanding of the issue and so a concise, persuasive Fact Sheet is needed to command attention and awaken or increase the reader's interest in doing something to solve the problem.

On the other hand, the Fact Sheet for decision-makers assumes some familiarity with the subject and aims to increase their understanding, or enhance their knowledge. Credible fact sheets avoid biased or inaccurate statements, focus on the critical questions, and reinforce the advocacy position.

For the media, the Fact Sheet that is written as the basis for a news story is most likely to be quoted. Writing in headlines, media fashion, with a peg or hook to grab attention helps the media reflect the advocacy position.

The Fact Sheet for distribution to supporters who will testify at the public hearing, write letters-to-the-editor, and phone their congressman, provides both an opportunity to articulate the advocacy rationale and to give directions for action in language that stimulates emotional commitment.

Adjusting the FACT SHEET to the Sophistication of the Audience

A local public hearing includes many first-nighters—persons with little experience in public hearings or political debate. But a hearing before a federal Administrative Law Judge (ALJ) in the EPA, for instance, includes knowledgeable specialists and is covered by media representatives who have acquired more than passing knowledge of the problem. Fact sheets should recognize these differences.

For example, the uninitiated are confused when a bill is mentioned only by number (e.g., HB2220) or a regulation only by its acronym (RPAR—Rebuttal Presumption Against Registration). The

Figure 4–15

Rudolf Flesch's "Reading Ease" Formula*

Rudolf Flesch developed this formula or rule-of-thumb for checking copy for understandability.

Take a random selection from the copy being tested of five 100-word samples. Start each sample with the beginning of a paragraph. Avoid introductory paragraphs.

•Count contractions (such as: don't) and hyphenated words (such as: non-technical) as one word.

•Count numbers, acronyms, symbols, and letters as words of one syllable.

•Count the words in each sentence; divide by the number of sentences to determine the average sentence length.

•Count the number of syllables in 100 words.

Use the following formula:

Multiply the average sentence length by 1.015   _____

Multiply the number of syllables per 100 words by .846   _____

Add   _____

Subtract this sum from   206.835

The "reading ease" score is   _____

A score of 90 to 100 indicates very easy reading. A score of 0 to 30 is very difficult reading. Standard is about 60 to 70.

_____

*Adapted from "How To Use The Readability Formula" from *The Art of Readable Writing,* 25th Anniversary Edition (Revised and Enlarged) by Rudolf Flesch. Copyright 1949, © 1974 by Rudolf Flesch. Reprinted by permission of Harper & Row, Publishers. Inc more sophisticated EPA hearing participants may roll these initials trippingly off their tongues and refer knowingly to Section 6(f) or 102. Therefore, the fact sheets for the first group should explain appropriate numbers and acronyms while this is not as necessary for fact sheets for the second group.

Reporters who cover the state or federal scene acquire land-use vocabulary or energy terminology as they repeatedly report their beats. Reporters for the local media must become instant experts in whatever topic currently captures the public attention. Fact sheets for the local media need to be, as the computer trade says "user friendly," or they won't be used.

5

Public Hearing Tactics

Strategy without tactics is comparable to cooking a meal and neglecting to serve it. Tactics carry out the strategy. Tactics translate strategy into action, transform potential into achievement.

HOW TO SELECT APPROPRIATE TACTICS

Successful advocates select tactics to meet the requirements of both the strategy and the advocacy group. Tactics that make members feel uncomfortable or self-conscious are neither fun nor effective. Five factors should be weighed in selecting tactics:

1. *The group's leaders*—Some leaders have the verve, charisma and experience to induce members to adopt tactics that go outside their accepted social norms. Members readily follow such leaders in executing clever Alinsky-style confrontational tactics—staging an occupation of the lavatories at O'Hare Airport Terminal in Chicago, obstructing public paths with chewed bubble gum, or causing other public inconvenience or embarrassment. The group with that type of charismatic leadership is willing to risk tactics that scare others.

2. *The group members*—Some group members are ready to barter personal safety or inconvenience for results. Parents angry at the threatened closure of a school might be sufficiently agitated to picket the school board or stage a sit-in, but not angry enough to stage a recall. "Never go outside the experience of your people." This one of activist Saul Alinsky's admonitions is a wise guide for determining what activism members can use comfortably. Attempting to transform a businessman into a raging "Poor People's" activist usually fails because it goes outside his conventional social norms.

3. *The issue*—Nuclear energy and the nuclear freeze evoke a high degree of emotion; advocates may be prepared to use tactics in opposing nuclear activities that they would consider unacceptable for

opposing a local zone change. Environmental issues generate a similar depth of commitment.

4. *The level of government*—Chaining oneself to the White House fence would be overkill for someone attempting to persuade the school board to reverse a decision on an athletic program. But that tactic does focus media attention on national issues. However, tactics that put officials at a disadvantage sometimes generate sympathy for the officials, rather than for the advocates. A march on city hall to lower the state sales tax that is obviously contrived for media attention because the city fathers have no jurisdiction in the state sales tax, may impair a group's credibility.

5. *The tactics of the opposition*—Activist tactics of adversaries may act as a spur to encourage groups to use as counter tactics what they would otherwise prefer to avoid.

Tactics Styles

In addition to specific tactics for each strategy, interest groups adopt their own tactics styles, or combination of tactics. Five styles have been observed: (1) confrontation tactics; (2) system sponsored tactics; (3) public advocacy tactics; (4) community alternative tactics; and (5) social alternative tactics. These styles are illustrated by options available to a hypothetical League of Handicapped Persons in attempting to reverse a budget cut:

1. Confrontation tactics, often called Alinsky-style tactics, focus on inconveniencing or embarrassing adversaries to the point where they are vulnerable and polarized. Confrontation tactics often isolate a key person with whom to negotiate. They also devise actions outside the social norms of adversaries. Confrontation tactics depend on the leadership's ability to induce members to assume risks.

An example of the confrontation style is a League of Handicapped Persons wheelchair march-in at a public hearing to demonstrate the difficulties of handicapped children in getting around school. Selecting a husky, healthy football-playing mayor as the target, the advocacy group attempts to embarrass him for proposing budget cuts for special services for handicapped children.

2. System sponsored tactics make vigorous use of the existing system to increase official awareness of their advocacy. Usually non-confrontational, the system sponsored style leans to communication through media campaigns, debates, forums, pamphlets, petitions, and letters to officials. Using the system sponsored style, the League

of Handicapped Persons would flood city officials with letters and communication protesting budget cuts for special health services for handicapped children.

3. The public advocacy style centers on the issue. It depends on research and documentation to prove its point and disseminates its findings through education and lobbying. By building coalitions, it is able to pack public hearings with supporters. When the League of Handicapped Persons uses the public advocacy style it studies the number of students affected, the school architecture, comparisons with other areas, and the cost effectiveness of removing architectural barriers. Preparing and publishing a report on its findings, it asks the Parent Teacher Association (PTA) and other groups to testify at the public hearing on behalf of restoring the budget appropriation.

4. Community alternative styles are proactive and collaborative. Often coming in from left field, advocates selecting this style propose alternative solutions. Using the community alternative style, the League of Handicapped Persons would propose at the public hearing that three-quarters of the budget cut for handicapped children be restored, with the remainder to come from other identified sources.

5. The social alternative style considers the cultural basis of problems. It views problems as culturally induced and emphasizes cultural changes by the process of consciousness-raising. If the League of Handicapped Persons embraced the social alternative style, it would first embark on a program of making the community conscious of the problems of handicapped children; then it would use this heightened awareness as a tool for marshalling support at the public hearing.

Considerations in Selecting Tactics

In selecting specific tactics or a tactics style consideration should be given to the following factors:

1. Resources available (manpower, time, money) to carry out the tactics
2. Motivation for using the tactics
3. Possibility that the tactics will alienate decision-makers, the public, or the media
4. The power to be gained from the tactics
5. The consequences of using the tactics
6. The appropriateness of the tactics for the decision
7. The members' skills for these tactics

8. Whether the tactics sacrifice short-term advantages for long-term gain or vice versa
9. The members' commitment for these tactics
10. Whether the tactics will make a difference in the outcome

Weighing each tactic against the pros and cons of these factors helps planners maintain an objective focus on the purpose of the tactic. Suppose, for example, that the League of Handicapped Persons has decided to base its public hearing planning on the Fairness Strategy. In considering tactics, the group has determined that public consciousness has already been raised; the need now is to promote action. The group evaluates using confrontational style tactics to force officials to restore the rights to special education of the handicapped. The wheelchair march-in sounds exciting: it certainly would attract attention; the group has the resources; the members have the skills and the commitment; it would make officials uncomfortable about being unfair. But on analysis the planners decide that, although confrontational tactics would probably be effective with this official body, they might sacrifice long-term credibility for short-term gain. The group determines to adopt the system sponsored style instead.

Some tactics and tactics styles implement certain strategies better than others. Consciousness-raising and confrontation tactics support the Fairness Strategy more effectively than they do the Legal Theory Strategy. Coalition-forming tactics and the Public Advocacy style are more appropriate for the Public Consensus Strategy than for the Mitigation Strategy. All strategies are more likely to affect the outcome if they link with the political power of the Public Consensus Strategy. The following discussion of tactics addresses first those tactics shared by all strategies and follows with aspects unique to implementing each strategy.

TACTICS SHARED BY ALL STRATEGIES

The success a strategy achieves in influencing a decision depends on two types of tactics: tactics used *prior* to the public hearing to develop public support; and tactics used *during* the hearing to demonstrate public support.

Prior to the public hearing, tactics serve two purposes: (1) setting the stage; and (2) finding supporters. The purpose of setting the stage is to create a perception, an opinion environment favorable to the advocacy's position. Setting the stage focuses on transmitting the advocacy message to the media and through the media to the public, using communication techniques ranging from letters-to-the-editor to creating media events. Finding supporters includes identifying grass-roots groups with compatible objectives, locating individuals and allies, and forming a coalitional network.

Tactics used during the hearing are managerial: assure that supporters appear at the hearing; assure that the testimony is orchestrated to carry out the strategy; handle adversary tactics; meet procedural requirements; and, provide information to the decision-makers and media.

Although all strategies do not depend on developing and demonstrating public support to accomplish their mission, public support ameliorates the politics of all strategies. But the essence of the Public Consensus Strategy is a show of public support. Therefore, the tactics to be engaged prior to the hearing and during the public hearing are described under the Public Consensus Strategy.

TACTICS FOR THE PUBLIC CONSENSUS STRATEGY

The most powerful strategy in influencing public hearings, the Public Consensus Strategy is doubly effective: used alone it adds felicity to the decision-maker's task and enhances popular approval of an outcome; linked with other strategies it has a symbiotic effect.

The essence of the Public Consensus Strategy is showing officials that constituents favor a particular outcome. All tactics for the Public Consensus Strategy serve this purpose. To demonstrate constituency support, tactics for the Public Consensus Strategy center on:

1. Mobilizing supporters—to contact public officials and the media and carry out the public hearing process.
2. Enlisting allies and sympathizers—to contact public officials and the media and to add clout to the advocacy.
3. Developing media recognition—of broad support for the advocacy.
4. Managing the hearing—to orchestrate support and testimony for establishing the record.

Broad public support promises officials the opportunity to emerge as heroes by favoring a popular position. For example, authorities making a decision on custom auto license plates can do so with little direction from the public when the media report on a hearing on rules to keep offensive words off license plates has as its headline, "NO COMPLAINTS ABOUT CUSTOM PLATES." No such comfort eases the lot of the council in a hearing that demonstrates public opposition as the following instance:

"ANGRY RESIDENTS SHOUT 'NO' AT CHEM HEARING"

"Arthursboro—More than 400 residents of this suburban area crowded into City Hall last night to tell the Council what they thought about CHEM's plans to expand. Most did not approve. When the CHEM manager explained the plans he was interrupted by a chorus of 'No! No!'. . . ."

Tactics Prior to the Public Hearing

The public hearing process begins long before the public hearing. As in producing a play, the stage must be set and the cast assembled.

Setting the Stage

Setting the stage develops public awareness and acceptance of the advocacy position. It reinforces the perception that the advocacy position represents the position of the public.

Communicating with Public Officials and the Media

The public hearing process provides a ready-made opportunity for manipulating public opinion—an opportunity seized by some groups to effect profound social changes. Developing the perception of public support is straightforward and includes:

1. *Letters and other direct communication* to the public and media—inexpensive and within everyone's reach. Persons who drag their feet on writing letters may be encouraged to write letters-to-the-editor of local, statewide, or national newspapers by making the letter writing as painless as possible. One method for expediting letters is to draft a sample letter, invite the letter-writing volunteers for coffee in the evening, and ask each to write a letter during the meeting based on the sample and the Fact Sheet and allocating the facts to be covered among the letter writers. To develop the advocacy

perception each letter should be short, concentrate on one point, establish the writer's credibility on the subject, be persuasive and avoid distractions of sarcasm or wit. Figure 5–1 illustrates a letter-to-the-editor that meets these requirements.

Letters to public officials—equally important to establish public consensus. A campaign urging officials to grant a permit for an energy facility would include letters to officials of the State Department of Energy, Environmental Quality, Public Utilities and other departments with input in the decision.

2. *Petitions*—to provide further evidence of public support if used to bolster the demonstration of public support. For instance, by a dramatic presentation at the hearing of petitions signed by thousands of supporters.

3. *Personal message dissemination*—another form of communication to develop the perception of public support and to broadcast the advocacy message. Supporters who wear identification buttons, tags, or T-shirts bearing the advocacy message help develop the perception of broad public support.

4. *A Communication Campaign* to inform the media and public of the advocacy message—the heart of developing public support. Activities range from distributing the Fact Sheet to holding a media conference. The activities available for a communication campaign are limited only by the time, talent and funds available. Additional information activities are described in Chapter 6, Communication Techniques for Public Hearings.

5. *Holding media events* to compete for media attention—to capture the competitive edge in winning media space. Media events frequently used are:

   a. A workshop that invites the public to suggest solutions to problems.
   b. A debate on the issue at a public meeting, Chamber of Commerce forum, or club meeting.
   c. A celebrity making a statement in support of the advocacy.
   d. A Teach-In, using well-known professors, citizens and others interested in the advocacy.
   e. A series of events leading to a climactic event. "Earth Week," held in the spring of 1970, was a highly publicized series of events on the environment, culminating in "Earth Day." Many political observers credit "Earth Week" with the impetus for the environmental era of the 1970's. "Ground Zero" played a similar role in the Nuclear-Freeze movement.

Figure 5-1

A Letter to the Editor

Editor
Capitol City Journal
Capitol City, State

Dear Sir:

On September 7, the Planning Commission is holding a public hearing on permitting the Wright Research Laboratory to locate in the Northwest area.

As a resident of that area I was skeptical about having the laboratory so close. But after attending the two neighborhood meetings held by the Commission I have changed my mind. The main question everyone asked was: Will the laboratory encourage other development in the area?

From what I heard the answer to that question is "No." The Wright Company is buying all 250 acres in the area for its own use. The model they had showed a lot of landscaping—trees and bushes. It seems to me the best protection for the neighborhood is to have the land owned by one responsible company, like Wright, which has a reputation for keeping their property like a park. If we don't let Wright get it, I'm afraid it will be broken up into a lot of small ownerships and who knows what we'll get.

The agreement the Wright Company has with the city says they cannot subdivide the property and they are required to keep most of the land as open space.

I hope any neighbors who still question the research laboratory will take the time to look at the models. I'm sure they will be as convinced as I am that Wright will be an asset for our neighborhood and will join me at the hearing Wednesday to urge the Planning Commission to approve Wright's application.

Sincerely,

John Q. Citizen

These proactive methods for making news conform to the accepted social norms of most organizations. More aggressive newsmaking ideas are listed later in this chapter in the Catalog of Activist Tactics and in Chapter 6, Communication Techniques for Public Hearings.

Finding Supporters

The Public Consensus Strategy needs many workers to demonstrate broad-based support. Supporters are found in grass-roots groups, allies, and coalitions:

1. *Grass-roots groups* are representatives of the common people, persons who do not apparently benefit directly from the outcome, but who benefit from the perception that they are "people's" groups as differentiated from "special interest" groups. However most modern grass-roots groups represent an "interest."

Environmental grass-roots groups instigated legislation to protect the environment. The Wilderness Society is a grass-roots group advocating wilderness; Save-the-Redwoods League is a grass-roots group responsible for preserving California Redwood trees, and the Citizens' League Against the Sonic Boom (CLASB) was the grass-roots group that led the defeat of the SST.

A roster of "round earth" societies is listed in *Ecotactics*, by John G. Mitchell and Constance L. Stallings.[1] The National Wildlife Federation publishes an annual Conservation Directory, listing organizations, agencies, and officials concerned with natural resource use and management. (Obtainable from The National Wildlife Federation at 1412 Sixteenth St., N.W., Washington, D.C. 20036.) Although environmental and similar special interest grass-roots groups have long enjoyed high visibility, many pro-industry grass-roots groups have organized in recent years. These groups can be located in "The Directory of Pro-Industry Citizen Organizations," edited and published by Ron and Janet Arnold, 12605 N.E. Second St. Bellevue, Washington, 98005.

2. *Other advocacy groups* who are promoting or opposing a similar issue or project are also a source of supporters. An advocacy group—for instance, the Central Association of Neighbors (CAN), which is promoting a shopping center—might contact the North Citizens' Advisory Council (NCAC) which had previously helped a shopping center developer.

---

[1]John G. Mitchell and Constance L. Stallings, *Ecotactics* (New York: Pocket Books).

3. *Allies* should be sought from traditional and non-traditional "strange bedfellow" sources:

• *Traditional sources* imply allies who would be expected to favor the same outcome. A manufacturer seeking a zone change for a factory expansion expects the Chamber of Commerce, labor unions, the State Economic Development Department, and other groups interested in preserving payrolls to support his request. Neighbors urging denial of the request expect assistance from environmental groups, land-use preservation organizations, other neighborhoods and groups interested in maintaining a low-growth profile for the community.

• *The "strange bedfellows"* are supporters who come from unexpected sources. In the "Battle of the Indiana Dunes," a 50-year effort to set aside some 25 miles of the Indiana Dunes as a national park, organizers picked up some strange bedfellows—steel companies and steel workers' unions who recognized that if the Dunes were not preserved in a national park, the area would be the site of a deep draft port which would favor competitors.

Strange bedfellows in jobs versus environment battles might be: school-teachers—who recognize that the revenue from a job-creating venture will maintain their jobs; librarians—who understand the municipalities' need for increasing the tax base; possibly the Boy Scouts—whose camp will benefit from extending the road to accommodate the factory, etc.

4. *A coalitional network* of interconnected, cooperating individuals who support each other provides a structured system for locating supporters. Differing in scope from the personal support networks such as the "Women's Networks" or the "Old Boy Networks," the coalitional networks consist of people (or organizations) who share the same stake in an issue and who will work together to promote a decision favoring that issue. The work includes testifying at public hearings, writing letters, contacting public officials, lobbying, wearing the identifying buttons, and participating in the many tasks necessary to influence a decision.

Coalition Networks call upon each other for support on a sort of honor system: "I'll help you now, if you'll help me later." A developer in California reported that he had spotted the same anti-growth advocates testifying against his developments in two cities almost 100 miles apart. "They come out of the woodwork," he sputtered. These public hearing participants were the products of an organized network.

5. *Individual supporters* may be discovered through the advocacy group Speaker's Bureau. Talks to civic clubs (such as Rotary, Lions, Altrusa), Chambers of Commerce, and special interest groups of all types may inspire interest in speaking on behalf of the advocacy at a public hearing. A Speaker's Bureau might contact groups such as:

— Service (Rotary, Lions, Altrusa, Soroptimist, etc.)
— Civic (League of Women Voters)
— Business and Trade (Chamber of Commerce)
— Agriculture (Women in Agriculture, Cattle Growers Association)
— Racial (National Association for the Advancement of Colored People)
— Conservation (Friends of the Earth)
— Labor (unions, company organizations)
— Fraternal (Elks, Eagles)
— Religious (churches)
— Women (National Organization for Women)
— Social (country club)
— Education (Parent Teachers Association; teacher's groups)
— Age-centered (senior citizens, youth groups, university students)
— Cause-centered (peace groups, Gay Rights)
— Neighborhood Groups

Demonstrating Public Support at the Hearing

The coalition, allies, networks and individual supporters constitute the troops whose task it is to demonstrate public consensus at the hearing. These are not persons who can be "whipped into shape," in military parlance, but volunteers who need to be cajoled, encouraged and reminded to sacrifice evenings preparing for and appearing at a public hearing. Getting out the troops is a five-step effort:

1. A hearing floor manager is appointed to orchestrate and manage the public hearing. Specific duties of the floor manager are listed in Figure 5-2 and a typical participant checklist is shown in Figure 5-3. As the conductor of the orchestration the floor manager is also responsible for correlating the planning with the hearing. A 25-point Checklist for Planning a Public Hearing is shown in Figure 5-4.

Figure 5-2

Duties of the Hearing Floor Manager

- 1. Maintain a checklist of persons who agree to testify and the emphasis of their testimony.
- 2. "Count the house," noting the number of opponents and proponents.
- 3. Act as the command post for supporters who must leave if the hearing drags until a late hour (hearings on controversial projects frequently do!), locate substitutes, or arrange to notify participants if the hearing is carried over.
- 4. Note new material or new ideas which should be rebutted.
- 5. If rebuttal is precluded at the hearing, arrange for written comments and distribute comments to decision-makers and the media.
- 6. Arrange to record hearing comments. Hearing minutes are not always complete.
- 7. Determine the effective moment for such activities as presenting that petition with 2100 signatures, or for whipping out the rack of a six-point elk to set on the hearing table. (A maneuver used to emphasize the contention that a land-use change would halt hunting in the area. The antlers were the only testimony to be shown on the 6:00 o'clock news.)
- 8. Facilitate the submission of written statements, the presentation of visual aids, the media coverage.
- 9. Check the meeting room logistics, directing supporters to the locations most likely to be photographed, or closest to the microphone.
- 10. Determine in advance the order of speaking—by first-come, first served; sign-up; rows; standing in place; or random selection—and place supporters for maximum impact.
- 11. Furnish information to the media that cannot be provided before the hearing including the names and background of supporters who deliver quotable or persuasive presentations.

Figure 5-3

A Participant Checklist for a Public Hearing

Public Hearing on _____

Hearing Floor Manager _____   Date _____

No.	Name	Telephone No.	Date Called	Will Write	Will Testify	Reminded	Material Prepared	Subject

Figure 5–4

A Checklist for Planning a Public Hearing

1. Have you described the project?   _____
2. What are the major issues?   _____
3. Are there hidden agendas?   _____
4. Have you investigated the history?   _____
5. Have you listed specific benefits of the project? Ad-
    verse effects?   _____
6. Have you decided the importance of the project?   _____
7. Have you determined applicable regulations?   _____
8. Do you know the required hearing procedures?   _____
9. Have you prepared a FACT SHEET?   _____
10. Have you prepared a distribution list for the FACT
    SHEET?   _____
11. Has the FACT SHEET been distributed to sup-
    porters?   _____
12. Have you made the FACT SHEET available to the
    media?   _____
13. Have you included details of the hearing time, place,
    allotted time, and sign-up in the FACT SHEET?   _____
14. Have you prepared an Action Plan?   _____
    a. Created an advocacy group?   _____
    b. Identified your supporters?   _____
    c. Searched for less obvious allies?   _____
    d. Started a letter-to-the-editor campaign?   _____
    e. Initiated a petition?   _____
    f. Devised an identification?   _____
    g. Provided identification to supporters?   _____
    h. Located experts to present testimony?   _____
    i. Planned media strategies?   _____
        News releases?   _____
        Interviews?   _____
        Press Conferences?   _____
        Confrontational event?   _____
    j. Demonstrated public support?   _____
        Speaker's Bureau?   _____
        Circulated the FACT SHEET?   _____
        Planned seminar, forum?   _____

Figure 5-4 (continued)

k. Arranged personal contacts?
   door knocking
   neighborhood coffees ____
   telephone blitzes ____
   lobbying ____
15. How many supporters should attend? ____
16. How many testify? ____
17. Have supporters been supplied with instructions for preparing testimony? ____
18. Do they know where to sit? ____
19. Has testimony been coordinated? ____
20. Has a floor manager been appointed? ____
21. Has he been trained in his duties? ____
22. Has the floor manager been included in the planning? ____
23. Do supporters know the floor manager and his duties? ____
24. Does your testimony make a record for appeals or litigation? ____
25. Have you obtained legal advice? ____

2. The advocacy group appoints a special public hearing committee whose functions are:

   a. Assist the floor manager in compiling a list of supporters.
   b. Form a telephone tree to remind supporters of the hearing deadlines.
   c. Distribute fact sheets to supporters.
   d. Assist in preparing testimony. (See "Testimony as Communication")
   e. Distribute identifying buttons, placards, or other identifiers to supporters at the hearing.
   f. Distribute fact sheets or other advocacy literature at the hearing.
   g. Act as "gofers" to the hearing floor manager.
   h. Assist in operating visual aids, if used.

3. A meeting is called of all supporters who have agreed to testify shortly before the hearing. The points of the testimony to be inserted in the record are reviewed and any gaps in the record filled.

4. All supporters are telephoned on the day of the hearing as a reminder and to provide a question-answer opportunity.

5. The process is repeated if a hearing is carried over, postponed, moved to another location, or continued.

Activist Tactics

A difficult decision facing public hearing planners is the use of activist tactics—tactics that grab media attention and help create the appearance of public consensus. Although many persons equate activist tactics with civil disobedience and fringe group actions, these tactics also include innocuous aggressive activity such as lobbying a Congressman, as well as those that exceed accepted social norms such as bringing goats into a meeting room. Many of the activist tactics as shown in Figure 5–5 are merely aggressive, assertive actions undertaken with more energy and vigor than most individuals care to in-

---

Figure 5–5

A Catalog of Activist Tactics

• Actions within accepted social norms:
   — Hold a letter-writing work session
   — Lobby a public official
   — Hold a Bike-a-thon
   — Purchase shares of stock to legitimize a protest at a stockholder meeting
   — Form a "human billboard" (several people stand at busy intersections with large picket signs on long poles)
   — Conduct a tour of a site or project
   — Hold a vigil in a public place
   — Conduct a teach-in
   — Initiate a recall of a public official
   — Organize a march
   — Hold a seminar

Figure 5-5 (continued)

— Organize a work shop
— Make a survey; publicize results
— Enlist the support of a celebrity
— Threaten litigation
— Initiate litigation
— Pack a public hearing with supporters
— File a petition to deny broadcaster license renewal
— Set up a mock public officials board to challenge a public decision

•Actions outside accepted social norms:
— Occupy public lavatories at airports, bus stations until officials agree to a proposed action
— Hold a sit-in
— Hold a sleep-in
— Boycott an activity
— Hold a demonstration
— Organize a truck parade
— Hold a mock trial
— Hold a call-in (tie up the telephone lines)
— Expose political connections of public officials
— Cause inconvenience in a public place (a mass "shop in" to immobilize a shopping center)

•Actions that may involve civil disobedience (and the risk of arrest):
— Throw a cream pie at a public official
— Bring goats to a public hearing
— Bring dogs to a public hearing
— Heave manure at public officials
— Occupy a public place, preventing its peaceful use by others
— Climb over the fence surrounding an off-limits facility
— Obstruct the use of a public path by littering
— Take over a public building
— Camp out in a public place where camping is not allowed
— Hold a truck blockade

vest in citizenship—impolite, perhaps, but not as disruptive as civil disobedience.

Handling Adversary Activist Tactics at a Public Hearing

One of the most vexing challenges in a public hearing is the adversary who goes outside the accepted social norms—picketing, shouting, using confrontation tactics or outright civil disobedience. Non-activists find themselves in the predicament of the person dancing a disciplined minuet with a partner doing free-wheeling swing steps. Experience shows that the group which elects to act within the social norms when an adversary throws a cream pie or disrupts the hearing with motorcycles faces these consequences:

1. Most certainly, the non-activist group will be upstaged. Television cameras and newspaper photographers will focus on the activist tactics.

2. The excitement generated by the activist tactics will distract the decision-makers.

3. The activist tactics consume more time than rightfully allotted to the adversary position precluding a logical, orderly presentation, probably eliminating the use of audio-visuals.

4. The activist tactics may develop a climate of opinion that will influence lawmakers, the courts who hear appeals, and the public.

5. The activist tactics may prompt decision-makers to favor the activist position.

6. Officials may conclude that "We can't ignore all those people out there" and favor the activist advocacy because the tactics create a strong impression of public consensus.

Options for handling adversary activist techniques range from doing nothing to outdoing the activists. Doing nothing risks adverse consequences. Becoming a super-activist risks pitting inexperienced non-activists against experienced, street-wise activists. When they anticipate adversary activist action at the hearing, some groups select these middle-ground options:

•More aggressively use tactics within accepted social norms; for example, double the efforts of a letter-writing campaign; obtain 4000 names on a petition instead of 2000; create news.

•Release statements to the media prior to the public hearing, urging that the hearing be conducted with dignity and consideration for the decision-makers. This tactic puts the advocacy on the side of reason and law and order in contrast to adversaries who act outside normal behavior.

•Co-opt the activists by piggy backing on adversary tactics. A group opposed to the nuclear freeze activists co-opted their adversaries' tactic of a sign parade in front of the state capitol. Organizing their own sign parade, the antis marched around the pro-nuclear freeze parade. The television cameras recorded both groups.

•When confronted by "street politics," they call upon a street-wise consultant. For example, a federal agency applied for a routine permit to demolish an old, vacated building to make room for a new federal building. On behalf of transients who used the old building for shelter, a young attorney petitioned to deny the demolition. The transients staged a sit-in, organized a shouting picket line, and crowded the hearing room. The permit was denied. The agency responded by sending in a team of corporate attorneys who had not previously dealt with the Demolition Board. The demolition permit was again denied. As a last resort, a former political office-holder representing that ward was consulted. Calling for another public hearing, the street-wise office-holder negotiated with the Demolition Board to permit transients to use another building; the federal agency won its permit.

•They replace activist methods with drama techniques, using "show," rather than "tell" methods. To emphasize that the evidence supports the advocacy position, they don't merely state— "The weight of evidence is in favor of this position." They dramatize the point by displaying the impressive stack of evidentiary reports. They dramatize a noise problem by having an acoustical engineer record the offending noise and play it back at the hearing. In a budget hearing on an appropriation for the blind, they dramatize the plight of the blind by providing cloth blinders for decision-makers. Dramatization provides the media with that hook for grabbing the reader's attention.

When deliberating whether to adopt activist tactics for the public hearing process, the advice in activist Saul Alinsky's *Rules for Radicals* should be considered. *The Nation* called Saul Alinsky "This country's leading hell-raiser" and many observers regard him as the dean of American organizers of the poor. Alinsky advises:

— "Never go outside the experience of your people."
— "Whenever possible, go outside the experience of the enemy."

— "Make the enemy live up to their own book of rules."
— "A good tactic is one that your people enjoy. If your people are not having a ball doing it, there's something very wrong with the tactic."[2]

Using the Public Consensus Strategy in Appeals

Most public decisions can be appealed to some higher or different authority. The original public hearing decision is reversed frequently enough to make the appeals process an attractive alternative to accepting defeat. The Public Consensus Strategy may help in appealing the decision, especially if the media reports of the public hearing results indicate that officials paid little attention to the public voice.

The Public Consensus Strategy is also used in initiating legislation to legitimize an advocacy. An example is the mass demonstration of public support to promote stricter regulations for the storage of hazardous waste, thereby limiting the opportunity for public officials to approve hazardous waste sites.

TACTICS FOR THE PUBLIC INTEREST STRATEGY

The Public Interest Strategy attempts to persuade decision-makers that an advocacy is in the public interest. The Public Interest Strategy is useful for such technical matters as toxic chemical utilization or endangered species that are understood only by a few experts. It is also used when the predicted consequences of an action (or a product) instill a sense of public fear or insecurity. The Public Interest Strategy leans heavily on experts to define the public interest based on the assumption that the public, unfamiliar with the risks, dangers or opportunities, is unable to otherwise discover what is in its interest.

The Public Interest is, therefore, defined by special interests. In the prolonged controversy over how much federally owned forest land should be set aside as "wilderness," the public interest has been defined by the relatively few persons in the United States who value the wilderness areas—back-packers, naturalists, biologists and scientists

---

[2]Saul D. Alinsky, *Rules for Radicals* (New York: Random House, Inc., 1971), pp. 125–130.

who view wilderness as a public good and worry about losing the last herd of mountain caribou or the disappearance of pristine nature. Ralph Nader's "Big Business Day" promotion defined the public interest as increased government control of corporations. The citizen's lobby, Common Cause, defines the public interest as the reform of the federal government.

Sources of information for tactics for the Public Interest Strategy are available from:

1. The mailbox—many public interest groups solicit support through the mails. These solicitations explain goals, objectives and tactics used.

2. Public Interest Groups—Public Interest Groups are organized to promote special interests which they maintain are the public good. From environment to consumer credit, national parks to nuclear energy, public interest groups provide information and promote legislation to further their particular interests. Many public interest groups are prolific publishers. Garrett De Bell's *The Environmental Handbook* was prepared by Friends of the Earth. Ralph Nader's affiliates and their offspring publish extensively—Donald K. Ross' *A Public Citizen's Action Manual* was prepared by Public Citizen, Inc., a Nader organization.

3. Reference libraries—Some reference books for the Public Interest Strategy are:

— Gale's *Encyclopedia of Associations* which provides information on approximately 15,000 associations.
— Gale's *Consumer Sourcebook* which provides information for consumer protection and guidance.
— The Council of Planning Librarians (P.O. Box 229, Monticello, Illinois 61856) publishes exchange bibliographies, a resource for specialists in land-use and social planning.
— The media—news reported in the press, on radio and TV covers tactics for the Public Interest Strategy. Books by or about the environmental movement describe the tactics utilized to accomplish their objectives. *Citizens and the Environment—Case Studies in Popular Action,* by Lynton K. Caldwell, Lynton R. Hayes and Isabel MacWhirter typifies environmental action books.
— University Extension Offices and University Extension Services, funded by individual states or jointly with federal and local governments, include experts in many resource fields who

are also trained communicators and can assist the layman on technical subjects.

— *The Calendar of Federal Regulations*—published by the United States Regulatory Council summarizes information on proposed public interest legislation. For example, the listing on the Channel Island Marine Sanctuary Regulations under the authority of the Marine Protection, Research and Sanctuaries Act of 1972, covering several islands off the coast of California defines the public interests as commercial fishing, recreational fishers, boaters, tourists, endangered species, marine life and the general public.

Elements of Proof of the Public Interest

The tactic of documentation marks the Public Interest Strategy. Documentation includes statistical evidence, anecdotal evidence, or research evidence. Hearsay evidence has also been used with this strategy.

•*Statistical evidence* uses the persuasive magic of numbers. "Worst case" scenarios extrapolate existing data to compute statistics for "What if the worst imaginable catastrophe occurs." An example of the persuasion of statistics is Arthur Godfrey's introduction to his 1969 *The Arthur Godfrey Environmental Reader*.[3] Based on the extrapolation of then current population statistics, he concluded: "It is predicted, scientifically that we shall export our last grain of wheat in 1976—just six years away! Why? Because we will have no more surpluses to export. In fact, we won't have enough for ourselves." (As every farmer knows, Godfrey's scientific prediction of the death of wheat surpluses turned out to be grossly exaggerated.)

In the footnotes to a section he reprints from Robert and Leona Train Rienow's *Moment in the Sun*, Godfrey cites this statistical legerdemain as evidence of American overconsumption: "One American may consume more paper in one trip to a supermarket than an inhabitant of East or South Asia may consume in several months. Gross annual consumption of paper and paper board has now reached . . . about six times the paper consumption of any other industrial country."

---

[3]Arthur Godfrey, *The Arthur Godfrey Environmental Reader* (New York: Ballantine Books, 1969).

Statistical evidence provides "hard" data—or the appearance of hard data—that is difficult to refute, except with another set of "hard data."

•*Anecdotal evidence* carries the persuasion of human experience. The public more readily relates to the experience of other humans than to statistics. Rachel Carson's monumental *Silent Spring* published in 1962—credited with the genesis of the environmental era—used anecdotal data with consummate skill. "From the town of Hinsdale, Illinois, a housewife wrote in despair," Carson says, introducing a personal experience on the disappearance of bird life in her area. Again, "An Alabama woman wrote," Carson begins in describing another bird sanctuary experience. The influence of *Silent Spring* was considerably enhanced by Carson's ability to translate statistics to anecdotal evidence. Witness: "There are now only two or three dozen robins to be found each spring on the entire 185-acre campus of Michigan State University, compared with a conservatively estimated 370 adults in this area before spraying.[4]

Anecdotal evidence has been used extensively in the herbicide controversy, the nuclear energy controversy, and the effects of hazardous wastes.

•*Research evidence* utilizes or extrapolates research results as a tactic for demonstrating the public interest. Especially adapted to introducing a new worry, research results are the basis of "the scare of the week" phenomenon. New reports of a research project, a report on scientifically conducted tests, or a new government study provide the basis for research evidence.

•*Hearsay evidence,* wherein someone repeats without first-hand knowledge, or without technical qualifications for understanding, the evidence produced by others, is cited frequently. In a local controversy involving a permit to operate a manufacturing facility, opponents based their opposition on possible health hazards to the public. Opponents cited articles in the popular press reporting the research of one scientist which supported the contention that the manufacturing process was a health hazard; they avoided citing the research results that refuted their claim.

---

[4]From *Silent Spring* by Rachel Carson. Copyright © 1962 by Rachel Carson. Reprinted by permission of Houghton Mifflin Company.

Experts and the Public Interest Strategy

Tactics used to establish the public interest include forming alliances, educating by holding conferences (for example, "Earth Week"), organizing training courses, publishing advocacy books, introducing and promoting legislation, creating news, and litigation, but the tactic unique to the Public Interest Strategy is the dependence on experts—both trained and instant to establish the public interest.

The willingness of decision-makers to be persuaded that a proposal is in the public interest rests with the credibility of the experts citing the evidence, or on the persuasive ability of those who are not experts. The controversy over reopening the Three-Mile Island Nuclear plant near Harrisburg, Pennsylvania posed the credibility of nuclear scientists and engineers against the credibility of popular celebrities. The nuclear engineers and scientists who worked for the utility, the Nuclear Regulatory Commission and the local, state and federal governments were not as persuasive as Jane Fonda and other celebrities who disputed their conclusions. (Chapter 10 "Managing Public Hearings" includes a checklist to assist public officials in gauging the relative credibility of experts who present testimony. The checklist is equally useful to assist experts in preparing their testimony.)

The success of the promoters of such esoteric legislation as the Endangered Species Act (1975) or the Archaeological and Historic Data Conservation Act (1974) in persuading American lawmakers that these laws represent the public interest (although very few citizens are interested) rests with their ability to locate credible spokespersons—both public and expert, who testify on the complex concepts.

Interested citizens have demonstrated remarkable facility at acquiring instant expertise in complex and technical subjects. Credible public figures whose only qualification is immediate identification acquire instant expertise by reading and listening to the opinions of experts. They provide corroboration to puzzled decision-makers that the proposal is truly the public interest. Credible spokespersons include teachers, professors, and leaders with regional or national standing. Celebrities who espouse an action in the public interest become surrogate experts. Robert Redford, Jane Fonda, Joan Baez and the late Arthur Godfrey exemplify celebrities who have influenced the outcome of public hearings. The 1979 public hearings before the California Coastal Commission on the expansion of the deluxe Ventana Inn at Big Sur were called a "battle of the stars" because the five stormy public hearings featured singer John Denver supporting the expansion, singer Johnny Rivers opposing it, and actor Robert Redford urging denial on the grounds that "the unique quality of Big Sur has been overly abused."

An expert with a string of advanced degrees to his credit usually makes an impressive witness. The expert who also is able to clarify the complex concepts for non-technical decision-makers is a persuasive witness. Experts who communicate effectively follow these ground rules:

1. They deliberately avoid talking over the heads of decision-makers (or the public and media) by eliminating technical jargon, acronyms, and unfamiliar terms.

2. They resist the scientific format technical professionals use for preparing reports. They relate conclusions to concepts laymen understand.

3. They say exactly what they mean, avoiding obfuscation such as "the proper functioning of this component is critically dependent on its maintaining dimensional integrity" when they mean "the component won't work when it's bent."

4. They use only as many facts and figures as needed to make the point and no more.

5. They state clearly the explicit conclusion the audience should reach from the facts presented. They do not rely on simply reciting the facts and expecting the audience to supply the conclusion.

6. Some experts use the technique of a "Napoleon's Idiot" to assure that their testimony is understandable to lay decision-makers. Legend has it that before French leader Napoleon Bonaparte sent an order to his generals in the field, he would have his not-too-bright orderly read it and repeat what he thought the order meant. If the "idiot" could distort the meaning in any way Napoleon would rewrite it. While professional idiots are probably not for hire, some of the benefits of using an idiot are realized when persons from different disciplines review each other's testimony. A professional botanist who reviews an engineer's testimony and an engineer who reviews a botanist's testimony would be expected to quiz each other with the type of questions an intelligent lay person might ask.

7. Articulate experts shun inflicting the exhibits or figures from their scientific reports on a non-technical audience, using graphs and mathematical illustrations sparingly if at all, explicitly stating the conclusions to be drawn. Persuasive engineers use three-dimensional sketches rather than the engineering drawings few laymen understand.

8. Articulate experts make every effort to be understood. They avoid cut-away models that require an engineering degree for interpretation, using working miniatures and three-dimensional scale models instead.

A Classification of Special Interest Groups
Who Use Public Interest Tactics

Certain special interest groups use Public Interest Tactics with notable skill:

1. Environmentalists—organizations who consider the protection of the environment to be the public interest. These organizations range from conservative to those who propose revolutionary action. There are approximately 3,000 environmental groups in the United States. The top ten, based on membership and annual income:

— National Wildlife Federation
— National Audubon Society
— Sierra Club
— The Wilderness Society
— Izaak Walton League
— National Parks and Conservation Association
— Environmental Defense Fund
— Natural Resources Defense Council
— The Nature Conservancy
— Friends of the Earth

2. Conservationists—groups who view the public interest as conserving the land, saving trees or historic buildings, and preserving artifacts and history. (Environmental groups were at one time called conservationists. A distinction began to emerge between environmentalists and conservationists in the 1970's.) Conservationists have successfully promoted land-use regulation at levels of government higher than the traditional local zoning boards. Planning in the public interest and centralism (e.g. centralized planning by the federal or state government) are key to conservationist's tenets. Conservation organizations include such diverse groups as:

— National Association of Conservation Districts (NACD)
— California Coastal Alliance (over 100 component organizations with 1400 local chapters)
— One Thousand Friends of Oregon—a land-use watchdog group
— Save the Palm Trees

— The Conservation Foundation
— Save the (Train) Depot Committee
— Save the Covered Bridges Alliance

3. Minimum Risk-takers—diverse groups who believe that the public interest is to minimize perceived hazards to health, safety, and the quality of life. Dedicated to minimizing risks from technology and progress, these organizations carry the burden of protecting people from themselves. Risk minimizers include:

— Anti-nuclear groups, e.g. the "Clams," the Ground Zero group
— Anti-toxic spray groups, e.g. Citizens Against Toxic Sprays
— Anti garbage-burning plant groups, e.g. Families for Responsible Government
— Clean air groups, e.g. Action for Clean Air, Inc.
— Chemical poisoning, e.g. Citizens to End Lead Poisoning (CELP)

4. Consumerists—organizations who consider the public interest as protecting consumers (from business, their own follies, and the government). These powerful organizations have been responsible for introducing important legislation in the public interest. The consumer protection organizations include:

— Consumer Federation of America
— Student Public Interest Research Groups (SPIRGs)
— Common Cause
— Center for Science in the Public Interest
— Consumer Action Now (CAN)
— Ralph Nader Groups

TACTICS FOR THE LEGAL THEORY STRATEGY

The Legal Theory Strategy—one of the more expensive strategies—is a back-burner strategy, often used as a second line of attack when other strategies aren't working. For instance, Citizens for Equitable Housing (CEH), a group advocating construction of public housing, organizes testimony around the Fairness Strategy. Their request is denied. CEH then switches to the Legal Theory Strategy demanding another public hearing by claiming improper notification for the first hearing.

Tactics for the Legal Theory Strategy are investigation, monitoring, selection of a legal theory, and litigation.

—Investigation is a tactic for identifying applicable regulations and procedures. The techniques and sources of information for determining the regulations and procedures that apply were described in a previous chapter.

—Monitoring is a tactic for tracking conformance with regulations and procedures. Monitors personally watchdog procedure in every phase of the decision process, including maintaining independent records and keeping minutes of the hearings. Although state and federal hearings are usually taped or recorded by a court reporter or secretary, the printed minutes may not accurately reflect the testimony. Agencies at all levels of government are sometimes guilty of sloppy recordkeeping—documents kept loosely in folders with no method for recording whether papers have been removed or copied. Successful application of the Legal Theory Strategy requires meticulous recordkeeping.

—Selection of the legal theory is the tactic of isolating the particular technical elements of procedure, statutes or ordinances to be challenged.

Hinds[4] suggests six categories of legal theories to justify challenges:

1) Procedural denials of due process. (Insufficient notice of the hearing, denial of opportunity to testify, improper conduct of public officials.)
2) Technical challenges to jurisdiction or standing. (Statute of limitations, rights or propriety of parties to testify.)
3) Challenges to the authority of government to act. (Jurisdiction of the hearings board.)
4) Substantive challenges relating to denial of due process or equal protection. (Denial of equal protection, unreasonable use of government power.)
5) Substantive challenges to the police power of the government. (Use of government power to infringe on community health, safety, welfare or morality.)
6) Other constitutional attacks based on various grounds of public policy.

---

[4]Dudley S. Hinds, Neil G. Carn, and Nicholas Ordway, *Winning At Zoning* (New York: McGraw-Hill Book Company, 1979), pp. 151–152.

—Litigation is the tactic of appealing to the courts. Litigation usually is initiated by the party dissatisfied with the public decision. Based upon the challenges categorized above, litigation has become a powerful tactic in recent years. The National Environmental Policy Act and other legislation have enlarged the scope of public decisions subject to challenge by citizens. Aided by public funding of legal services for politicized power-shifting and of environmental activists, litigation has become the ultimate weapon in public decision-making.

Is an Attorney Required for the Legal Theory Tactics?

If the monitoring tactic discloses a minor breach—i.e. the seven-day notification period was only three days, or the 30-day appeal period had expired—the threat of going to court may be sufficient to influence a hearings board. A State Commission that otherwise might have been sympathetic to reopening a public hearing for new evidence might decide not to risk the legal consequences when it is pointed out that the 30-day time limit for reopening the hearing had elapsed. These monitoring activities, while important, do not require a lawyer.

But litigation requires the services of an attorney. Public Interest law firms, i.e. the Natural Resources Defense Council, the Center for Law and Social Policy, Mountain States Legal Foundation, Pacific Legal Foundation and others provide legal services for significant issues. The federally funded Legal Services Corporation provides free legal services to citizens who are otherwise unable to pay for legal assistance. In addition, a growing number of private attorneys specialize in government procedures and represent clients before government agencies. Each facet of government regulation has spawned new specialists, e.g. land use, energy, environmental protection, mining, social services, and other specialist attorneys. It is not uncommon for a hearings board in land-use, for instance, to hear one attorney who represents three or four different clients in succession.

Legal Theory Tactics differ from those used in a courtroom. The Legal Theory tactics lay the groundwork for litigation, but at the public hearing they focus attention on procedure and regulations. Legal Theory tactics serve to inhibit the hearings board from adopting procedures that may favor one party over the other. Nevertheless, the citizen who dreams of playing Perry Mason to impair the testimony of witnesses by pressure or other tactics is out of line in a public hearing because the public hearing does not attempt to establish guilt or innocence of parties. Tooth and fang courtroom procedures, bullying of witnesses, and threats of legal action are inappropriate. Sensitivity to the rights of witnesses is even more important in public hearings than in the courtroom as most hearings, including quasi-judicial and contested case hearings, are not legal proceedings and parties are not always represented or protected by an attorney.

Examples of Legal Theory Tactics

Tactics use for the Legal Strategy Theory include allegations of:

1. Inadequate environmental impact statement
2. Omission of the required public hearing
3. Improper notification, conduct or error in the hearing process
4. Questionable jurisdiction or standing
5. Questionable authority of the government to act
6. Questionable interpretation of the law
7. Deprivation of *due process*
8. Violation of civil rights.

How these allegations are used is illustrated by the case history of a public hearing on a hazardous waste disposal site. Several hearings were conducted with more than 100 citizens testifying, most opposing the disposal site. The vehemence of public opposition collided with the importance of the industry to the community. As a compromise, the Board approved the site, requiring the company to provide extensive and expensive mitigation. The hard-core opposition, dissatisfied with the mitigation, demanded that the hearing be reopened because the hearings officer deprived them of due process in the hearing.

Risks in the Legal Theory Tactics

Time, cost, and possible reversal of the decision are major risks of using Legal Theory tactics. But tactics such as investigation and monitoring, are readily handled by most groups and act as insurance if the Legal Theory Strategy must be used.

•*Time* represents delays if the decision is litigated. When a decision gets into the courts, months or years elapse until a project gets on line or a problem is solved.

•*Costs* are twofold: (1) the expense of preparing a case and fighting in the courts, and (2) the costs associated with inflation as projects are delayed. Expert witnesses, attorney's fees, tests and other expenses consume thousands of dollars. Even a minor zoning dispute will probably cost more than $25,000 to litigate the first round. Hundreds of thousands of dollars may be required to resolve matters in the courts.

•*A decision may be reversed by a higher authority.* Some decisions go through three or four higher authorities with as many reversals. The possibility of reversal encourages continued litigation.

If a public decision is litigated, the hearing testimony, how the public hearing was conducted, and who testified constitute the record. Public consensus, the public interest, fairness, equity and other considerations influence the final decision. The record of every public hearing should be established to form the basis of possible future litigation.

TACTICS FOR THE FAIRNESS STRATEGY

When a constituent cries, "Unfair!" public officials shudder. Few persons accept with equanimity the accusation of "unfair." The Fairness Strategy attempts to persuade decision-makers that outcomes advocated are fair. Social changes and social movements are built around the Fairness Strategy, focusing on what has been termed "suffering situations." Both confrontation styles and public advocacy tactics styles are used for the Fairness Strategy.

Consider a public hearing on the establishment of a local Rape Crisis Center. In the 1970's, promoters of such a center would have devoted a period of time—a considerable time—to consciousness-raising. The consciousness-raising tactic would be needed to legitimize culturally induced problems of sexism, discrimination against women, and problems of women who were raped, as community problems. Then, after these were identified as community problems, a Rape Crisis Center could be introduced as a solution. Community consciousness would be raised by conferences, newsletters, support networks, media campaigns, speaker's bureaus and other educational and informational techniques.

By the 1980's consciousness-raising had taken hold: culturally-induced problems of women had acquired legitimacy. The principle of treating women fairly had been established. A public hearing on a Rape Crisis Center could focus on helping decision-makers demonstrate that they were treating women fairly by allocating financial and other resources to the Center

The tactics style adopted would depend on the consciousness-scale of the community. The tactics vary with the position of the community (or state or nation) on the consciousness-scale. The consciousness-scale is a qualitative estimate of the community consciousness of the problem: Is the community conscious of the problem? Is it ready to acknowledge that the problem requires a solution? Is it a culturally induced problem (racism, sexism, ethnic) or an economically induced problem (high rents, high utility bills, welfare rights)? These techniques are used to determine the consciousness-scale:

•*Participant observation*—viewing the community by participating in it as an insider. The participant making the observations does so inconspicuously, listening and questioning inobtrusively. The participant observer attends meetings and interviews leaders, but does not take the role of an advocate or activist.

•*Surveys*—collecting data about citizen attitudes. If the surveys are to be used only to guide planning, volunteer surveyors may provide the information. To use the survey as the basis of testimony or news releases, recognized survey experts should be consulted. In either case:

— The survey sample should be representative of the population.
— The questions should be framed to elicit specific answers.
— The questions should be clear to assure unambiguous answers.
— The interviewers should be trained.
— The survey should be pre-tested on a representative sample.

The consciousness-scale survey may show that the community is (1) very conscious of the problem and its equities, or (2) quite conscious of the problem but not ready to accept solutions, or (3) oblivious to the existence of the problem and therefore not ready to consider solutions. If the community is very conscious of the problem the Fairness Strategy can comfortably use the system sponsored tactic style and rely on media campaigns, debates, forums and pamphlets. If it is quite conscious of the problem but not ready to accept solutions, the Fairness Strategy increases acceptance of solutions by public advocacy style tactics of research, education, documentation and massing supporters at the public hearing. Community alternative tactic styles may also be used.

However, if the community appears oblivious to the problem, two tactic styles are available: Consciousness-raising or Confrontation styles. Confrontation styles are used when consciousness-raising has been attempted, but the values of the community are so polarized that coercing decision-makers remains the only method of solving the problem.

The Fairness Strategy is often used to oppose the public interest as proclaimed by special interests. The prolonged debate on setting aside national wilderness areas is an example of the conflict between the Public Interest Strategy and the Fairness Strategy: The wilderness advocates proclaim that it is in the public interest to set aside areas as untouched wilderness. The communities and forest industry claim that setting aside wilderness unfairly deprives them of jobs.

Three tactics effectively serve the Fairness Strategy:

1) *The underdog.* This tactic is common in the siting of hazardous waste facilities. Opponents question the fairness of having their community bear a disproportionate share of the environmental pollution and pollution abatement costs of modern industry. The question of equity or fairness often overrides other concerns.

2) *Mistreatment.* This tactic is used to demonstrate that a group has been mistreated through no fault of its own. Workers requesting a permit to reopen a closed facility as a worker-owned factory utilize this tactic.

3) *Deprived.* This tactic is used by the Poor People's Movements, Women's Rights, the handicapped, and ethnic minority movements to demonstrate that persons have been deprived of their rights. Many federal Grants-in-Aid require representation of these special interests on councils and committees to assure that these persons have a say in protecting their rights.

Fair to Whom?

The word "fair" implies that all sides are treated alike and impartially, suggesting a compromise or negotiation. But in public hearing strategy *fair* is the product of a power struggle between single-issue groups who attempt to establish a perception of equity that coincides with their interest. An "interest" is defined as any entity who shares a consistent value system on a specific project or issue. Each single issue or special interest group demands treatment according to a rather narrow definition of *fair*. Special interest groups include right-to-lifers and pro-abortionists, "union busters" and "labor baiters," "big-spending liberals" and "tight-fisted conservatives," pro-gun and anti-gun forces.

Special interest groups who use Fairness tactics may be classified as:

—Physically impaired, including seven major organizations for the blind, 30 million physically handicapped (who successfully promoted Section 504 of the Rehabilitation Act of 1973, causing the expenditure of millions of dollars to provide access for the handicapped.

—Economically disadvantaged, including the rural poor (e.g. OBRC-Organization for a Better Rice County), the Urban poor (ACORN and FAIR SHARE).

—System sufferers, including groups who have been deprived by the social system (e.g. Gay Rights, Pro-abortionists).

—Wrong-Righters, including feminist organizations, civil rights organizations (National Organization of Women [NOW], National Association of Colored Persons [NAACP]).

—Age disadvantaged, including senior citizens, retired groups, youth groups (Gray Panthers, Aging Advisory Councils, National Youth Employment Coalition, Youth Action Program).

—Humanists, including groups promoting humane treatment for animals, babies, whales (Greenpeace).

How Citizens Use Fairness Strategy Tactics

Citizens use Fairness Strategy tactics to develop the public perception that they have been treated unfairly. The following three examples are gleaned from media reports (tactics used follow each example in parentheses):

1. A media release: "Supporters of gay rights defeated in a key Senate vote Monday, returned to the Legislature Thursday night. . . Representatives from the Privacy Coalition, a lobby group for Gay Rights, told the House Human Resources hearing that homosexuals are discriminated against by the state Children's Services Division, the Mental Health Division and the Liquor Control Commission." (Tactics used: Deprived; system sponsored style.)

2. From another news story: Hundreds of federal employees waving signs in front of the White House bearing the legend, "Federal employees want to be treated fairly!" protested the proposal to require future government workers to join the Social Security System. (Tactics used: Underdog; confrontation style.)

3. And yet another story: Youth groups lobbied Congress not to lower the minimum wage for youths 22 years old and under on the grounds of unfair exploitation of young people. The lobbyists cited data which they maintained proved that lowering the minimum wage was unfair, took advantage of youth and would not lead employers

to hire more young people. (Tactics used: Mistreatment; public advocacy style.)

How Governments Use Fairness Tactics

Governments recognize the need for citizen support or "Substantial Effective Agreement on a Course of Action" (SEACA) as The Institute for Participatory Planning calls it. In deciding which trade-offs to settle for, they consider the effect on the various interest's sense of fairness. When a government allows controversies to degenerate into polarized symbolic politics where one side appears to be treated unfairly as compared to the other, the government becomes the loser.

An example of how the Fairness Strategy generated a difficult and losing decision game for the mayor and city hall policy makers was the City of New York Transit Strike of 1966. Invoking the Fairness Strategy, Mayor Lindsay maintained that New York was being victimized by power brokers (the Transit Workers Union) who were seeking private gain at the expense of the citizens. "Not so," claimed Mike Quill, the leader of the Transit Workers Union, insisting that the fight was really between the upper-class elite and the little guys seeking a decent wage and that transit workers were the victims of unfair treatment. Mike Quill's claim that the little guys were the victims was bolstered when the union leadership was marched off to jail, martyrs to the cause. Quill's use of the Fairness Strategy influenced the decision in the Transit Workers' favor.

TACTICS FOR THE MISTAKE STRATEGY

The Mistake Strategy feeds upon the reluctance of public officials to make mistakes and their greater reluctance to admit mistakes. The Mistake Strategy combines the tactics of the Public Consensus Strategy, the Public Interest Strategy and the Fairness Strategy to demonstrate that the public consensus believes that it is in the public interest and fair to most citizens to avoid or promote a specific mistake. Tactics for the Mistake Strategy include research, documentation, communication and lobbying. Avoiding confrontation tactics, the Mistake Strategy usually stays with the public advocacy style.

Two examples of the Mistake Strategy tell how authorities and the public were persuaded that an affirmative decision was a mistake:

• *The Defeat of the Supersonic Transport (SST)* blended several public advocacy tactics to induce Congress to reverse its decision to fund the SST—in the face of massive support from powerful sources. Tactics used by opponents to persuade Congress that funding the SST would be a mistake included the public advocacy tactics of research, education, lobbying, and coalition building. The public hearings were carefully planned and skillfully orchestrated, using aggressive activist tactics sparingly. The campaign to defeat the SST achieved a major victory using tactics within the accepted social norms:

— Organizing an advocacy group (Citizens' League Against the Sonic Boom—CLASB).
— Forming a coalition with environmental groups to demonstrate public support (The SST Handbook Appendix 1 listed 21 Anti-Boom Groups).
— Preparing and distributing educational material (*The SST and Sonic Boom Handbook*) which succeeded in arousing public fears about excessive noise from SST aircraft.
— Supporting legislation (the Aircraft Noise Abatement Act of 1968) directing the government to abate excessive aircraft noise.
— Locating technical experts to establish that the public interest lay in preventing sonic booms rather than accepting them as the price of progress; clarifying the complex concepts for instant understandability by the public and media.
— Raising questions on the accuracy of the cost estimates for the project and persuading the public that the cost to the taxpayer would be greater than anticipated.
— Winning strong media support.
— Persuading the public that they would be paying unfairly for the advantage of the few who would gain from the SST.
— Impugning the credibility of the government by alleging five misleading statements by the Federal Aviation Administration and publishing the report and comments of the Ad Hoc Review Committee appointed by President Nixon. (The report was allegedly withheld from the public for six months.)

The second example of the Mistake Strategy was the defeat of the proposal to hold the 1976 Winter Olympics in a western state. Although strongly supported by the governor of the state as well as by business and political leaders, the Olympics were called a "mistake" at the public hearings. A citizen-led anti-Olympic movement bypassed the legislature, garnering a sufficient number of signatures to place the issue to a direct public vote. By a 5-to-3 margin the voters defeated funding for the Olympics, showing unquestionably that they were persuaded that hosting the Winter Olympics would be a mistake. The tactics used to defeat the Olympics included:

— Demonstration of public consensus in opposition to hosting the games by collecting 25,000 signatures on a petition.
— Demonstration of the public interest by raising environmental considerations that would have long-range impacts on the state.
— Winning the support of the Mexican-American and Black communities by indicating that it was unfair to spend the money for the Olympics which could be better invested in improving social programs on their behalf.
— Winning the support of homeowners in the affected community by pointing out that they would be bearing an unfair adverse impact of the Olympics while gaining nothing in return.
— Forming a coalition with anti-growth advocates.
— Revealing that cost estimates were mistaken and that the potential cost would have to be borne by the taxpayers.
— Impugning the integrity, credibility and capability of the organizers of the Olympics.

Many of the organizers of the anti-Olympic effort were veterans of Senator Eugene McCarthy's unsuccessful presidential bid. They brought to the fight organizational skills and knowledge of the public hearing process that far exceeded the skills of the Olympic promoters. They attacked aggressively from every angle, boring in whenever they discovered a weak spot. Few confrontational tactics were noted by the media. The anti-Olympic group stayed mostly within accepted social norms using those tactics aggressively to persuade the voters that the Olympics would be a mistake.

TACTICS FOR THE MITIGATION STRATEGY

The Mitigation Strategy plays upon the preference of public officials to please as many constituents as possible. The tactics for this strategy involve discovering the divisive issues, devising options to resolve the issues, and establishing a workable procedure for all parties to accept the options.

Mediation is a tactic for the Mitigation Strategy. Mediation assumes that the parties involved in a dispute have the most information concerning the issues and will, under appropriate conditions, provide the best solution to a conflict. For Mediation to work, all parties must feel that they have something to gain. Public officials welcome citizen mediation in an otherwise win-lose conflict.

Inviting all parties to a meeting is the smoothest way to initiate Mediation. In a bitter conflict, getting the parties to meet is often the most difficult task. A mediator assists the parties to lay out the issues of the conflict. A skilled mediator helps the parties realize that the conflict could be in the perception rather than the reality. But if the conflict is real, the mediator tries to find interests that all parties share, some value or concern they have in common. Building on these commonalities, the mediator leads the parties to enlarge upon the areas of agreement and to invent solutions to the conflict. The parties retain full control of the conflict while seeking an agreeable solution.

Mediation Through a Third-Party is a tactic for resolving conflicts resulting from a continuing difference between groups. Finding an independent third party acceptable to all groups is a major challenge. When the third party has been selected, he can suggest and conduct trade-off negotiations at a formal public hearing where competing interests meet face to face, or he can act as a go-between at separate meetings. Either method can be time-consuming and expensive.

The tactic of *Negotiation* requires that both parties to a conflict be ready and willing to discuss giving up something to reach a solution. Roger Fisher and William Ury[5] point out that people usually see only two ways to negotiate: soft or hard. The soft negotiator makes concessions readily in order to avoid personal conflict. The hard negotiator sees any negotiation as a contest of wills and holds out longer in an attempt to maintain his position. Fisher and Ury propose a third method—*principled negotiation* in which issues are decided on their merits rather than on the positions of the negotiators.

Arbitration, in which parties agree to submit their dispute to an independent third party who has authority to find a solution, is a Mitigation Theory tactic. Rarely used because decision-makers feel that decisions are their responsibility, two sides who can present an agreed-upon outcome to a hearings board have a reasonable expectation that a decision favoring that outcome will be recommended.

Preventive mitigation is the objective of the Public Acceptance Assessment described previously. Step eight of this ten-step assess-

---

[5]Roger Fisher and William Ury, *Getting To Yes* (Boston: Hougton Mifflin Company, 1981), page xii.

ment evaluates which impacts can be altered or controlled in order to reduce public opposition. Mitigating these perceived or actual adverse impacts in the planning process before they become a focus for public agitation minimizes and, sometimes, avoids controversy.

Sources of Information for Mitigation Tactics

Recognition of the dimensions of the conflict is basic to the Mitigation Strategy. Information on the conflict can be obtained by the Public Acceptance Assessment, participant observation and surveys, or other citizen participation techniques including:

- Fishbowl planning—asking citizens to react to several alternatives.
- Conducting a charette—directly involving citizens in the development of a plan.
- Brainstorming—encouraging participants to express their ideas on needs, goals and values.
- Conducting a working session retreat—providing groups an opportunity to apply innovative thinking.

Example of the Mitigation Theory Tactics

Mitigation Theory tactics were applied by the Kansas Industrial Environmental Services (KIES) in obtaining a permit to operate a waste disposal facility about 15 miles from Wichita, Kansas. An information meeting about the site was attended by about 200 angry residents, many fighting mad and vowing to take any steps necessary to stop KIES. To mitigate the conflict, the Kansas Department of Health and Environment (KDHE), the agency responsible for issuing the permit, worked with a study group established by the Kansas legislature and a citizen group to develop extremely stringent restrictions that responded to opponents' concerns. The strict regulations, described by the EPA Region VII staff as among the tightest in the nation, helped allay the fears of residents. Increased confidence in KIES as well as trust that their government through KDHE was protecting them, reassured citizens and reduced their opposition to the project.

Mitigation tactics are unlikely to succeed in the absence of communication and trust between citizens and their government. If the leaders of any of the interests believe they will gain by continuing the conflict, there is little incentive to mitigate. Mitigation tactics have been applied to larger environmental issues on a state or federal level where interests are less likely to discover an immediate personal stake.

6

Communication Techniques for Public Hearings

"News just isn't news until it's reported as such," observed Ellen Stern Harris, leader of the fight to clean the polluted California Los Angeles-Long Beach harbor area. "If you didn't read it in the paper, see it on TV, or hear it on the radio, it's as if it never happened."

The media influence the outcome of public hearings. If the media ignore a problem, the public hearing is likely to be a perfunctory exercise. If the media report extensively on the issue or project, the public hearing becomes an event luring citizens and reporters from firesides and TV. The media's selection of the persons to quote, attitudes on issues, and the judgments they make create the public perception which influences the decision.

This chapter discusses the methods of obtaining fair and accurate media coverage and how to generate news. It includes preparation of news stories for public hearings, media mechanics, orchestrating testimony for media coverage, testimony as communication and other communication techniques for the public hearing process.

HOW TO OBTAIN FAIR AND ACCURATE MEDIA COVERAGE

Headlines and news emphasis can create adversaries out of interests who merely disagree with each other and transform vague ideas to polarized perceptions. Consider the following excerpt from a by-lined news story in a major newspaper:

"ALUMINUM COMPANY GETS POLLUTION PERMIT FOR SMELTER"

"Despite local fears about potential acid rain and crop damage, state officials have granted an air pollution permit to the Aluminum Company for a proposed $500-million aluminum smelter in the northeastern part of the State . . . The terms of the permit have been challenged by environmentalists and by farming corporations because of concerns about the potential for acid rain and excessive emissions of fluorides with the potential to damage crops. . . ."

The story quoted organizations and individuals opposed to the permit elaborating the reasons for opposition. The report omitted the evidence cited by the state officials as the basis for the permit. Not surprisingly, the public demanded another hearing after the story appeared, and the second hearing was stormy.

Lester Markel, a retired editor of the *New York Times* comments: "Admittedly, the ideal of objectivity is hard to realize. Lapses into non-objectivity are more easily, and much more frequently, achieved by editing tricks and word manipulation." Attempts at objective newswriting are scorned by disciples of "advocacy journalism" as barriers to reporting the truth.

Few media professionals dispute that "slanting" of the news is practiced. The concern in the public hearing process is how to best handle the reality of slanted news.

"Give us *fair and accurate coverage*," plead participants in a conflict. But *fair and accurate coverage* is difficult to achieve—a difficulty compounded by the media's problems in obtaining accurate information and by the organization's problems in providing accurate information.

Most advocates concede that fair coverage affords an opportunity for all views to be heard and read. Activists define fair coverage as that which promotes their ideology. Some reporters attempt to cover public hearings fairly by quoting an equal number of opponents and proponents. But is a story fair when 30 persons have spoken for a proposal and only two have spoken against it, and the report quotes but two of the proponents and all two of the opponents? Accurate coverage is difficult to assess, especially when reputable experts cite contradictory facts. How does the media determine which facts are indeed factual?

The media present special problems in obtaining fair and accurate coverage, ideological biases aside. A reporter preparing a story on a public hearing must meet a tight deadline. The reporter deciphers the scribbled notes of the four- or five-hour hearing to quickly get at the who, what, when, where and why. He searches for the controversy, for the colorful quotes, for the unique bit of appeal that qualifies his story for space and optimum location. He rarely enjoys the luxury of time to verify a quote, or the spelling of a name, or the accuracy of the data. In addition to the problem of inaccuracies due to bias, the inadvertent errors due to the way news is gathered and transmitted lead one to marvel when a name *is* spelled correctly. Media requirements are less frustrating when there is a good working relationship with the editors, TV stations, radio talk show hosts, "stringers" (correspondents for statewide or regional newspapers), and local authors. Any group who leaves an information vacuum by not providing accurate information forces the media to stress the emotional responses resulting in a public perception that may not represent the facts.

The most satisfactory method for preventing inaccurate reporting is to provide the media with credible data and ample information following these rules:

1. Double check facts
2. Attribute information to sources
3. Use names, quotes, specifics
4. Supply background material
5. Provide a glossary that defines the technical or special terms
6. Provide typed lists of names, titles, affiliations
7. Help the media understand the problems and the position advocated
8. Avoid setting up an adversary position with media persons who are merely doing their jobs.

FIVE TECHNIQUES FOR FAIR AND ACCURATE COVERAGE

Five communication techniques increase the probability that a position will be fairly and accurately reported: (1) acquire instant identification; (2) generate news; (3) think and write headlines; (4) provide credible information; and (5) be assertive.

Acquire Instant Identification

The advocacy group provides the instant identification, the adjectival tag, the media need for the "who" in a news story. A newspaper report on a court order banning herbicide spraying in the forest begins: "Anti-herbicide activist Sam Jones has won a federal court-ordered ban on all government forest spraying near his home." A by-lined story on President Reagan's trip to Pittsburgh is headlined "Jobless Protesters Jeer President in Pittsburgh." (The 6th paragraph of the article explains that the protesters were largely unemployed steelworkers.) "Scared Neighbors Leave Dioxin Town," another story begins.

If a group does not tag itself the media will. The best protection against an objectionable tag is to establish an identity. An appropriate name lends itself to a creative acronym that accurately describes an advocacy: There's no mistaking the purpose of Group Against Smelter Pollution (GASP) or Environmental Action for Survival (ENACT). But Citizens for Food and Fiber requires further identification.

A useful technique in acquiring instant identification is a concise, comprehensive statement of the advocacy organization's objective. ENACT (Environmental Action for Survival) at the University of Michigan identified itself with this statement:

> "ENACT seeks to stimulate increasingly widespread awareness of the delicate balance upon which life depends, and of the rapidity with which man is destroying this vital balance. We will take action to halt this destruction. By providing accurate information and guidelines to effective action we will work to encourage commitment, by individuals and by institutions, to attack these critical problems with a sense of urgency and priority."

Emotive media words are used throughout: stimulate, awareness, vital, action, guidelines, commitment, attack, urgency, priority.

A spokesperson facilitates instant identification, especially one whose personal credibility adds credence to the organization—a popular minister, political figure, educator, or community leader. An articulate or colorful spokesperson gains additional media attention for an advocacy. When a spokesperson is named, a safeguard is to provide the media with a listing of the group's leadership structure including telephone numbers where they can be reached for further information if the spokesperson is unavailable.

An advocacy may appeal to and enlist the services of an identifiable celebrity with access to talk shows, television interviews, and reporters. Robert Redford is credited with a significant role in the defeat of the Kaiparowits Project—an electrical generation plant in the Southwest which was cancelled after environmentalist protests. Robert Redford has been associated with numerous environmental projects, to the extent that some observers feel that he now provides a "knee-jerk" reaction that diminishes his value to causes. The Associated Press reported that Washington State University and the University of Idaho, who jointly landed Robert Redford's Institute for Research Management, also landed complaints from numerous prominent individuals. Branding Redford a "radical environmentalist," these persons felt that Redford's Institute would heighten rather than defuse the emotional battle between industrialists and environmentalists.

Lacking an identifiable celebrity, one can be created. By speaking at public hearings, by issuing statements to the press and initiating aggressive action—litigation or accusations—a person can acquire celebrity status. Land-use "watchdogs" who attend and speak at every state land-use meeting, environmental "watchdogs", etc. quickly become news figures. TV cameras aim in their direction, reporters flock to them for statements, the hearings board listens expectantly. The person may make the same or similar statements each time, but no matter, he or she has become a celebrity.

Generate News

If an average citizen speaks at a local planning commission hearing, the media may not notice. If the governor of the state speaks, that's news to the local paper and state papers. If the same governor speaks at a public hearing in Washington, D.C., his position doesn't automatically qualify him as a newsmaker; he competes with other important officials for space. Only an unusual statement will qualify as news.

What's news varies with the level of government involved. A request for rezoning to construct a hotel is major news in the local media. If that hotel is in an area under the federal Coastal Zone Management Act of 1972, the rezone request expands to state or even national status. Any action in which Congress is involved has national status.

An issue of importance to an advocacy may end in the media waste basket. Figure 6-1, When a News Story Isn't Published, illustrates how to determine whether the story really qualifies as news.

If it does not qualify as news, news can be generated. The medium may be the message but the media won't transmit a message unless it qualifies as news.

Figure 6-1

When a News Story Isn't Published

If a story isn't published consider the following:

1. Is the story important to the area? Closing of the local widget manufacturing plant idling 50 workers may be local headline news, but have no interest for the *Times*. If the plant closed is an asbestos producing facility, the *Times* may feature the closure as part of a national trend. A speech by a prominent expert to the local Rotary Club is news to a small town. The same expert may be ignored by a large city newspaper—unless he is very prominent.

2. Is the story about a well-known person? Identifiable people make news.

3. Is the story timely? Has it just happened, or is it going to happen in the near future?

4. Will the story seize the imagination of the public? Does it concern some element of the human condition—conflict, age, fear, sympathy, uniqueness—to which people can relate?

5. Does the story reflect the passions of love, hate, deceit, disappointment, ambition or other commonly shared feelings?

If a story fails to meet any of these criteria, it probably won't pass for news.

How to Generate News

Symbolic actions or news hooks attract media attention. For example, leaders of a new government program to train and find jobs found the local press inhospitable to their news releases. As far as the press was concerned the program did not exist. Ignored by the press the public hearings for the program became non-events. However, during the funding designation, elected officials engaged in a bitter turf battle. The conflict immediately aroused interest in the program. The media assigned reporters to cover the battle; editors personally read future news releases.

Conflict, dramatization, actions outside the accepted social norms, and activist techniques generate news. Conflicts can be created and events staged within or outside the social norms:

•*Create a conflict*. Environmentalists "wage" a cleanup campaign against an industry polluting a stream. Social activists "accuse" business of insensitivity. "Against," "Accuse," "Attack," "Dissent," "Cram," "Snags," "Raps," "Oppose," "Fight," "Tangle"—are the currency of conflict. For example, this article from the *Las Vegas Sun*:

> (Headline) PROTESTS LEAD NUKE HEARING
> BRYAN HEADS DISSENT
> (Lead paragraphs)   Hundreds of Nevadans told the federal government Wednesday to keep a national high-level nuclear repository out of the Silver State during the nation's second public hearing on the issue.
>
> Gov. Richard Bryan vowed to veto a presidential decision to develop the Nevada Test Site as a crypt for radioactive wastes spawned by the nation's 72 operating nuclear power plants. . . .

And this headline from the (Portland) *Oregonian*:

> REAGAN BLASTS EPA CRITICS,
> ENVIRONMENTALISTS

and from the Eugene *Register Guard*:

> ANTI-ARMS PROTESTS MARK GOOD FRIDAY

•*Create an event*. Pack a public hearing, stage a demonstration, hold a news conference, hold a seminar—preferably an event described by an active verb: The Seminar can "reveal"; the demonstrators "denounce"; the news conference "expose." The more dramatic the event, the better news generator. The activist tactics described in the previous chapter are news generators. Civil disobedience and actions outside the accepted social norms win more media space than mere aggressive actions.

•*Personify and localize the target*. Another method of generating news is to personify and localize a target for the advocacy activity.

Attacking city hall is vague and abstract but a dirty pool attack on the mayor generates news for the advocacy. An attack on a company president is more newsworthy than attacking the company.

Think and Write Headlines

News writers struggle to explain controversies in the fewest words and with minimum discussion. To achieve this objective they think and write headline style. The media is more likely to report the story as submitted if the news is written this way. An Associated Press story about two men who chained themselves near the banks of the Stanislaus River in order to force President Carter to declare the area a national monument illustrates instant understanding through headline thinking:

> "Two protestors, one of them disabled, who shackled themselves by the banks of the Stanislaus River in an attempt to block flooding of a stretch of white water, left their hiding spot Sunday."

It is clear that these persons were protestors, that one of them was disabled and that the news is important. The story might have begun: "Robert Metts and Jeanne Marlow chained themselves together near the Stanislaus River on January 6 and did not unchain themselves until January 11 in order to convince President Carter to declare a national monument." This beginning included the five "w's" but it would not have created instant understanding or interest.

Another example of instant understanding is a story from the *New York Times* News Service:

> "Concern is growing among public health officials, environmentalists, scientists and legislators that contamination by dioxin, one of the most toxic substances created by humans, may turn out to be a serious national problem for which they are ill-prepared."

The entire meaning of this paragraph could have been altered by changing the description of dioxin. The phrase "one of the most toxic substances created by humans" could have been restated as: "believed to be one of the most toxic substances created by humans"; "claimed by some scientists to be one of the most toxic substances created by humans"; "a toxic substance found in nature and believed to be one of the most toxic substances created by humans"; or "a chemical which has been the focus of considerable controversy." The qualifier "one of the most toxic substances created by humans" is bound to frighten the public. Preceding the statement by "believed to be" or "claimed" modifies the fright to serious concern. In the sixth paragraph of the story, dioxin is finally put in perspective: "There is no reliable information about how much dioxin has been produced or where it is, and there is considerable controversy over what danger it poses to health and the environment. Nobody knows for sure."

Provide the Media with Credible Information

Providing the media with credible information establishes an advocacy as a media resource. In this day of high technology, the media depends on technically trained specialists to condense complex information for the non-technical public. Complicated charts and scientific jargon stand in the way. Media personnel welcome the advocate who makes a point of:

— Being available to answer questions.
— Answering candidly and honestly.
— Providing complete background information.
— Discussing pros and cons of controversies.
— Providing references, statistical material, quotations.
— Avoiding "No comment" answers.
— Interpreting technology in lay terms.
— Risking "off the record" answers.
— Providing a summary of testimony by experts or celebrities.

Be Assertive

Being assertive with the media means aggressively earning media friendship: telephoning to express appreciation for a good story (very few persons do, forgetting that reporters are people too; they appreciate praise) and telephoning to express disapproval in a polite, professional manner. Meeting media deadlines is also an assertive action, indicating intent to work with the media.

MEDIA COVERAGE OF PUBLIC HEARINGS

Experienced advocacy groups know how to capture the TV spots and column-inches: they orchestrate public hearings for media coverage, putting on newsworthy presentations with the media present. If forced to choose between producing the most dramatic testimony for the media, or saving it for the final clinching persuasion for the decision-makers, they select media exposure. At the Congressional hearings on energy, the media ignored testimony by eminent scientists and prominent industry officials. But an environmental leader made first-page national news by setting his three-year-old daughter and her dolls on the hearing table and stating simply, "This is why we must conserve energy."

Fresh faces, fresh ideas, and celebrities catch media attention. In the perennial jobs versus environment public hearings, the wife whose husband's job is at risk is more effective than the plant manager who speaks abstractly about 50 jobs. Grass-roots groups are good at presenting the dramatic testimony that attracts media coverage. At public hearings that allow speakers to appear in order of sign up, an orchestrated hearing brings in newsmakers early for media exposure. In a morning hearing, the television cameras leave by 10:30 a.m.; the newspaper reporters by noon. Testifying after the media leaves sacrifices the opportunity to appear on the 6:00 o'clock news. Experienced groups know this and fight for prime time. Sometimes all that is required is a phone call to the staff member in charge of the hearing asking for an early spot on the agenda. In a "showcase" hearing, some political clout may need to be added to the request.

The leader of a social services group with a history of successfully influencing decisions confided this advice: "You'll never fail to grab a headline if you bring along a crier—someone who can really put on the tears. It will get them every time."

Newsmaking techniques range from identifying supporters with colorful T-shirts that catch the TV eye (The only TV coverage of an all day hearing on a hazardous waste site was devoted to the chests of opponents whose bright green T-shirts were emblazoned with the statement: "Don't make us the toilet of the State"), to presenting huge fish to the officials, or outsize deer antlers, or a forest of miniature trees, or whatever dramatizes and personifies the message. At a public hearing on remodeling buildings to improve access to the handicapped, a wheelchair brigade at the front of the room dramatized the problem of the handicapped. Four aged women carrying placards outside a hearing room dramatized the needs of the aged (and won TV and wire service coverage). Packing the hearing room with supporters readily identified by the TV camera helps demonstrate the numbers essential for the Public Consensus Strategy. The T-shirts or large slogan-bearing buttons add visibility to that support.

Handling a Media Set-up

The investigative reporter who searches for and writes about corruption by businessmen, public officials, individuals, or organizations may win a prize and can certainly count on an audience. Despite libel laws and back-page apologies for front-page errors, there is always danger that an innocent person may be "set-up" or cast in the villain role by being misquoted or quoted out of context. These are suggestions from a person who found himself set up once too often:

- 1. Learn which reporters or interviewers have set-up others with similar ideas. Prepare and rehearse answers to potential embarrassing questions.
- 2. Tape or video record the interview for comparison with the report. If broadcast, use discrepancies to appeal to the FCC.
- 3. Provide documented statistics, studies, supporting papers. Prepare to cite from reports rapidly and with confidence. If on television, prepare special graphics. Take the documents to the station; use them as TV props.
- 4. Obtain professional public relations assistance to build a counter image.

Encouraging a Media Blackout

Most advocacy groups are anxious for maximum media coverage. But on occasion they wish the media would forget the hearing. Some strategists have attempted to discourage the media by withholding information, a strategy that usually fails—the media resorts to quoting only opponents. Another strategy involves inundating the media with so much material they become wary of the technical nature of the hearing. A third strategy is to attempt to convince the media that the hearing will be a boring repetition of old material, a tired crisis not worth their time. This strategy may work for a group that has credibility with the media.

How to Get a Story Used

Crisp, newsworthy writing and meeting the technical requirements of the media are prerequisite to getting a story used. But when a story doesn't appear all is not lost:

- *News stories*: If the story doesn't appear, phoning the editor to ask if the story was received is in order. The editor may report that it has been put in the "holdover" or "carryover" for later use. If the story does not appear in reasonable time, the editor may be checked again. By this time he probably at least remembers the name. If the story is being carried over, asking some supporters to write letters to the editor on the topic alerts the editor to public interest and increases the probability that the story will finally appear in print.

•*Radio*: Phoning the news department and stating that the message will be of interest to their listeners increases the opportunity for getting heard. The manager will probably say, "I'll tape your message." After the message is used, he'll welcome a word of thanks for his help. Or, if he doesn't use it, a polite inquiry may indicate why.

•*Television*: To plan TV coverage, a brief presentation should be mailed to the assignment editor, followed with a phone call. If the item is timely, the editor may ask for additional information. This is the time to send the media Fact Sheet. A spokesperson, an alternate spokesperson and still another alternate should be designated to give the producer/director an immediate contact when and if he decides to use the story. The station executive needs help in assessing why his audience will be interested in the story. He also is interested in the number of people the organization has or represents and the names of the opposition.

•*The Wire Services*: The wire services distribute news, film, photographs and tapes to clients. Wire services are indicated by the initials in parentheses to the right of the origin. For example, "San Francisco (AP)" is an Associated Press release. "Salem (UPI)" is a United Press International release. The major wire services use a daybook which lists events from which assignment editors decide if staff coverage is warranted.

Mention in the daybook greatly extends contacts with the media. To enter an event into the daybook, the Fact Sheet or press release should be sent to the daybook assignment editor of the nearest wire service. The most credible release is on a letterhead, includes the name of a press contact and the who, what, when, where, and why of the event. The release should be sent a week ahead of time unless there's an urgent current development. If notification has missed the 3:00 p.m. deadline of the day before, the information can be telephoned to the daybook editor.

NEWS

How to Prepare a News Article*

There are two types of newspaper stories: the news story and the feature story. *The News Story* submitted to the editor as a news release competes for space with other releases. Major papers may be inundated by as many as 200 a day. An interesting and understandable release, in the proper format and conforming to technical requirements, attracts the editor's attention. The proper format is:

• *The news release's Front Page* immediately alerts the editor to a group's legitimacy and the nature of its advocacy. A properly designed News-Release Head tells the editor who is sending the release as well as who to contact for additional information or verification, and the release date. A pre-printed release form with unique artwork adds to the impression of legitimacy, but is not essential.

• A strong *Headline* attracts attention and indicates the substance of the story, although the editor may assign it to the headline writer for rewrite. The four or five words allotted to a Headline are crucial in grabbing the reader's interest.

• *The Lead Paragraph* encourages the editor to read on. The Lead Paragraph includes the most important of the five "w's" in the story—who, what, when, where and why.

• *The Subsequent Paragraphs* elaborate on the lead. The second or third paragraph may include a quotation from a spokesperson or from the major person in the story. The Associated Press story on the protesters quoted the disabled protester in the third paragraph: "Robert Metts said he and Jeanne Marlow had been chained together since last Tuesday in a 'small hole in the ground, and I had to lie on my back.' " Major details follow the lead with minor details at the end of the story. This provides the editor with an opportunity to chop the story without losing important details.

A release announcing an event or a publication includes the date of the meeting, where to obtain the publication and its price, and other details to encourage reader action.

A brief summary of the group's activities and the purpose of the

---

*This section applies news article writing fundamentals to promoting an advocacy in the public hearing process. Journalism texts explain the basics of news article writing, among them: Fred Fedler's *Reporting for the Print Media* (New York: Harcourt Brace Jovanovich, Inc., 1973) and Max Gunther's *Writing the Modern Magazine Article* (Boston: The Writer, Inc., 1976).

release—announcing a meeting, the results of a study, making an accusation, or throwing a challenge—helps the editor to decide whether to use the story. A professional looking story has "more" at the bottom of every page, each page is numbered, and the last page ends with traditional signals: "-30-," "-0-," "END," or "###." A story longer than 250 words may discourage an editor from reading the release.

The feature story resembles a magazine story—timeliness is less important; writing style more leisurely; and there are more opportunities for motivating and influencing the reader. The feature story is constructed differently from the news story:

•The *Title* of the feature story attracts or "hooks" the reader. Titles may summarize, narrate, describe, quote or question. They may consist of a startling statement, catchy alliteration or address the reader directly.

•The *Lead Paragraph* further captures the reader's attention. Lead paragraphs may contain:

A *Summary*—a statement with a startling conclusion.
A *Narrative*—a leisurely introduction to the subject.
A *Description*—another type of leisurely introduction.
A *Startling Statement*—a challenge that captures attention.
A *Quotation*—a challenge quoting a person.
Questions—a challenge in a question form.
Direct Address—personification of the reader.
Contrast—captures attention by comparing extremes.

•The *body* of the story develops the theme by providing details in a logical sequence; however, they do not need to be presented in order of importance as in a news story. Use the sequence that best will hold the reader's continued attention. An advantage of the feature article is the opportunity to quote, present statistics, relate anecdotes and other illustrations not appropriate for the terse news story.

•The *close* in a feature story performs the important function of reinforcing the objective of the story. Unlike the news story, it is not dispensable. A well-written feature story close can't be chopped without impairing the story.

Variations of News Releases

News releases for public hearings come in three styles: *sensational, factual,* or *boring.*

The *sensational* release may win newspaper space but lose supporters by impairing credibility. A release written in a sensational vein includes exaggeration and clichés and careful writers distinguish between the sensational release and the news release describing a sensational action. For example, sensational illegal but non-violent tactics used to dramatize an issue are often reported in a non-sensational style.

The *Factual* release states facts, avoiding exaggeration and symbolism. In the factual release, spokespersons "said," rather than "accused"; they act "unwisely" rather than "illegally." The factual release uses fewer, less emotive adjectives.

The *boring* release is so long, involved, or uninteresting that it discourages the reader from perusing the story. In an attempt to tell all in the first paragraph it loses its hook.

The following lead paragraphs on the same topic contrast the *sensational, factual,* and *boring* styles:

> *Sensational*: Citing "crooked dealing" and an "under the table racket," the East Lake Neighborhood Association charged the Lake Development Associates with blatant disregard of the public and with bribing two key Planning Commissioners to rig Tuesday's public hearing.

> *Factual*: The East Lake Neighborhood Association urged the County Commissioners to investigate alleged bribery of two Planning Commissioners whose votes are crucial in next Tuesday's decision on rezoning the East Lake south shore.

> *Boring*: The leaders of the East Lake Neighborhood Association, an association of residents who are aiming to prevent rezoning of the East Lake south shore, said in a news conference held at City Hall today that it is possible that there may have been an attempt at bribing two Planning Commissioners in order to get them to vote affirmative after the public hearing scheduled next week in the second floor hearing room at the Court House.

Some dos and don'ts for news releases are summarized in Figure 6–2.

Advocacy Reporting

Some observers believe that advocacy journalism serves the public by making reporters personally accountable for their work. Objectivity, they feel, cloaks a dangerous anonymity that encourages reporters to evade their responsibility for changing social conditions. Popular newscaster David Brinkley is reported to have said: "News is what I say it is. It's something worth knowing by my standards."

Figure 6-2

Dos and Don'ts of News Releases for Public Hearings

A. Determine the major objective of the news release: To encourage the public to attend? To report on the hearing when a reporter was not present? To elaborate the issues of the hearing?

B. Time the release to further this objective. Submit early enough to appear several days before the hearing if the objective is to encourage attendance. Submit immediately after the hearing in time for the next deadline, if the objective is to report the hearing. If the purpose is to elaborate issues to be discussed at the hearing submit the release as early as feasible to encourage letters-to-the-editor, discussion, and editorial support. Prepare and send releases at least two days before the release date.

C. If a release advocates a point of view, use quotations from the most credible or newsworthy sources.

D. Check data. Attribute information to sources whenever possible.

E. Use full names, first and last, double-checking the spelling of all names and affiliations.

F. Don't ignore the fact that there is opposition.

G. Include some of the questions that have been raised. Mention which questions will be answered.

H. Include as much background as can fit into the release space without losing the reader's interest.

I. Use news releases to reinforce the strategies selected to influence the decision.

Recognition that many reporters practice advocacy journalism warrants a study of media biases. Interest groups that influence public decisions maintain files of the biases, thinking styles and advocacies of the influential journalists and newscasters who cover their advocacy. Local reporters assigned to a public hearing may not be as widely read as syndicated columnists, but their biases are none the less important for local issues. Profiles should be discreet in the event they become subject to public scrutiny. These profiles can include the reporter's education, writing approach, previous articles, biases, etc.

MEDIA TECHNICAL REQUIREMENTS

Scheduling releases to meet media requirements helps assure publication. The following schedules are in general use:

Newspaper Deadlines

Sunday papers— file by Thursday, no later than noon Friday.

Morning papers— file in morning if possible, no later than 3:00 p.m.

Afternoon papers— file before 10:00 a.m.; some papers will take stories till noon.

Weeklies— four or five days before publication or as early as possible.

Saturday afternoon papers compete with other activities, but Sunday morning papers are usually well read.

Radio

Phoning the news release to the radio station late at night or very early in the morning increases the chances of reaching the largest daily radio audience—commuters driving to work. For current news, preparing ten or twenty words to introduce the topic and phoning as soon as possible gives the station a welcome edge on the news. The interview will be recorded when the interviewer says, "Go ahead." The interviewer will probably interrupt to ask questions or clarify a point. For brief explanations or announcements radio provides greater access than other electronic media.

A very brief announcement about an event of general community interest to the "community bulletin board" or its local equivalent sent about ten days before the event will probably be announced, as will a seminar or field trip, if written as general news.

Television

Television cameras from local stations set up in the morning for public hearings that have generated controversy, conflict or excitement. The cameras shoot the celebrities, colorful characters, or an incident for a few minutes. By 10:30 a.m., they quickly pack their gear and disappear, possibly to return later to record the decision and comments of participants.

News releases to TV stations and invitations to news conferences may catch a day when news is slow and the news director welcomes an interview. For example, phoning the news room the Thursday before a weekend release alerts the program manager that news will be available. As weekend news tends to be slower, a weekend release has a better chance of being broadcast. The program director is the key contact for ideas for special features, getting on a hosted program or requesting air time under the Fairness Doctrine.

In many communities the cable television franchise requires the cable company to provide public access to some channels. Federal Communication Commission (FCC) regulations affecting the cable industry are changing rapidly. Most communities hold public hearings before granting cable franchises. These hearings have provided citizen groups opportunities to request increased access to cable channels.

Public Service Announcements

Effective radio Public Service Announcements (PSA's) are catchy, concise, free of abbreviations or other impediments to easy reading, written in conversational style, with quotes used sparingly. Indicating the length on top of the script: 10 seconds (20-30 words), 30 seconds (75 words), and 60 seconds (150-200 words) assists the station in scheduling announcements.

Television PSA's add sight to hearing. New communication technologies offer an ever larger menu of visual techniques—35 mm slides, a short 16mm film (film clip), a videotape cartridge, slides, slides/voice over, teleconference techniques. PSA's running 30 seconds have a better chance to be used than other lengths.

Sources of Information on Media Requirements

The above overview of media requirements is intended only to familiarize persons with its problems and opportunities. It cannot substitute for the knowledge and experience of the professional public relations practitioner. Further information on media requirements is available in:

Broadcasting Yearbook, 1735 De Sales Street N.W., Washington, D.C. 20036

UPI Broadcast Stylebook, 360 N. Michigan Ave., Chicago, Ill. 60601

The Editor & Publisher Yearbook, 850 Third Avenue, New York, New York, 10022

Three books that include useful information on writing and publishing news stories:

•Philip Lesly, ed., *Lesly's Public Relations Handbook,* 3rd ed. (Englewood Cliffs, N.J.: Prentice-Hall, Inc., 1983).

•Ted Klein and Fred Danzig, *How to Be Heard* (New York: Mac-Millan Publishing Co., 1974).

•James R. Fazio and Douglas Gilbert, *Public Relations and Communications for Natural Resource Managers* (Dubuque, Iowa: Kendall/Hunt Publishing Company, 1981).

PUBLIC HEARING COMMUNICATION CAMPAIGNS

One of the first decisions public hearing planners make is the goal of the communication campaign because the goal determines the type of campaign. If the goal is simply to inform the public about the advocacy and its position, they adopt a "blanket campaign." If public response is the goal, then a "public participation" campaign is in order.

The blanket campaign tells the public who the advocacy is and what it stands for. The blanket campaign using television, radio, newspapers, brochures, and other communication techniques, fits the familiar "inform and educate" function of many organizations. Its purpose is simply to inform, to help make the public aware of the advocacy.

The public participation campaign aims to elicit a response from the public on a specific issue. The public participation campaign helps win the active support an advocacy needs at public hearings. Its end-product is *response*.

The steps to *response* are:

a. Determine the issue on which public response is desired.

b. Determine the specific audience who will be or can be responsive to the issue. A campaign for community support at the public hearing for a Certificate of Need for a new cancer treatment unit at the local hospital could target Cancer Society members, senior citizens, persons with a family history of cancer, the medical profession, members of DES groups, and the Parent Teachers Association (PTA).

c. Determine which communication channels reach these targets: the local newspaper or radio stations, TV stations; fact sheets distributed at the local library; feature stories on cancer patients who must travel out of town for treatment; speaker's bureau to reach the service clubs; action alerts—the menu is endless.

d. Provide communication channels for the target audience to feedback to the process: flyers distributed by the speaker's bureau with the date of the public hearing, and the address of officials to whom letters can be written; letter-writing parties. A citizen committee to contact persons to testify at the hearing. A radio panel. Petitions left at the public library. Any action that provides a mechanism for participation facilitates response. The public participation campaign is essential in the Public Consensus Strategy.

NEWS CONFERENCES

When the news deserves more attention than a news release it merits a media conference. Reserved for important stories, media conferences require meticulous attention to details. The media conference that fails to provide the promised information and news, that is held in a room too small or too large, with a spokesperson who does not seem to have learned the advocacy's position, discredits the group. In calling a news conference, the group risks more than it might gain if it doesn't first get its act together. A well-organized conference follows this plan:

— Define exactly why the conference is called: To present new data? To announce the results of a study? To announce an important decision?
— Summarize the key points to highlight.
— Decide who will speak for the advocacy. Should resource persons be available to answer questions?
— Locate a suitable place for the conference, preferably a setting that reinforces the purpose of the conference. A news conference to announce opposition to a school closure might be held at the school. Or, if unveiling a study on violations

of the building code in a new public building, the conference could be at the site. Most news conferences are held indoors where there is seating room for reporters, electrical outlets for TV cameras and tape recorders, away from the hectic noise of the hearing.

— Provide amenities—electrical adapters for the meeting room with two-prong outlets (most modern electrical equipment has three prongs); heat in the winter, air conditioning in the summer; coffee or lemonade.

— Set up separate rooms away from the interruptions and distractions of the meeting for interviewing VIP's—officers, celebrities, experts, spokespersons.

— Have telephone facilities available.

— Monitor the invitation list. The size of the invitation list depends upon the size of the story. A major story attracts media from other areas as well as regional media and the wire services. It is as poor economy to be stingy with invitations as to waste them. Events relating to nuclear energy, waste disposal, innovative legislation, cancer, the current "hazards of the week," and any local event that indicates a trend or a movement capture nationwide interest.

— Hold the meeting as early in the day as possible, in the morning unless it's a heavy news day. Hold the conference always *before* a Friday afternoon.

— Deliver invitations—an "editor's advisory," a brief announcement stating when and where and why the media conference will be held. Deliver this two days ahead of the conference unless there is a fast news break that calls for a spontaneous conference. A complicated report or information that requires study and analysis sent with the invitation, noting the date the information can be released, allows reporters time to read and prepare questions.

— Prepare a media kit with fact sheets, background material, statements, graphs, photographs and any other material that will help reporters prepare stories. Photographs and biographical highlights of spokespersons, experts and organization officials are a welcome addition. Provide a press badge and, most important if parking is a problem, a parking permit or a section reserved for the media.

— Rehearse spokespersons in answering difficult questions. A

news conference provides a rare opportunity to explain and amplify an advocacy position.
— A news conference in the nation's capitol or in a large city draws sophisticated reporters who have "heard it all." Professional public relations assistance to prepare spokespersons and an emcee to deliver the desired impression help form a bridge for the advocacy message.

How to Use a News Conference in Public Hearings

A news conference before a public hearing is an opportunity to beat media deadlines. Statements, visual aids, or other material that may get lost in the public hearing will receive undivided attention. For instance, the media conference is the opportunity to display a model that requires explanation and may be difficult for the media to see during the hearing. In addition, a news conference before the hearing is a method for handling a "showcase" hearing, where it is anticipated that an advocacy's position will not be accorded fair treatment.

A news conference held after the hearing, especially after the official decision has been announced, offers an opportunity to rebut testimony, to comment on the decision, and to alert the media to plans for further action. When the hearing drags into the early morning, it may be necessary to delay the news conference several hours. Announcing a scheduled news conference before the media personnel wearily pack their gear and leave helps them to decide whether to head for the office or home for a brief nap.

ENHANCING MEDIA ACCOUNTABILITY

The media is often called to account on its responsibility for shaping the ideas and values of the nation. Federal government regulations include procedures for citizen participation in keeping the broadcast media accountable. The "Fairness Doctrine" provides citizens a degree of control over the broadcast media. A 1959 amendment to Section 315 of the Communications Act of 1934, the Fairness Doctrine requires broadcast stations to operate in the public interest and "afford reasonable opportunity for the discussion of conflicting views on issues of public importance." The Fairness Doctrine provides an avenue by which citizens can access the broadcast media to balance discussions.

The federal government regulates the broadcast media through periodical renewal of the license of every station, which requires filing an application with supporting data. The Federal Communications Commission (FCC) reviews the application and determines whether the public interest is best served by renewing or denying the license. Opposition to renewal or the filing of a competing application may lead to denial. In the 1970's hundreds of citizen activists filed petitions to deny a license, alleging that stations had not acted in the public interest.

These regulations provide a pipeline from citizens to the government in handling inaccurate or biased broadcasts. The complaint process is outlined in Figure 6–3, How to Handle Inaccurate or Biased Broadcasts.

Figure 6–3

How to Handle Inaccurate or Biased Broadcasts

1. Write or call the networks. At this writing there are four major networks—American Broadcasting Co. (ABC), Columbia Broadcasting System (CBS), National Broadcasting Co. (NBC) (located in New York City), and Turner Broadcasting Co. (located in Atlanta, Georgia). Contact the network for the name of the individual to whom to write.

2. Write or call the local network affiliate for the same information. Phone books list addresses and telephone numbers of local affiliates.

3. Write or call the sponsor of the show in which the offense occurred. Sponsors shy away from controversy that may harm sales and their reputations.

4. Complain to the FCC about programming that isn't balanced. Tape or videotape offending material and be prepared to offer solid evidence. A monitoring team who counts the number of offenses and records them, comparing time allotments and treatment of both sides in the controversy, can provide the evidence. Allegations based on flimsy support detract

Figure 6-3 (continued)

from an organization's credibility. Note carefully the network and call letters of the station, the name of the commentator, and the time and date of the offense. The Federal Communications Commission can be reached at 1919 Street, N.W., Washington, D.C. 20554.

5. If a station takes sides in a public issue, the station is required to offer those with an opposing viewpoint a reasonable opportunity to respond within 24 hours. If there is evidence that that offer was not made, complain to the FCC.

6. The FCC also requires that a station get in touch with an identified individual or group whose "honesty, character, integrity, or like personal qualities" have been attacked and provide a "reasonable opportunity to respond over the licensee's facilities." The station must provide the date, time, and name of the broadcast, and a copy or accurate summary of the script or tape. Evidence that reasonable opportunity was not provided is a valid reason for complaining to the FCC.

7. General complaints can be voiced to the FCC, the networks, and affiliates in the license renewal process. Petitions can also be filed against license renewal—a potent weapon. When the network or affiliate has done a good job, win a friend by sending a letter to the FCC—with copies to the network and station—praising its fairness and response to community concerns.

The printed media provides fewer avenues for citizen monitoring. The citizen who believes that a news report is biased or inaccurate is left largely to devise his own techniques to hold the printed media accountable. Some of the methods used by citizens to enhance accurate reporting are listed in Figure 6-4, How to Handle Inaccurate or Biased Newspaper Reports.

USING OTHER COMMUNICATION CHANNELS TO INFLUENCE DECISIONS

Communication channels other than the newspapers and broadcast media are easily available, less costly and reach a broad spectrum of decision-makers and the public.

Figure 6-4

How to Handle Inaccurate or Biased Newspaper Reports

1. Write a letter to the editor.
2. Urge others to write a letter to the editor.
3. Request a meeting with the publisher or editor. Politely and objectively point out the error. Support your contention with data. These tactics work. For example, a citizen's group felt that the local newspaper provided considerably greater coverage of the ideas of the opposition. By assembling a scrapbook of stories on both sides, including the news releases sent but not used and counting lines of coverage, the group was able to provide convincing data that its ideas were being slighted. Following that meeting, the citizen's group releases were used regularly. It may not be possible to enjoy such success with the *New York Times* or the *Washington Post*, but local newspapers prefer to keep their reader's friendship.
4. If the error is significant and appears in a newspaper which is difficult to access, notify an organization called Accuracy in Media (AIM). AIM monitors news reporting practices and publicly calls attention to offenses. Reed Irvine, Editor of the *AIM REPORT*—a newsletter published twice monthly—vigorously pursues media biases including the press and broadcasters.
5. If the error concerns a particular industry or organization, notify the industry professional or trade association, e.g. American Chemical Society or the Manufacturing Chemists Association. (There are about 14 pages of the names and addresses of such associations in the *World Almanac Book of Facts*.)

Magazines and other periodicals are especially useful in influencing opinion leaders. The magazine format, often combining photographs with text, allows in-depth development of ideas. An article in a popular magazine can create a hero or heroine and fix a perception firmly in the public mind. When Bonnie Hill, a former schoolteacher in the small forest town of Alsea, Oregon, was hailed by *Good House-*

keeping magazine as the heroine who induced the Environmental Protection Agency to ban the use of 2,4,5,T herbicide in the forests, the home use of this herbicide was dramatically curtailed. Evidence may develop that the problems experienced by Ms. Hill were caused by other chemicals, but it will require another equally skilled magazine writer to persuade the public that 2,4,5,T was not the culprit.

It isn't necessary to break into *Reader's Digest* to publish a magazine article that influences public opinion. In addition to the many consumer magazines, there are thousands of publications for special interests. Bowker's *Literary Market Place* lists these publications. *Writer's Market*, an annual published by *Writer's Digest* also carries an extensive list. Providing a staff writer or a professional free-lance writer with information to write an article assures a professional piece that enjoys a high probability of appearing in print.

Shoppers, those grocery or retail advertising sheets, are widely circulated and often devote some space to announcements, meetings, or events of local interest. Usually free at the local market, contact telephone numbers are on the classified page.

Campus and *Underground* publications influence persons who are ready to commit energy to causes they advocate. The local campus newspaper carries the names of the current news staff. Much of the success of the environmental movement and the Ralph Nader consumer movement is attributable to reaching the college audience. High school publications carry stories and announcements as do underground newspapers.

House organs and the *Newsletters of Organizations* are too seldom used communication channels. Gale's *Standard Periodical Directory* includes names and addresses of house organs and newsletters. The publication potential of a news release is enhanced by emphasizing the relevancy of the advocacy to the organization publishing the house organ or newsletter.

Handbills, Posters, Lawn Signs and *Pamphlets* communicate. Posters and lawn signs are limited to headlines but are essential tactics in the Public Consensus Strategy. Handbills and pamphlets written as terse news releases offer the luxury of more space, but not much more. Before investing in this type of communication, the distribution should be arranged. Stacks of handbills or posters sitting in someone's family room don't communicate. If a team to place the lawn signs or distribute the handbills door-to-door can't be put together, other communication methods are preferable.

Speaker's Bureaus link an advocacy to community leaders.

Rotary, Kiwanis, Lions, Altrusa, Soroptimists, Zonta, JC's, Chamber of Commerce, League of Women Voters and other groups that meet regularly are hungry for interesting speakers on timely topics. Local newspapers and the Chambers of Commerce maintain lists of organizations including their current contact persons. Because many clubs plan their programs a year ahead, it may be possible to capture only two to five minutes to distribute a fact sheet and handbills but those few minutes are valuable.

Conferences, Symposiums, and *Seminars* focus attention on an advocacy. An informal meeting with speakers presenting both sides of a project and an opportunity for questioning is a communication channel. Meetings may be as small as neighborhood get-togethers or large enough to crowd the high school auditorium. A forum, with presentations from each interest, helps explain complex projects.

A symposium lends credibility. When the subject is complex and technical, a symposium of experts illuminates the problems. Symposiums featuring credible experts add legitimacy to public concerns and draw the media. A symposium should enlist equally persuasive speakers on both sides of the problem. A group anxious to alleviate public fears on the use of a chemical learned this lesson when they organized a symposium. The chemists who spoke on behalf of allowing the use of the chemical related scientific data, substantiated by imposing graphs and charts. Opposition provided by biologists related the chemical to human health problems that the media readily understood. Media coverage featured the biologists and the symposium failed to accomplish the purpose visualized by the sponsoring group.

Person-to-person is direct communication. Knocking on doors, neighborhood coffees, telephone blitzes, and organizing telephone trees are time-intensive but productive.

Lobbying communicates to legislators. An advocacy group may employ a lobbyist or use volunteers. Lobbyists are more influential when they represent a large constituency (the Public Consensus Strategy again). Many organizations believe that lobbying is the most effective method of influencing decision-makers. Environmental, consumer, business and special interest groups of every stripe lobby in the nation's capitol and state houses. Consumer groups have organized effective citizens' lobbies.

Special Events communicate ideas. A parent's group proposing a traffic light on a street near a school staged a "balloon in" the day before the public hearing, with 100 children flying balloons to communicate the danger of the street to children. A nuclear-freeze advocacy group staged a "nude in" with participants parading in their underwear to focus on the dangers of nuclear war. The possibilities are limited only by the imagination and the social norms of the group.

Site visits communicate the unique aspects of sites or projects. A builder requesting approval for a zone change eased concerns on a proposed housing development by inviting the public to a site walk-through held the Saturday before the scheduled hearing. A small advertisement and a news story attracted visitors and the media who walked around the site, experiencing for themselves the isolating effects of the natural barrier formed by a ring of trees around the property.

Site visits that help win friends for an advocacy are arranged so that no nagging inconvenience distracts from their purpose. The United States Forest Service has developed site visits into a science by following these principles:

1. Let everyone in the organization who may be involved in the visit participate in the planning.
2. Determine the points the visit should illustrate.
3. Plan the itinerary with an inclement weather contingency. Prepare an itinerary, including destinations, brief description of planned activities, estimated arrival and departure time, names of host personnel, and travel accommodations.
4. Furnish maps, names and addresses of contacts, special equipment, i.e. ear plugs for noise, hard hats, and briefing papers for the visitors.
5. Plan coffee stops, box lunches, rest stops.
6. Include the itinerary, travel arrangements, maps, and suggestions for clothing with the invitation (e.g. we will be walking through muddy fields; high boots are suggested).
7. Prepare background information on official decision-makers who join the tour: education, official position, committees on which they serve, special interests (environment, defense, urban problems, technology, etc.). Brief the tour guides on points to emphasize for each official.

TESTIMONY AS COMMUNICATION

Communication campaigns prior to the public hearing event set the stage and develop the perceptions that make the decision-makers and the public receptive to the outcome advocated. Testimony delivered at the hearing crowns the campaign, adding persuasion to influence the outcome.

Testimony implements the public hearing strategy. Testimony that influences the decision takes into account four factors: (1) the advocacy position; (2) the decision-makers; (3) the hearing record; and (4) the clarity and persuasiveness of the testimony itself.

• *1. The advocacy position:* The advocacy position should be explicitly stated. One method of developing the statement is to consider five key questions:

 a. What outcome do we advocate? (e.g. vote no, vote yes, delay vote, obtain further information.)
 b. Why should the decision-makers favor this outcome? (e.g. health and safety, costs, follows comprehensive plans, adverse affects, other reasons consistent with the strategy.)
 c. To what values should we appeal? (e.g. sense of fairness; public concern; responsibility to protect the public; environmental ethic.)
 d. Which techniques and tactics should frame the appeal? (e.g. ask questions; use statistics; quote from authorities; use a demonstration; apologize; express appreciation; be humorous; express a sense of urgency; use overt emotion, be persuasive, present facts only.)
 e. What specific points should we cover? (e.g. what the outcome should be; why; when; action that should be initiated.)

• *2. The decision-makers:* The opinions, biases, thinking-styles and history of the decision-makers clue the preparation of testimony. First, it is necessary to obtain the information to determine these opinions and thinking-styles. One method for organizing the information is to prepare a profile on each decision-maker. A typical profile includes background information on family, education, positions held, voting record, committee memberships, vote ratings, thinking-style, and other comments pertinent to the problem.

Armed with this information, testimony can be adjusted for decision-maker's proclivities and thinking-styles. C. Northcote Parkinson in his witty *Parkinson's Law*[1] states that "... in a cabinet (committee) of nine it will be found that policy is made by three, information supplied by two, and financial warning uttered by one. With

---

[1]C. Northcote Parkinson, *Parkinson's Law* (New York: Ballantine Books, 1957), p. 52–54.

the neutral chairman, that accounts for seven, the other two appearing at first glance to be merely ornamental." Parkinson adds: "There can be no doubt (of) . . . the folly of . . . more than three able and talkative men in one committee."

Parkinson's wit reflects experience in public decisions. Searching for the five thinking styles on Parkinson's nine-person committee it may be postulated that:

— The three policy makers are probably Idealists, Realists and possibly Pragmatists.
— The two who supply information may be Analysts or Synthesists.
— The financial warning will probably come from a Pragmatist.

Apply this wisdom to nine Planning Commissioners seated around a large table in the city hall courtroom. The meeting is called for public testimony on an extension of an airport runway on the south side of the airport, jogging into a township that has been previously unaffected by air traffic. Apprehensive neighbors crowd the room, split into hostile groups. Opposing the extension is a group called NAT (Neighbors Against Traffic). Supporting the proposal is the SAT (Safer Airport Travel) organization. To win, SAT must persuade five committee members to deliver "yes" votes for its position. SAT prepares the following testimony for each Thinking Style:

•SAT supports the proposed airport runway expansion because:

1. It is safer than expanding in the opposite, more populated, direction.
2. The land for the runway has poor swampy soil, unsuitable for intensive agriculture or housing.
3. The runway will accommodate only the traffic of smaller planes.
4. The flight pattern will avoid the township.

•SAT provides information to the Analysts and Synthesists— the length of the runway, the thickness of the concrete, how the length and thickness limit the size of the planes that land, the anticipated number of flights a day, the noise levels of the allowable planes compared to a 747.

•SAT focuses on the higher public interest to the Idealist: the high standards of safety this runway promotes, the human benefits of separating traffic of smaller planes from the large jets.

•To the Pragmatist SAT emphasizes that an urgent air traffic problem can be solved right now by constructing this runway; that we don't know what will happen in ten years, but we don't need to stop everything now because of the unknown future.

•SAT approaches the Realist by showing the opportunity to achieve a specific result with this runway; the facts are there for everyone to see. There really is no alternative solution that can accomplish what needs to be done as rapidly and efficiently as this runway.

• *3. The hearing record:* The hearing record is the nominal basis for a public decision. Practitioners of litigation tactics for the Legal Theory Strategy maintain that the hearing record is more important than testimony in influencing decisions. One value of orchestrating testimony is the assurance that the hearing record includes all the evidence necessary to carry forward the advocacy position.

The Hearing Floor Manager of an orchestrated hearing checks each presentation to assure that:

1. It forwards the strategy adopted.
2. All essential information to make the record is presented.
3. One point is not emphasized to the neglect of others.
4. The tactics used are appropriate for the presentation and group.
5. The total presentation leads to the outcome advocated.

• *4. Clarity and persuasiveness of the testimony:* Condensing to ten crisp sentences makes testimony more persuasive. Time may permit more, but passing *The Ten-Sentence Test* before elaborating the ideas with additional sentences assures clarity. Figure 6–5 is a step-by-step guide to writing testimony in ten sentences.

Figure 6–5

Ten-Sentence Guide to Writing Testimony

Condense and clarify testimony. The ten sentences selected can outline complicated testimony but should be framed to independently present your position without further explanation. (The sentences in parentheses are the actual testimony at a public hearing on a permit for a nursing home. Fictitious names are substituted for the real names.)

1. Summary Statement

Figure 6-5 (continued)

(Epton County residents should know that the Manor Nursing Home has rejected its commitment to extend community service to low income people.)

2. Specific Example
   (Last week another elderly infirm person was forced to find other care.)
3. Clinching Statement
   (This person is the eighth I've learned about in the past six months.)
4. General Conclusion
   (Persons with limited means who must live off capital in order to pay charges of $1,500 per month are accepted until their resources are exhausted.)
5. What Happens as a Result
   (When these people must accept Medicaid to make up the difference between their income and their cost for care, the management requires them to be cared for elsewhere.)
6. Emotional Reinforcement
   (Moving the infirm and aged after months or years is a disturbing and emotionally critical thing.)
7. Further Emotional Reinforcement
   (It is not only cruel to the aged, it is very difficult for the families to handle.)
8. Credibility
   (I know because as a minister I have had to comfort aged people with modest means who have had to move from the Manor Home when they were forced to rely on Medicaid.)
9. Consequences to Decision-Makers
   (You will not be able to live with yourselves if you let this condition continue.)
10. The Action Urged
    (I strongly recommend that the Manor Home not be permitted to expand in this location.)

Subjecting the ten-sentence testimony to the *Fog Index,* an index devised to show whether readers can readily grasp information, further assures that the testimony will be understood. Figure 6–6 illustrates how to apply the *Fog Index* to sharpen testimony.

Using Visual Aids at Public Hearings

Psychologists report that 83 percent of our learning depends upon what we see and only 11 percent on what we hear. Visual aids add the sense of sight and sometimes other senses to increase comprehension of the message. Visual aids used improperly are a disaster in public hearings. Officials groan over boring slide shows that consume too much time or unintelligible graphs projected on a corner screen out of everyone's visual range. When a visual aid can clarify a presentation, it is better to show than to tell. If the visual aid distracts, complicates or confuses the presentation, it is better to rely on telling, rather than showing.

Figure 6-6

Using the Fog Index

1. Select a passage from your writing or testimony (100 words or more).
2. Divide the total number of words by the number of sentences. Treat independent clauses as separate sentences. This is the sentence pattern.
3. Count the number of words with three or more syllables. Omit from this count (a) capitalized words, (b) combinations of short easy words like "manpower" and "insofar," and (c) verbs made into three syllables by adding "es" or "ed." Divide your total by the number of words in the selected passage. This is the polysyllable factor.
4. Add the two factors and multiply by 0.4. Ignore digits after the decimal point. Because few readers have more than 17 years' schooling, any passage higher than 17 is given a Fog Index of "17-plus."

TESTIMONY SHOULD NOT EXCEED A FOG INDEX OF 10.
EXAMPLE:

NOW TO CONGRESS. Now the issue has been put up to Congress. Members of the Senate and House who feel that not all clear-cutting should be banned are strug-

---

Figure 6-6 (continued)

gling to produce legislation that will settle the matter quickly.

In the Senate, a compromise bill was completed by a special committee on June 6. It would permit clear-cutting in national forests under tight regulation by the U.S. Forest Service and is to be brought to the Senate floor soon. A House bill is awaiting committee action. Final decision by Congress is expected this fall.

1. Number of words in passage: 95
2. Sentence pattern: 12
3. Polysyllable factor: 8 divided by 95 = .08 = 8 (Note polysyllables are marked with a ● above the word.)
4. Fog Index calculation: 12 + 8 = 20.

$$20 \times .4 = 8 \quad \text{FOG INDEX: 8}$$

Adapted from *The Technique of Clear Writing* by Robert Gunning; New York: McGraw-Hill Publishing Company, rev. ed. 1972. Copyright by Gunning-Mueller Clear Writing Institute, Santa Barbara, California. Fog Index is a service mark of Gunning-Mueller.

Risks in Visual Aids for Public Hearings

Unless pre-hearing scouting shows that the hearing room has adequate facilities for visual aids and prior rehearsal in the room can be arranged, projected visual aids are risky. Controversial local hearings frequently land in the public library, or high school cafeteria with folding chairs hastily set up for the crowd. The screen a clerk promised is locked in the janitor's closet. There are no curtains for darkening the room; light switches are behind the table. Participants move noisily in and out of the room. By the time the presenter fiddles with the projector his five minutes are up.

Visual Aids that Work in Public Hearings

Some visual aids adapt easily to the uncertainties of public hearings:

1. Actual objects—objects that can be seen, smelled, felt, heard:

a six-point antler, a fish, a small tree, a cackling hen, a motorcycle (A) motorcycle wheeled into the hearing room with the motor roaring helped persuade a board to close a city street to motorcyclists.), a plastic sack containing evil-smelling garbage.

2. Static graphics—photos, charts, maps, blown-up graphs: simple messages, clear, interesting and sufficiently large that they can be seen by all the officials and the media. THE MESSAGE THAT IS TO BE CONVEYED BY THE GRAPHICS SHOULD BE PRINTED ON THE DISPLAY IN THE LARGEST LETTERS FEASIBLE. A bar chart that shows an increase in recreation vehicles clearly conveys its message if it states the conclusion: "This chart shows that the use of recreation vehicles has doubled in the past five years." A photograph should state the reason it is being included in the presentation. Most persons have difficulty understanding the simplest graphs especially those flashed in rapid succession on the screen, and most particularly graphs lifted from scientific reports for a public hearing audience.

3. Models—three dimensional representations of the project or object under discussion. A model of a technical facility illustrating how it blends with the landscape. A model that demonstrates a point can diffuse a controversy. (Opponents of one project claimed that water would not permeate the type of soil in the area. The applicant set up a permeation test at the public hearing and ran water through a test panel, demonstrating the permeation. He won the permit.) At another public hearing a hand-operated working model of a mechanical device persuaded public officials that the device was safe. Models cost more than other visuals but are cost-effective if they make the point. Working models can be displayed for the audience before or after the hearing.

4. Active graphics—magnet boards, hook and loop boards, flannel boards, charts or graphs with moving parts hold the attention of the audience and lend themselves to dramatic conclusions. A portable easel placed for viewing by officials and the media is easily managed.

If the hearing room has the necessary facilities and it is possible to set up before the hearing, projected images are one of the most manageable visual aids:

1. The overhead projector projects transparencies onto a screen and is adaptable for most public hearing audiences without darkening the room or distracting the operator. Many copy machines make transparencies from line drawings and books. Letters at least one-

quarter inch high can be read by even a large audience *if* the transparency is not light and crowded. Manufacturers of transparencies and overhead projectors supply kits with instructions on preparing transparencies.

2. Slide talks are easy for speakers to manage. The slides and script need to be coordinated allowing an average of 30 seconds per slide. Slide talks tend to bumble if the hearing room cannot be darkened and the projector tried prior to the meeting.

3. Professional quality movies add dramatic emphasis and are in adjunct to testimony when the scenery is the message. As with other projected images, movies should be reserved for hearings where equipment can be set up, tested and kept intact.

4. Videotapes share the advantages of movies. They can be taken with special videocameras, made by a professional videotape company, or rented. Again, they should be used only when the equipment can be set up before the hearing and left intact until the presentation.

5. Telecommunications bring expert testimony and statements from other officials or celebrities directly to the hearing. Still innovative, telecommunications require special equipment. Newer public facilities may be equipped for telecommunications and many older hotels are remodeling meeting rooms to accommodate teleconferences.

Dos and Don'ts of Visual Aids for Public Hearings

There are precautions to note in preparing visual aids for public hearings:

1. Visit the hearing room before preparing visual aids.
2. If the location of the hearing has not been decided, assume the worst conditions.
3. If audience reaction is important, use only those visual aids that are visual to the entire audience.
4. Do not try to cram in too much detail.
5. Use contrasting colors boldly.
6. Check that all officials and the media can see the visual aids.
7. Don't fake impressions (e.g. landscaping, building style, signs) that will not be included in the project.
8. Get professional assistance for complicated visual aids.

Solving Some Public Hearing Problems

7

Coping With Difficult
Public Hearings

Some public hearings pose problems for which there are no easy textbook solutions: handling a "showcase" hearing: opposing a zoning request; turning around a smear campaign; presenting comprehensible technical testimony to non-technical decision-makers. This section describes how to adapt basic strategies, tactics and techniques to solve these special hearing problems:

HOW TO HANDLE A "SHOWCASE"
HEARING

A "showcase" is a public hearing called to give media exposure to a political entrepreneur or to promote a particular solution to a problem. The showcase hearing may proceed according to a hypothetical scenario as follows.

At the instigation of the recently organized Senior Citizen's Health Alliance, a prominent Senator introduces S. 1001, a bill to expand the rights of Senior Citizens to medical information. Popularly known as "The Right to Medical Information" Bill, S. 1001 has been referred to the Labor and Human Resources Committee, whose subcommittee schedules a public hearing. The Chairman of the subcommittee, rumor has it, is angling for the appointment as Secretary of the new Department of Aging.

The opponents of the Bill arrive armed with statistics, carefully reasoned reports and charts, accompanied by three attorneys to monitor their statements. About 10:00 a.m. proponents wheel an aged senior citizen into the hearing room to testify tearfully how the withholding of medical information has hindered her recovery. The next witness,

179

a dignified white-haired man, controls a sob as he recounts how a medical error cost him his wife of 55 years. The TV camera hones in on the tears of sympathy in the Chairman's eyes. Senior citizens wearing white armbands with red letters urging, "Don't bleed us" pack the hearing room.

The public hearing is a showcase for the Senator and his "Right to Medical Information" Bill. News reports of the hearing ignore the opposition testimony, except to note that the opposition is "rich and powerful." The evening TV news centers on the Chairman's tears of sympathy and the sobbing witnesses.

Some organizations who have been victims of showcase hearings ignore the manipulation, maintaining that the public hearing means little anyway; it is just politics. It is the public hearing record that counts. A few attempt to outclass the opposition with their own sensational "criers." Yet others invest in scathing full-page newspaper advertisements castigating the media for their part in the showcase.

Although there are no book solutions to the problem, there are methods that minimize adverse effects and may even turn the showcase to advantage. Some of the methods that have been used are:

• *1. Anticipate the "showcase."* Expect a showcase hearing when a public official wants media exposure. Running for higher office is a motive; keeping an office in a hotly contested race is another. Showcase hearings also serve the ambitions of appointed officials, agency heads, and others looking for a media event to promote themselves or their ideas.

Administrative assistants and lobbyists are in position to predict *federal* and *state* showcases. They know which interest groups are behind the bills and are on top of the rumor mills on current political posturing. *Local* showcases may be spotted by noting whether the official sponsoring the hearing has hidden political ambitions, or whether the mayor of a large city is playing power games.

In this hypothetical scenario additional clues would have indicated a showcase hearing:

— Three months before the public hearing, the Senior Citizen's Health Alliance had sponsored a "Recapture Health Week," holding information programs for senior citizen clubs on medical records, medi-alerts, and other medical care topics. The Alliance sponsored a poster contest for grade school children; first prize was a trip to Washington, D.C. "Recapture Health Week" unfolded horror stories of medical practice and provided the preliminary bombardment of the media and public.

- "Recapture Health Week" concluded with a petition-signing campaign. Petitions bearing 11,000 signatures urged the Senator to introduce the "Rights to Medical Information" Bill.
- The crusading former editor of a popular health magazine had organized the Senior Citizen's Health Alliance about six months earlier. The Board of Directors of the Alliance includes two attorneys with experience in allocating community resources, a prominent professor, a formerly highly placed federal government official with access to many influential members of Congress. (The full-time paid executive is known as one of the most skilled citizen-action organizers in the United States.)
- The former editor is now a consultant and writer for the health magazine (circulation 400,000). Surveys indicate that the magazine's readers have upper middle-class incomes, 75 percent own their homes, 65 percent belong to several organizations and 92 percent respect the opinions of the former editor.
- A nation-wide senior citizens organization has joined with the Alliance. It has held bake sales and raffles to raise money. The proceeds of these efforts plus some grant money the executive director has been able to raise will pay the expenses of some fifty members to travel to Washington during the week of the public hearing.
- The executive director of the Alliance has presented more than fifty training workshops to senior citizen clubs on small group and one-on-one techniques, how to present opinions effectively, and how to work with the media.
- "Recapture Health Week," the bake sales, and debates were reported by the press, the morning TV news shows, and several late-night radio talk shows.

• 2. *Plan an anticipated showcase hearing as a media event* and recognize the congregation of reporters and broadcasters as a media opportunity for both sides. Opponents of "The Right to Medical Information" Bill could have taken advantage of the opportunities for a slice of the media pie by transforming their opposition from a scattered humdrum effort lacking identifiable character, into a credible action group. The transformation could have been effected by:

- Anticipating the purpose of the hearing (what do the various players expect to accomplish).

— Evaluating the objectives of the Bill (what problems is it attempting to solve?).
— Anticipating the Senior Citizen's Health Alliance strategy and tactics.
— Forming an appropriately named coalition or alliance (for example, Citizens for Privacy or Citizens Concerned about Information) with other groups who oppose "The Right to Medical Information" Bill.
— Organizing and activating a grass-roots group to oppose the Bill: including citizens who cherish the right to privacy, auxiliaries to the medical profession, pharmacists and hospital personnel. Women in Health (similar to Women in Agriculture, Women in Timber, etc.) could be organized as an educational grass-roots group.
— Setting the stage by using tactics to demonstrate constituent consensus against the Bill: letters-to-the-editor of local and state papers; letters to public officials; petitions; news stories about the grass-roots group activities. Clipping services employed by most legislators clip items in local or state papers in addition to those printed in the *New York Times, The Washington Post* and other prestigious newspapers.

• *3. Pack the public hearing with grass-roots and coalition members*—a difficult feat in Washington or the state capitol unless there is a grass-roots group network within a day's travel time, or if travel funds are raised. Badges, buttons, T-shirts and other identifying methods add to the visibility of the advocacy.

• *4. Encourage fair and accurate media coverage* by aggressively pursuing national recognition of opposition to the Bill. National recognition is developed by providing information to local media as well to as national media. Restricting contacts to Washington or state capitol media is a disservice to an advocacy. When grass-roots groups hold meetings and events in their towns, local media interest encourages national coverage. Each story used by the media adds another notch in the fight for legitimacy and credibility. If the "Rights to Privacy" advocacy group is the only one covered by local media they will probably be the only group recognized by the national media.

An information-only Fact Sheet helps establish credibility with Washington officials and the national media. Dramatic examples add persuasion to the Fact Sheet. Emotive words that make good copy should be quoted from others. The information-and-advocacy Fact Sheet format is better reserved for local public distribution and the information-and-directions-for-action Fact Sheet for local grass-roots and advocacy groups.

 • *5. Catch media attention* by using the same tactics as to influence decision-makers:

— Prepare a *Media Package* with copies of clippings from the local press, petitions, press-quality photographs of local meetings or celebrity spokespersons, local fact sheets, statistical data on the number of meetings held throughout the nation, quotations from speeches, and Congressional staff counts of the number of letters received on the topic.
— Provide the media with copies of the information given to decision-makers.
— Arrange for physical facilities (rooms for interviews, telephones, including the amenities discussed under news conferences).
— Use the tactics for obtaining media coverage discussed in the chapter on Communication.
— Provide information requested in the form and at the time the media needs it as described in "Communication Techniques."

 • *6. Orchestrate testimony* to insert all pertinent information into the record. Although the showcase hearing is a media event, the hearing record is the basis for subsequent appeals to reverse the decision.

 • *7. Prevent outbursts or gratuitous remarks* that undo the careful planning. Alert and prepare the persons presenting testimony at the showcase hearing for possible disconcerting incidents:

a. Being ignored by the media.
b. Allotted time curtailed.
c. Inattentive officials.
d. Testimony delayed till a late hour (after media have departed).
e. Interruptions from other participants.
f. Testimony held over to a later hearing.
g. Lack of time or facilities for audio visuals.
h. Questions on peripheral controversial issues.
i. Entrapment questions. (Five questions used to trap witnesses

at public hearings and suggested answers are included in Figure 7-1, "How to Handle Entrapment Questions.")

Figure 7-1

How to Handle Entrapment Questions

1. Does your company agree to . . . ?
   (Answer: I don't have the authority to say.)
2. Do you believe . . . ?
   (Answer: Sorry, I can't answer that question "yes" or "no." Let me explain. . . .)
3. Didn't your company make a profit of 28 percent last year?
   (Answer: I don't believe I understand the question. Do you mean before or after taxes? Do you mean what each stockholder made?)
4. Don't you agree that . . . ?
   (Answer: I can't categorically say.)
5. Don't you believe people have a right to . . . ?
   (Answer: Please explain what you mean.)

Sometimes entrapment can be avoided by presenting testimony with firmness, authority, and conviction. Rehearse personnel to answer worst case questions. Some tests have indicated that statements delivered rapidly are more convincing than slow deliberate statements.

HOW TO TURN AROUND A "SMEAR" CAMPAIGN AT A PUBLIC HEARING

When several thousand members of the Mobilization for Animals—a coalition of animal welfare and protection groups—marched to the Wisconsin Regional Primate Center at Madison, Wisconsin to protest "the brutality, waste, greed and savagery of the animal experimentation industry" they were merely applying the technique of dramatizing a problem with standard moralistic rhetoric. Most controversial issues breed similar dichotomizing invectives. But if the invective becomes personal and maligns, defames or slanders the reputation of an organization or individual, the rhetoric becomes a "smear."

The group or individual victimized by a smear responds by either ignoring the entire matter hoping it will blow itself out, or angrily denouncing the smear and hauling the offenders into court. Neither response is satisfactory, as the Switzerland-based Nestlé Co. learned when consumer activists accused the firm of killing babies by marketing its infant formula in developing nations. A successful suit against the original activists who initiated the accusation was a legal victory for Nestlé but a public relations disaster, framing the problem of feeding babies in poor countries in emotional and political terms, which the company attempted to counter on a nutritional science level.

Scientific nutritional information proved no match for the skilled activism of the umbrella group called Infant Formula Action Coalition (INFACT), which gathered almost 40,000 signatures to organize a boycott of all Nestlé products. After several failures, Nestlé decided to change its approach. The company then arranged to meet directly with protesters and mounted an intensive effort to answer the charges, and also to demonstrate compliance with the World Health Organization (WHO) code for infant formula marketing. To restore its credibility, the Nestlé Company submitted to a social audit of its operation, providing information to the impartial Nestlé Infant Formula Audit Commission, chaired by former Senator Edmund S. Muskie. Nestlé's aggressive action was expensive and consumed management time but it slowly did make inroads on the boycott support of some of the 44 organizations, including many church groups.

Smearing the opposition is one of the tactics that gives politics a bad name. Unfortunately, there are controversies in which an advocacy group enters the public hearing lists handicapped by an accusation that could prejudice its chances for a favorable decision. But the damages of the smear campaign can be diminished, as Nestlé's experience shows, by following these rules:

1. Resist the temptation to retaliate by smearing or ridiculing the attacker.
2. Never respond directly to the smear.
3. Address legitimate issues brought out by the smear without direct reference to the smear.
4. When the smear contains gross inaccuracies, firmly state the

accurate information. Do not repeat the inaccuracies.

5. Refocus attention on different, relevant issues.

6. Counter the smear tactic as soon as it appears. Do not wait for the public hearing.

7. Probe for the hidden agenda in any smear campaign. Address the hidden agenda.

8. Review changing the strategy and tactics to counter the smear campaign as did the residents of the affluent neighborhood called, for this illustration, the Fairlee area, who protested a rezoning exception to allow a home to be used for religious services. They organized the Keep Fairlee Private (KFP) group and selected the Fairness Strategy as the basis for their opposition. The members of the religious group accused the neighbors of opposing the rezone because of religious prejudice. After reviewing its strategy, KFP switched to the Legal Theory strategy.

9. If the strategy is changed, issue a new Fact Sheet to reflect the new strategy. When KFP changed strategies, it put together a new Fact Sheet using the information-and-directions-for-action format. KFP claimed that the Planning Commission did not provide due notice, as required by law, and maintained that the Commission in considering the rezone disregarded the zoning ordinance provisions. The Fact Sheet emphasized that the home proposed as a Church was inappropriate for any type of community use. Located on a narrow, winding road with no parking facilities, the house was served by a septic system designed to serve a single family. The Fact Sheet urged the public to visit the neighborhood and to attend the public hearing, giving dates, location, and time.

10. Use news releases, letters-to-the-editor and other communication to reinforce the new strategy. KFP's news releases and letters-to-the-editor focused on the procedural irregularities and the appropriate use of the property.

11. Use citizen participation techniques to demonstrate the inaccuracy of the smear. KFP leaders invited the Church Board and the media to a meeting in the local library. The meeting objective was to learn the physical requirements of the Church and to assist the Church group in locating a home to meet its needs. By this positive action KFP defused the prejudice smear. Noting that few media representatives covered the library meeting, the Church and neighborhood lead-

ers called a joint news conference to announce the conclusion of the meeting—that the Fairlee Neighborhood Association would assist the Church in locating a more suitable home.

12. Concentrate on relevant issues in the public hearing. By focusing on the appropriate use of the neighborhood, the hearing testimony was kept free of defamation and slander. Both sides avoided mentioning the smear. The Church leaders devoted their testimony to how they would cope with the sewage problem and handle the traffic. The Commission turned down the rezone, but with the assistance of the Fairlee Neighborhood Association, the Church located another home serviced by a traffic artery and the city sewer system.

OPPOSING A ZONING REQUEST

Individual citizens attend more public hearings on zone changes than for any other purpose. As cities reach out into the suburbs and suburbs intrude into the countryside, requests for zone changes pit citizens against citizens and citizens against governments in controversies ranging from a simple zoning variance to accommodate aging parents to complex development projects involving millions of dollars. These conflicts surface at the public hearing, where citizen action has demonstrated that there is no stronger deterrent to the enactment of any zoning proposition than a well-organized, vociferous group of objectors who want to see the proposal killed. Let a developer propose a local zone change, and the neighborhood blossoms with a formidable barrier of impassioned activists. One study showed that opposition to a zoning request decreased its chance of winning approval to less than half.[1] Upon a show of overwhelming opposition from surrounding property owners, some city councils will disapprove almost any proposal.

The Institute for Participatory Planning[2] concludes that "citizens have learned that no issue is impossible to fight if it threatens the stability of a neighborhood." Citizens no longer accept an action they don't like in the name of progress. If they believe the action will have an adverse impact, they will fight to stop, or at least delay, the project.

---

[1]Dudley S. Hinds, Neil G. Carn, and Nicholas Ordway, *Winning at Zoning* (New York: McGraw-Hill, 1979), p. 138.

[2]IPP, *Citizen Participation Handbook* (Laramie, Wyoming: Institute for Participatory Planning, 1981), pp. III-1.

You Can Fight City Hall

The 1960's environmental movement and the 1970's land-use reform movement heightened public awareness that individual citizens can "fight city hall," not only the local city hall in the town square, but the state and federal governments. Citizens now have standing in court to sue federal agencies. The balance of power belongs to the opposition. Jack Shepherd in *The Forest Killers*[3] states his view of the trend: "Before 1970 the federal government could roll into any part of America and blast, dig, haul, dam, cut, cement, dredge, tar—do *anything* it wanted. Local people would have to put up with it, or get out. Thanks largely to the recent environmental awareness and the National Environmental Policy Act of 1969, local people aren't getting pushed around as much anymore."

The land-use reform movement has encouraged and provided mechanisms for citizens to propose and challenge land-use changes. When the Oregon Land Conservation and Development Commission (LCDC) was created in 1973, the State appropriated more than $6 million to help cities, counties and regions develop land-use plans and regulations. An important by-product of the LCDC was the development of strong neighborhood groups, who gained experience in public hearing tactics and became skilled participants in influencing social action in their immediate environs.

Citizen Opposition Is Effective

This heightened awareness has facilitated opposition to rezoning. Herbert H. Smith in *The Citizen's Guide to Planning*[4] concludes that: "There is nothing more effective for quickly changing the mind of a public official, especially an elected one, than a sizeable number of well-organized people who . . . have gotten their act together . . . Unified, well-founded public opinion is still the most effective weapon in participatory democracy."

Prior to 1970, "neighborhood power" was a theory in planner's books. The 1970's saw a remarkable growth of neighborhood associations reasserting control over their own neighborhoods. Neighborhood

---

[3]Jack Shepherd, *The Forest Killers* (New York: Weybright and Talley, 1975), p. 193.

[4]Reprinted with permission from *The Citizen's Guide to Planning* by Herbert H. Smith, p. 139. Copyright © 1979 by the American Planning Association, 1313 E. 60th St., Chicago, IL 60637.

groups as diverse as the neighborhoods themselves are directly account-able to their constituencies. Born in the heady atmosphere of confronta-tion politics, neighborhood groups have poured energy and skill into combating freeways, obtaining health care, defining tenants' rights and even to taking a stand on nuclear power.

For the most part, neighborhood groups are intent on preserv-ing the integrity of their neighborhoods. "Not in our backyard, you don't!" is the instant reaction to proposals for a zone change for many construction projects from a condominium, supermarket or a waste disposal plant—no matter how desperate the economic situation of the area. Some experts claim that "build elsewhere" ordinances add as much as 25 percent to the cost of homes.

The power of citizen opposition in influencing decisions on re-zoning requests is illustrated by such headlines as: "District Suspends Work on Garbage-Burner" or "Land Developer gives in." At the mini-mum, articulation of citizen concerns at public hearings frequently wins concessions that make the projects less objectionable:

— A neighborhood request to delay a zone change for an office building was rejected, but the hearing officer recommended a special design overlay to respond to neighborhood concerns.
— Friends of the Earth requested a State Environmental Quali-ty Commission to allow opposition groups to appeal permit terms. Friends of the Earth's request was turned down but the Commission instituted a study on broadening the appeals system to allow increased participation of opposition groups.

Industries have become aware that they can "no longer quietly buy parcels of land and set up facilities at will or expect to be greeted with open arms by local government . . . Even communities that need industry are likely to demand that it conform to predetermined stan-dards."[5] Neighborhood opposition is head-on or takes an end-run, depending on the situation. One neighborhood, distressed over the expansion of a nearby manufacturing facility, adopted the Public Inter-est Strategy plunging head-on into a quarrel with the environmental agencies who issued the permits, with the Health and Safety inspectors who approved the project, and with local political authorities. When this strategy proved unsuitable, they switched to the Mistake Strategy with an end-run at the zoning, claiming that the facility was incon-

---

[5]Arnold R. Deutsch, *The Human Resources Revolution* (New York: McGraw-Hill Book Company, Inc., 1979), p. 86.

sistent with the definition of permitted uses. The end-run was likewise unsuccessful in preventing the expansion, but the neighborhood persistence extracted mitigating actions from the company increasing its desirability as a neighbor.

Opposition to rezoning may resort to attacking the Environmental Impact Statements—a useful tactic when adverse impacts on the natural environment are suspected *especially* if federal regulations or funds are involved. Failure to hold public hearings may invalidate the Environmental Impact Statement findings.

Tactics for Opposing a Zoning Request

Numerous tactics have been successful in opposing zone requests. Some of the most useful tactics are:

• 1. Question the interpretation of the law(s) and the legitimacy of the zoning ordinance. An example is the finding of a lower court that the zoning ordinance in the town of Beverly Shores, Indiana (part of the Indiana Dunes) was invalid on the grounds of "procedural deficiencies" during adoption. Therefore, the decision based on that ordinance was not valid.

• 2. Search for a violation of the law or public hearing procedures noting especially whether:

— Notification met deadlines.
— The advertisements appeared in the newspapers the required number of days.
— There were any violations of quasi-judicial rules.
— The hearing complied with the open-meeting law. (The media oppose closed meetings. Reports that an official decision was discussed at a closed or secret meeting sparks editorials.)

• 3. Initiate new legislation to cause the proposed expansion to be a violation of the law.

• 4. Bring up any proven past misdeeds of the applicant.

• 5. Search for evidence that the expansion will: overload public facilities—roads, schools, water lines, sewer lines, drainage, streets; cause traffic problems, noise, pollution; or compete for available water supplies.

• 6. Examine the project for detrimental affects on public health or safety.

• 7. Look for suspected adverse impacts on the natural environment. Will the traffic, glaring headlights, or noise impair the quiet enjoyment of property?

• 8. Organize a protest group with a descriptive name: Margaret District Association of Neighbors (opposing rezoning for a shopping center), South Citizens Alliance (opposing a rezone for apartments), West Community Action Committee (opposing a condominium), Crest Community Association (opposing rezoning for a hotel).

• 9. Win media support by providing information and reporting events that make news.

• 10. Prepare to fund studies, experts, and attorneys to provide substantive detailed challenges to the proposal. Include consideration of:

— The characteristics of the district or area and how these characteristics compare to other districts or areas in the city.
— The suitability of the area for particular land uses and improvements.
— The conservation of property values.
— The land uses and improvements in the area.
— Trends in land development in the area.
— Density of development.
— The needs of economic enterprises in the future development of the area.
— Questionable access to sites in the area.
— Natural resources and prospective needs for development.
— The public need for healthful, safe and aesthetic surroundings.
— Proof of change in a neighborhood or area.
— Mistake in the planning or zoning for the property.
— Conformance with the comprehensive land-use plan.
— The need for the proposed use.
— Effect of the rezone on taxes.

• 11. Question the accuracy of the applicant's exhibits and the credibility of his experts, especially question whether the statistics cited are consistent with the findings and whether the data is accurate.

• 12. Question the appropriateness of the criteria used in reaching the decision.

Most neighborhood groups prefer non-confrontational strategies and tactics. However, in issues where feelings run high and reasonable, polite tactics appear ineffective, these groups have been known to adopt the Alinsky confrontational-style. An example of a neighborhood who resorted to these tactics is the 1971 campaign against U. S. Steel's South Works Plant in Chicago. U. S. Steel had earlier obtained a variance. In 1971, the Appeals Board held twenty public hearings on revoking the variance. Alinsky organized the Campaign Against Pollution (CAP) and, using typical confrontation tactics, personalized the conflict by targeting an individual. Discovering that one of the U.S. Steel Directors was Chairman of the Board of Sears, Roebuck and Company, CAP picketed Sears and distributed leaflets in front of the store.

Further sleuthing revealed that the then President of U. S. Steel was a candidate for the moderator of the United Presbyterian Church. CAP's charges that he was unfit to be the church moderator because he avoided his "moral responsibility for pollution" are believed to have contributed to his defeat for the honor.

PRESENTING EXPERT TESTIMONY

A *Wall Street Journal* article on media problems in reporting high technology reported, "If gaining access is one problem for reporters, digesting and conveying complex information are another. GPU [General Public Utility Corp.] officials 'show you charts, all of that stuff,' says Robert Janis, the news director of WHTM-TV in Harrisburg, 'but it's very hard to condense so a guy at home drinking beer and eating spaghetti can understand.' "[6]

George Keyworth, Director of the Office of Science and Technology Policy and chief science advisor to President Reagan, speaking to an annual meeting of the American Association for the Advancement of Science, confirms Janis' predicament: "We need a scientifically literate public to deal effectively with the difficulties and decisions of a high technology society . . . important decisions about our future are increasingly going to involve complex technical matters . . . we may find ourselves making poor decisions."

Neither the public nor the media nor most public officials are scientifically literate. Nevertheless, public officials make decisions involving complicated technical matters. Consider the plight of the county planning commission caught in a tug of war between experts who disagree about the ecological importance of a 130-acre wetland, or the federal agency groping with accusations that the insulation it once promoted to help conserve energy is now perceived as a source of toxic

---

chemicals. Public officials without the requisite training are expected to become arbiters of substantive questions of science and technology.

Officials, the public and the media look to the expert for answers. The expert, in turn, is backed to the wall by a public disenchanted with science, technology and government management. As he struggles to meet zero-risk demands he becomes the technical Chicken Little, creating the crisis of the week, the carcinogen of the month.

The very training which endows professionals with expertise works against their effectiveness at public hearings. Technical experts often disdain politics and the necessity for explaining their views. They do not understand the politics of public decisions and many feel demeaned by political posturing. Nevertheless the skill of the expert in interpreting his vast knowledge to decision-makers is the key to wise public policy.

Expert Testimony at Hearings

Expert testimony at public hearings is restricted by fundamental limitations:

—The limitations of decision-makers. Most persons are not trained to follow mathematical presentations, formulae, charts and graphs.

—The limitations of time. At a public hearing the expert is granted less than 10 to 20 minutes to summarize the technical information acquired in a lifetime. This time constriction is deadly for the academic professional geared to a 50 minute class presentation, especially when he is called upon for his presentation at a late hour, by which time his audience has been lulled to a soporific state.

—The limitations of the public and media. The public and media tend to tune out technical material with which they are uncomfortable. Audiences become impatient with what they don't understand and begin to whisper to each other.

The physical limitations. Many public hearings are held in deplorable facilities. The carefully prepared audio visuals may not be seen or heard. There may be no suitable place to hang a map. The slides are out of range of the media and the public.

—The limitations of language. An immediate language barrier is set up when experts use the mysterious vocabulary of their discipline. The language barrier is created by:

- *Scholarly Prattle* Words or combinations of words that are purposefully difficult to understand. Consider this gem from The

Directive Committee on Regional Planning:[7] "Thus, we conclude, as we began, that both of the two common and superficially different modes of defining a region express useful, if not indispensable truths. The less metaphorical mode is content to delimit a region as that contiguous one having the necessary geographic unities; the people with sufficiently homogeneous desires, attitudes, and wants; the sufficient bases in natural and man-made resources and technology; and the appropriate voluntary institutions and governmental organization to achieve, within the limits and opportunities of the structure of external political power, the utmost efficiency in the fullest attainment of the major human values of the people of the area." Elegant prose, but what does it mean to the decision-maker at 11:00 p.m.?

- *Complex Language* Too many thoughts included in one sentence prevent the listener from following the reasoning. He loses the train of thought on unfamiliar words and references to Section 4628 or Article 6a. By the time he deciphers Section 4628 the speaker is on to another topic.
- *Learned Obfuscation* Deliberately daring the layman to understand, the expert throws in a vocabulary of unfamiliar words. Take this example from a weather expert testifying in an air purity debate: "Temperature is the most important factor in determining the ecological optimum . . . and therefore the agricultural exploitation of our water and soil resources . . . temperature is probably measured within the present accuracy of our knowledge of temperature effects on resource utilization, and provides us with a standard measurement which can be linked empirically or theoretically to specific environmental applications."
- *Professional Slang* "Buzz words" that appear to add legitimacy to statements are supposed to show that the expert is really "in."

Clarifying complex concepts

A communications consultant reported midnight sessions with a group of nuclear experts who were attempting to devise an adequate

---

[7]The Directive Committee on Regional Planning, *The Case for Regional Planning* (New Haven: Yale University Press, 1947), pp. 35-36.

substitute for the word "dose." They failed to agree on a word which both scientists and the communicators could accept.

Language can be clarified using the same method that clarifies murky water: running it through a filter. For understandable testimony, experts need to filter the stuffiness out of each sentence, using the "Fog Index" and other clarifying techniques. The following example is taken from a valuable little book which should be in the library of every expert: *Gobbledygook Has Gotta Go*, written by John O'Hayre of the Bureau of Land Management (U.S. Department of the Interior):

> The original sentence as written by the entymologist read "Endemic insect populations cause little-realized amounts of damage to forage and timber."
>
> Rewritten for clarity, the sentence read "Native insects do more damage to trees and grass than we realize."

An appropriate comparison helps clarify a complex concept. In explaining a new technology to extract iron from taconite rock, Professor E.W. Davis, then director of the Mines Experiment Station at the University of Minnesota, likened the Mesabi iron deposits to raisin cake. The raisins were analogous to high-grade iron which could be plucked from the ore; the remainder of the cake was taconite. By the late 1940's the raisins were gone.[8]

Gobbledygook Has Gotta Go describes the clarification of a complex philosophical concept by Benjamin Franklin. In the early days of the United States, Federalists insisted on property ownership as a voter qualification. The Franklinites opposed this concept, maintaining:

> "It cannot be adhered to with any reasonable degree of intellectual or moral certainty that the inalienable right man possesses to exercise his political preferences by employing his vote in referendums is rooted in anything other than man's own nature, and is, therefore, properly called a natural right. To hold, for instance, that this natural right can be limited externally by making its exercise dependent on a prior condition of ownership of property, is to wrongly suppose that man's natural right to vote is somehow more inherent in and more dependent on the property of man than it is on the nature of man. It is obvious that such belief is unreasonable, for it reverses the order of rights intended by nature."

---

[8]Frank D. Schaumburg, *Judgment Reserved* (Reston, Virginia: Reston Publishing Company, 1976), p. 28.

Ben Franklin recognized that the public would not understand that statement and he clarified it thus:

> "To require property of voters leads us to this dilemma: I own a jackass; I can vote. The jackass dies; I cannot vote. Therefore, the vote represents not me but the jackass."

Experts should approach audio visuals cautiously. Peter B. Dorram counsels experts to avoid the use of color slides. "Some experts," he states ". . .have a passion for documenting . . .with color slides. They insist on going through the song and dance of screening windows, turning off lights, erecting screens, and projecting a collection of slides with accompanying prepared and canned narrative. . . . .The witness. . .is bound to lose eye contact—and any other contact—with his audience . . .we will just enjoy the darkness for a brief nap."[9]

Graphics help clarify a technical presentation when the following principles are applied:

1. Feature only one idea on each exhibit.
2. Use bold colors to highlight the idea.
3. Avoid a glossy, slick presentation.
4. Caption every graph, figure, photograph or map with the conclusion it illustrates.

In a public hearing on a sign ordinance, experts testified on the social implications of the law, utilizing glossy photographs, slick charts and slides. However, the most effective presentation was a long sheet of butcher paper, prepared with bright children's crayons, illustrating how the sign ordinance would affect each of the businesses in the downtown area. The objective—to persuade the Council to send the ordinance back for rewording—was handily accomplished, especially when some of the Council members noted that the proposed wording would bring their businesses into a costly violation.

Show, rather than say applies to expert testimony as well as to lay presentations. Models of complex projects clarify traffic flows, or the relation of a buffer to a neighborhood, or how something works. Letting the officials and the audience play with the toy cars, or operate the machine also gives them a chance to ask questions and to understand and adopt the advocacy view.

A demonstration is even more effective. To demonstrate the

---

[9]Reprinted with permission from *The Expert Witness* by Peter B. Dorram, p. 29. Copyright © 1982 by the American Planning Association, 1313 E. 60th St., Chicago, IL 60637.

formation of potholes, civil engineers at Pennsylvania State University use gelatin mixed with water poured over a fine steel mesh. Gelatin happens to share many physical properties with concrete and makes a handy inexpensive demonstration tool—especially for potholes.

Emphasizing the conclusions rather than the methods helps listeners understand. Education researchers have found that listeners recall the conclusions rather than how the conclusions were reached.

EXPERT MANNERS

Experts rarely enjoy the good fortune to make presentations at opportune times. They may be called upon at 11:30 a.m. when the audience is hungry, or at 11:30 p.m. when the audience is fatigued. An expert's manners adds leverage to his testimony or detracts from his expertise. The following "dont's" have been compiled for experts:

• 1. Don't lecture the audience. A long, professorial lecture loses good will, attention and credibility.

• 2. Don't talk down to the audience—cutesy allusions to the little housewife, the golf-playing businessman, the sweet little old lady antagonize listeners.

• 3. Don't volunteer unsolicited information, particularly out of one's discipline. Above all, don't comment on the legality, constitutionality, or other aspects of the controversy.

• 4. Don't assume the responsibility for views, opinions, or findings outside one's own field. One brilliant chemist lost credibility when he commented on the health aspects of a herbicide. "Are you an expert on health?," he was asked by a commission member. Forced to answer "No," he was subjected to the embarrassment of the media impeaching his entire testimony.

• 5. Don't let a question elicit gratuitous statements.

• 6. Don't state that a reference book, map, or text or report is correct unless all of it has been personally examined.

• 7. Don't speak too rapidly, nor with hesitancy.

• 8. Speak clearly. Expert testimony is frequently recorded by the official stenographer who cannot record the pointed finger, the shrugged shoulder, or other non-verbal communication.

• 9. Provide the decision-makers, media, and other officials with written copies of the testimony, including a concise, complete, organized summary.

• 10. Conclude the presentation with a brief review of the points made. Avoid adding new evidence or material in the conclusion.

8

Proposing and Opposing Proposals

THE PROPOSER'S CHALLENGE

W. Bernard Richland in *You Can Beat City Hall*[1], describes the efforts of a pickler to expand his pickle plant. He relates how the pickler must conduct a campaign of persuasion before making a formal application; and leak the news that he is moving his operation out of the city. "Well-placed stories . . . reach local newspapers," Richland writes, "and perhaps even generate editorials asking why the city is doing nothing to protect its economy and the jobs of 250 picklers. The appropriate city agency will move in . . . and try to induce the pickler to stay in the area by facilitating an appropriate zone change. The pickler, with the proper appearance of reluctance, will express a willingness to reconsider if the government will pave the way."

Sierra Club authors dismiss such actions as "job backmail," and warn their members to fight companies who use these tactics. Whatever the tactics employed, the jobs versus environment battle is an ever-present conflict between public officials, workers, and those citizens anxious to preserve the constantly endangered fragile "quality of life." Even in periods of severe unemployment it is not easy for picklers to build or expand their plants, especially in smaller communities and in the sections of the United States where environmental concerns rate a high priority. Announce plans for a pickle plant and the public hearing is apt to consist of a parade of complaining citizens: the chemicals from the plant will impair the health of the community; the odors create foul smells; the traffic imperil children and older peo-

---

[1]W. Bernard Richland, *You Can Beat City Hall* (New York: Rawson, Wade Publishers, Inc., 1980), pp. 130–131.

198

ple; property values will be depressed; and the waste hazardous.

As John Quarles points out ". . . a major expansion [Author's note: i.e., pickle works] obviously must now concentrate on environmental factors from the outset. Because many of the environmental approvals require a public hearing, the views of local elected officials and the general public are also interjected. . . . To an unprecedented degree the political acceptability of a project may be critical."[2]

A "pickle works" represents almost any type of facility—a plywood plant, a high technology plant, or a landfill. Some pickle works, i.e., high technology industries, are generally greeted hospitably; others find hostility everywhere they go. A report by the United States Environmental Protection Agency concluded that public opposition to the siting of hazardous waste management facilities is the most critical problem in developing new facilities: "The controversies have reached levels of stridency impossible to convey in reports."

The problem of acceptance is widespread: a hospital planning to add a radiation unit is required to demonstrate need; a utility requesting a rate increase must prove necessity; the citizen down the street desiring a zone variance to construct a home for his handicapped son is asked to prove the validity of his project. That the request is presented by a public body does not immunize it from this proving process. Government initiated requests encounter similar problems. Even the U. S. Corps of Engineers must assure the public that the dam it recommends will protect people, wildlife, and scenery and is really necessary.

The Citizen Participation (CP) Principle No. 1 that is taught to public officials by the Laramie, Wyoming Institute for Participatory Planning (IPP) states the problem: "Today it is very easy to stop a project; it is even easier to stall a project. By the same token, it is quite difficult today to get a project—*any* project—implemented." IPP states further, "Another lesson that has been learned by the public is that the bigger an agency or corporation is, the more vulnerable they are!"[3]

Because it is relatively easy for opponents to erect roadblocks to the construction of "pickle works," anyone proposing such a project should be forewarned. He may face a battle with the most formid-

---

[2]John R. Quarles, Jr., *Federal Regulation of New Industrial Plants* (Washington, D. C.: John R. Quarles, Jr., 1979), p. 2.

[3]IPP, *Citizen Participation Handbook* (Laramie, Wyoming: Institute for Participatory Planning, 1978), pp. III-1.

able of opponents—irate citizens. The realistic proposer prepares himself for a fight. The public hearing process becomes a war, with the proposer attempting to minimize the possibility and the consequences of defeat. The weapons in this war are hostile words, not bullets; but the conflict can be bitter. In keeping with the war concept, the experienced developer recognizes that the war is not over until the last battle is fought—that is, appeal of the decision to higher authorities, the courts.

The strategies available to the proposer are the Public Interest Strategy, reinforced by the Public Consensus Strategy. The Legal Theory Strategy may be a refuge or a fallback for appealing to the courts. The burden of proof is on the proposer to demonstrate that the proposition is in the public interest and that the public concurs. Although a community may want and need the jobs and the expanded tax base, today the burden of proof that these jobs can be provided without impairing the community or the environment lies with the proponent. To implement a project it is essential to obtain, in the words of the Institute for Participatory Planning, "*substantial effective agreement on a course of action,*"—an agreement good enough, broad enough, and strong enough to allow proceeding with the project.

The experienced project proposer has learned that obtaining public acceptance of a project is another obstacle of the many that must be overcome to expand a business or construct public projects. Despite the challenges and problems (and in the face of the experience that even one determined opponent can indefinitely delay a proposition) projects that are proposed with public acceptance in mind do obtain approval from decision-makers.

Crafting the Public Interest Strategy in a Proposal

Most business propositions build their case on supplying jobs and paying taxes. Although these benefits would appear so significant as to dwarf others, the burden of proof in the Public Interest Strategy in the current social environment demands additional benefits. Activist community leaders may be more impressed by such benefits as:

— Revival of a decaying neighborhood.
— Homes for the poor or elderly.
— Provision of needed sewers or water systems for the community.
— Money to pay additional teachers.

— Funds to build a school or library.
— Grants for road improvements.
— Pride in affiliation with a specific product.
— Reduction of crime.
— Benefits to the general welfare.
— Consistency with good community planning.

These positive public interest aspects are more persuasive than some of the stale arguments frequently relied upon by proposers:

— The original city plan was a mistake.
— Denial of the proposal would deprive the applicant of the highest and best use of the property.
— Denial deprives the applicant of his or her constitutional rights.
— The opposition is weak.
— The opposition is selfish.
— The opposition is dishonest.
— Delay will be costly to the proposer and the stockholders.
— If the project isn't approved, the property will be used for a less desirable purpose.
— The project will be profitable for the proposer.

The tactic of pointing out that the property might be used for a less desirable purpose, though it falls into the polite blackmail category, sometimes works. When faced with the possibility that a property will be used for half-way houses for the Criminal Corrections Department, or another unpopular use, if it is not approved for a grocery store, a community may decide to choose the store.

As important as proving that the project is in the public interest is demonstrating that it is not *against* the public interest—that it will bring no adverse consequences to the community. If noise is a problem, the proposer had better be prepared with plans for mitigating the noise, reinforced by acoustical engineering experts who show that the mitigation plan will work. If someone raises the problem of the odor from the pickle plant, detailed plans on how the odor will be confined to the plant or eliminated should be readied, accompanied by a demonstration at the public hearing to persuade the decision-makers, the media, and the public that the scheme works.

Dramatizing Jobs and Tax Benefits

Not relying solely on jobs and taxes to gain acceptance, does not infer that these benefits should be ignored or glossed over. These benefits cry out for innovative, dramatic demonstration but they are usually dismissed with the blunt statement that "This project will supply jobs and taxes for the community." The assumption that everyone understands these benefits is unwarranted. Jobs and taxes do not automatically assure a welcome. In many communities it is necessary to prove their value. Some techniques for dramatizing the value of the jobs and taxes will fill the gap between public understanding of economics and the realities.

- 1. Pay workers in $2 dollar bills, Susan B. Anthony dollar coins, or with different types of checks to illustrate the impact of the payroll in the community.
- 2. Translate jobs in terms of persons affected, rather than persons employed. A plant payroll of 1200 people involves 3600 to 4800 family members in the community, who may represent a significant percentage of the population of a small town. If the factory will bring in some workers with families, the schools might add additional students and therefore create jobs for school teachers. (This effect may be considered good or bad depending on whether the local school system is looking for students to maintain the school level, or will have to raise taxes to build additional schools.)
- 3. Relate the jobs supplied to changing trends in employment. A new high technology industry may be welcome in a town whose economy has depended on a declining industry.
- 4. Translate the increased tax dollars anticipated from the project to specific benefits for the community: $420,000 to construct those badly needed sewers; $250,000 for improving an old school; $140,000 for improving a road; $95,000 for a new library wing for senior citizens and the handicapped. An anticipated tax increase of $100,000 may rescue a failing public works department.

The fate of a project should not rest on assumptions. For instance, assuming that each of the 1200 workers is the breadwinner with two children risks credibility if the industry is one that employs many women or multiple members in one family. Also, the opposition can be counted on to fish out some of the studies that "prove" new or expanded industries cost towns more dollars than they bring. Keep in mind that many of the studies used for this purpose are out of date and are based on concessions made by communities to lure industries. Investing the time and money to obtain surveys that show otherwise may save the project.

Proposing a Project

The following narrative is intended to serve as a model for proposing a project. The process used to expand the Tech-Widget plant is the route to approval for projects of any magnitude from small struggling companies to national corporations. The principles are also appropriate for public projects such as sewer systems, dams, and libraries.

Tom Harrold, president of a company named, for the purpose of this narrative, Tech-Widget knew how to obtain timely acceptance of his company's expansion. As the Tech-Widget Directors drifted out of the spring Board meeting their smiles indicated good news. Tech-Widget's new product, Tech-Angle, had proven a great success and the Board authorized immediate facility expansion to take advantage of the current brisk market. "We'd better apply for a building expansion permit right away," the plant engineer suggested. "You know how long it takes."

"Not right away," Tom cautioned. "We'll wait till the time is ripe."

Tom arranged a meeting that afternoon with his key executives and the company attorney. "Remember what happened to the Markman plant last year," he reminded. "They applied for a building permit and that Committee to Preserve Center City held up the permit for over a year. I think it's still in the courts. I don't want that to happen to us."

Devise an Action Plan

Tom concluded the meeting by directing Jack Horton to take charge of the project with instructions to: "Assemble the team you need and do whatever is necessary to get approval for the expansion when we ask for it. No delays!" Jack pulled together a team including the Public Relations manager, an outside consultant on public hearings, the head of the engineering department, and the company attorney. Together they drafted an action plan.

First, the Public Relations manager issued a news story about the Tech-Angle breakthrough as new technology, its use in the Space Program and its implications for medicine and education. The Associated Press picked up the announcement and the local TV station prepared a documentary, with assistance from the PR manager, on the promise of Tech-Angle in the health field. A Fact Sheet on Tech-Angle was widely distributed at local meetings. Plant expansion was *not* mentioned. A Chamber of Commerce Vice President wrote a letter-to-the-editor stating that "We should all be proud that Tech-Widget is in Center City." An elderly resident wrote that she remembered when Tech-Widget started in a garage in town. One letter came from a person who thought we shouldn't be in the space program and urged Tech-Widget not to sell its products to the government.

Meanwhile, Tech-Widget's engineering consultants began preliminary engineering for the expansion. The public hearings consultant initiated a Public Acceptance Assessment to assess how the people in town perceived Tech-Widget and Tech-Angle, and to predict who, if anyone, might oppose the plant expansion and why.

Tom invited the Planning Commission, Mayor, City Council and the local media to lunch and to tour the plant. This invitation was not unusual: Tech-Widget invited local public officials to lunch at the plant cafeteria once or twice a year to discuss community affairs. A tour of the Tech-Angle manufacturing facilities proved especially interesting. A Councilwomen noted the beehive activity and asked if the plant wouldn't soon have to expand its facilities. Tom agreed that it looked that way. On hearing "expansion" the editor of the local paper rejoined the group. The next evening's editorial lauded the achievements of Tech-Widget and surmised that the plant might have to expand.

Prepare for Opposition

At the next monthly meeting of the Committee to Preserve Center City (CPCC), the agenda included a discussion of possible Tech-Widget expansion. Although most of the members opposed the expansion, the Committee decided not to organize opposition. Tech-Widget's record as a supporter of town activities and as an employer was good. Other employers in the town were laying off people and it would be poor strategy to publicly oppose the company at this time. These sentiments were not shared by Mason Hander, who lived in the Tech-Widget area and opposed any expansion of Center City.

When the City Manager read the editorial on the possible expansion, he phoned the Mayor, suggesting that they visit Tom Harrold and assure him of assistance if the plant expanded in Center City. The Mayor felt that his major supporters would not favor the expansion and decided not to go himself. The City Manager arranged a lunch date with Tom Harrold who suggested that Jack Horton join them. The luncheon conversation focused on the worsening unemployment problem in the city—a situation on which Jack Horton had compiled some worrisome statistics. Armed with these statistics, the City Manager talked with the *Center City Sentinel* editor about a series of in-depth stories on the employment situation. Jack Horton proved a valuable resource for the articles.

The public hearing consultant showed Jack Horton the results of the just completed Public Acceptance Assessment, which concluded that most residents hoped that Tech-Widget would expand in Center City. The leaders of the influential CPCC worried about the traffic bottleneck around the plant. In addition they were opposed to any action that would increase the city population and urbanize the area. One CPCC member (Mason Hander) vowed to fight any expansion through the courts if necessary. Though others would not publicly support his position they said they would contribute funds for the appeals. Traffic and urbanization concerned the City Planning staff also.

Mitigate Adverse Perceptions and Conditions

Project leader Jack Horton met with the engineers. "Is the traffic problem legitimate?," he asked. "If so, what can we do about it?" The engineers agreed that traffic did tend to bottleneck in that area. One solution to mitigate the problem would be to provide an access road and parking lot through the back of the property, which would not only handle new employees but would actually relieve the existing traffic problem. The new access road would add about 10 percent to the project cost. Another additional cost was a suggested buffer strip around the periphery of the entire property, attractively landscaped with trees and shrubs. The landscape buffer would conceal the parking lot from public view and maintain the country-like environment. Jack's analysis estimated that the cost-benefits favored the additional expenditure for the road and landscape buffer; this took into account the cost of delays if the permit were appealed.

President Tom Harrold agreed with the mitigation concept. Jack suggested that the PR manager issue a news release about plans for a new back access road to relieve the traffic on the major artery and the proposed landscape buffer. Jack continued to collect information from the City concerning its unemployment: the school superintendent was concerned about empty classrooms due to lost population; the Public Works Department was unable to maintain the roads on its reduced budget; the City Comprehensive plan called for a population increase of 5,000 persons in the next ten years and all city planning was based on that projection.

The announcement of the proposed back access road elicited little comment and Jack felt they were ready to apply for the building permit. The public relations team prepared a release on the application for the permit, emphasizing the contribution of the expansion to maintaining employment, the new road, and the landscape buffer. The company attorney advised against rocking the boat with a news release: "I think it will just go through and no one will know anything about it," he said. Jack decided to issue the release anyway.

The building permit application was duly filed: the Planning Commission scheduled consideration after the 30-day legal filing period. Everyone expected the Planning Commission meeting to routinely approve the permit, allowing construction to begin immediately. Jack was out of town and no one represented the company. The routine meeting was disrupted when the CPCC member, Mason Hander who had vowed to fight expansion at any cost, accused the Commission of bypassing the required public hearing and called for an Environmental Impact Statement. Although assured by the City Attorney that the process complied with legal requirements, the Commission, voting four to three, deemed it politically expedient to advertise a public hearing to be held in three weeks, the earliest legal date. This action set construction back three weeks and confirmed the finding of the Public Acceptance Assessment that one person intended to jeopardize the expansion program.

Use an Information Campaign

Jack put his team to work. Although the community favored the expansion, he recognized that it would now require a concerted effort to show overwhelming support at the Commission meeting. If the support was not demonstrated, a Planning Commission recommendation might be overturned in a subsequent City Council hearing. The Center City Economic Development Council offered to help. Organizing business, unions, and several neighborhoods into a coalition called "Expand Tech-Widget" (ETW), they immediately set about recruiting supporters for the public hearing. The PR manager developed an Information-and-Directions-for-Action Fact Sheet which was used by the ETW's newly organized Speaker's Bureau in two-minute talks to service clubs. Blue ETW buttons became prize possessions. Jack appointed his assistant as the Public Hearings Floor Manager. Adopting the Public Interest Strategy, backed by the Public Consensus Strategy, the Fact Sheet and the Speaker's Bureau emphasized that the expansion of Tech-Widget would maintain the level of employment in Center City and not bring new people into the community. Artist's drawings of the new access road and landscaping were displayed in the local banks and library.

Organize Support

The Public Acceptance Assessment revealed that the members of the current Planning Commission and City Council had a record of voting against industrial expansions. Jack and ETW determined that public support would need to overwhelm the decision-makers' personal inclinations. Supporters were asked to write letters to the editor on why they favored the expansion. One ETW member held an ice-cream social at his home to assist letter writers and help prepare testimony for the public hearing. Twenty-three supporters attended. The week before the hearing, an ETW calling committee personally phoned community leaders and persons who had indicated an interest, asking them to attend and testify at the hearing. The list included 84 persons who agreed to testify. The evening before almost 40 supporters showed up at a pre-hearing question and answer period at the Center City fairgrounds. Tom Harrold personally thanked each of the supporters for their help.

Prepare all Relevant Information

The call for an Environmental Impact Statement (EIS) posed another problem. Both the City and company attorneys said an EIS was not a legal requirement in this permit, but Jack did not want to risk the possibility of an intimidated Commission asking for one anyway, possibly leading to years of litigation. Engineering put together an Environmental Impact Statement addressing each of the questions, weighing all "significant adverse and beneficial effects of the proposed project . . . on the environmental, social, and economic characteristics of the affected area." The 76-page EIS covered all factors, though not as extensively as a standard EIS.

Make the Public Hearing the Climax of Your Strategy

Jack had noted 15 letters-to-the-editor on the expansion. Using the Letters-to-the-Editor-Index (See Chapter 10, Managing Public Hearings), he estimated that as many as 300 persons would attend the hearing and suggested moving to a larger room. The Commission Chairman reluctantly agreed to holding the hearing in the Junior High cafeteria. The night of the hearing more than 300 persons jammed the room, most sporting the blue ETW buttons. Jack, as the company spokesman, surprised the Commission with the Environmental Impact Statement and extensive statistical documentation in his brief presentation. Noting with satisfaction the puzzled look of one of the Commission members, Jack felt that his hunch that the EIS could have become an issue was confirmed. After Jack's presentation, CPCC member Mason Hander made an impassioned plea to not let the town grow, telling of his youth in the area which is now one of the new neighborhoods, talking of crowded, impersonal schools and lines of traffic. He concluded with the threat to appeal the Commission's decision if they approved the permit.

There followed a stream of citizens speaking in support of the expansion. Testimony covered every facet needed to make the record. The Committee to Preserve Center City sat together on one side of the cafeteria, whispering comments. But, although nine members had signed the testifying sheet and the Chair asked several times if anyone wanted to speak in opposition, each passed his turn.

By 11:15 p.m. the last citizen was heard. The Chairman closed the hearing. Commission members were seen referring to their fact sheets. During the discussion one Commission member wondered why they had to devote an entire evening to a hearing with such wide-based support. Another member was not satisfied that the Environmental Impact Statement was thorough. Fifteen minutes later the Commission voted, recommending approval of the permit by a vote of six to one. After the verdict, the local press flocked around Mason Hander, who had become a local celebrity figure. When asked if he would appeal, he said he'd have to think about it.

The postscript to this account was that he intended to appeal, but could not raise the funds from CPCC. The President of CPCC stated in an interview that the public so obviously supported the expansion his organization did not want to take on the entire town.

Acceptance of a Proposal

The Tech-Widget expansion illustrates ten important factors in winning acceptance of a proposal at a public hearing:

- 1. Vest responsibility and authority for shepherding the project through the public hearing process in one competent individual.
- 2. Prepare for each proposal as if it will be opposed. No project is ever assured, no matter how minor the opposition.
- 3. Search for elements of the public interest to justify approval. Select strategies and tactics to demonstrate public interest.
- 4. Invest in careful, thorough research. Dig out all relevant information; document all statements.
- 5. Assess the public perception on the project, especially perceptions of opinion leaders.
- 6. Make every effort to mitigate adverse perceptions and to remove adverse conditions from the project.

- 7. Use an information campaign to set the stage for acceptance at the hearing. Assist the media. Emphasize the mitigation in the news releases.
- 8. Form a coalition to promote and support the project.
- 9. Give the coalition high visibility.
- 10. Recruit, train and assist supporters to present testimony at the hearing. Make the public hearing the climax of the strategic effort.

Who Should Be Delegated to Present a Proposal at the Public Hearing?

Individuals who hesitate to speak in public often prefer that their attorneys make the presentation for a proposal. Sometimes the engineer, developer or other specialist presents the testimony. However, unless he is too ill-at-ease to speak out at a hearing, the person requesting the permit, zone change, or rate increase is the most effective advocate for his proposal. This is especially true if the public officials are volunteers from the area appointed to fill the decision-making positions. The farmer appealing to fellow farmers on the planning commission enjoys greater credibility than an out-of-town attorney. The small businessman requesting permission to issue industrial revenue bonds for a business expansion shares a common interest with the other small businessmen appointed to the port commission. Attorneys, engineers and other experts are the best to testify on the technical aspects, but the applicant, properly coached, should be the most persuasive advocate for the project.

OPPOSING A PROPOSAL

Herbert H. Smith[4] observes that: " 'You can't fight city hall' . . . has been (and is) true in many cases, but only because of the lack of an informed public, ineffective approaches, or disorganization."

Smith advises anyone opposing a proposal to:

---

[4]Reprinted with permission from *The Citizen's Guide to Planning* by Herbert H. Smith, pp. 138, 139, 141–142. Copyright © 1979 by the American Planning Association, 1313 E. 60th St., Chicago, IL 60637.

1. Make sure you have a real issue, not just a personal ax to grind.

2. Once you believe you have an issue, check it out to see how inclusive of others it is and make certain that it is a valid concern, not just something founded on rumors.

3. If there is no neighborhood council already in existence, get others together who should be interested and find out if they are informed and have some facts, not conjecture, to further inform them.

4. Assuming the issue is genuine and has held up through discussion and interest arousal, program carefully how you are going to get your act together.

5. Pick out any expertise in your group and get acceptance of responsibility for data collection, analysis, and presentation preparation. If possible, supplement this with aid from other citizen action groups, advocacy agencies, or a community design center (these exist in many cities).

6. Organize and plan your strategy, your timing, and your approach, making certain that you stay away from emotion and stick with facts. Avoid threats and implied intimidation. [Author's note: see Chapter 4 on persuasion.]

7. As soon as you have enough data to begin to formulate a position, assign effective individuals to personal contact with key local officials and members of the "power structure," if they are known. No one in a position of influence or decision making likes to be surprised.

8. Get the troops out for the presentation, but be sure you have them well informed and under strict orders to stick with the "game plan" of your presentation. An effective maneuver is to have the opening speaker ask all of those interested in this issue and being represented to stand up. Keep them standing for a few minutes so that the "pros" can get a good idea of the head count.

9. Proceed with your informative and persuasive presentation keeping it as concise and brief as possible. Have graphic materials and visual aids to help make points. Prepare something to leave with the hearing body, but keep it short and in summary form. Interestingly, one of the least effective things to leave is a petition. Too many of these have been shown to have been signed by those who will sign anything without knowing what it is about. There is no substitute for personal appearances for effectiveness.

10. Get a decision or get a definite timetable for action. Follow up and make certain that commitments are carried through. If

and when favorable results occur don't forget to thank those who caused them to happen.

Opposing a Project

Richland[5], whose advice on proposing a pickle plant was quoted in "Proposing a Project," also has advice for those opposing the pickle plant project.

"The first principle to recognize is that a pickle mogul, however rich and influential, has only one vote in an election . . . the ancillary principle is that the main goal of elected officials is to be reelected. Therefore, your first step is to form a pressure group of the pickle factory despisers in your area".

In practice, the tendency to form pressure groups may in itself stop or delay the pickle works. Roger W. Schemner[6], in his examination of plant location decisions, is persuaded that "business climate" plays a role in some location decisions. "Business climate" is the sum total of an area's attitude toward business, including labor's and government's attitudes, regulations, managing services and schools. An area that readily gives birth to anti-pickle works pressure groups develops an unfavorable business climate. Schemner observes that "a location's perceived business climate is markedly self-perpetuating and hence difficult to turn around, but there is no doubt that it does exert influence on new plant location decisions."

Anti-pickle works groups use the public hearing as the opportunity to demonstrate opposition, poking and probing for holes in the proposal to point out problems to decision-makers: violation of procedures; conflict with the public interest; lack of need; concern over adverse impacts. Skillfully presented and well-documented objections weaken the case for the proposal.

The tactics for opposing zoning requests were examined in the section on Opposing a Zoning Request and many of these tactics apply to opposing any project. Additionally, Figure 8-1, A Checklist for Opposing a Project, lists forty specific questions to raise in opposing projects. These forty questions help identify the appropriate strategy for opposing the project.

---

[5]Richland, *You Can Beat City Hall,* p. 129.
[6]Roger W. Schemner, *Making Business Location Decisions* (Englewood Cliffs, N. J.: Prentice-Hall, Inc., 1982), p. 53.

Figure 8-1

A Checklist for Opposing a Project

1. Does the project comply, rigorously with all applicable regulations?
    a. Land use
    b. Zoning—Uses permitted in the zone
    c. Environmental: Air; Water; Noise; Odor
    d. Historic preservation
    e. Endangered species
    f. Citizen input
2. Does the project require an environmental impact statement, according to NEPA requirements, or any other type of impact statement?
3. What licenses and permits will the project require?
4. Does the project fill all the requirements for licenses and permits?
5. What are the possible adverse effects of the project?
    — Traffic
    — Odor
    — Endanger children
    — Create hazards in the area
    — Overload existing sewers
    — Overload existing school system
    — Devalue land or homes
    — "Quality of life"
6. What are notification procedures for the permits, public hearings, etc.?
7. Have notification procedures been followed? Have any procedural requirements been ignored or poorly handled?
8. What studies applicable to the siting have been made by public bodies?
    — Flood studies
    — Geological studies
    — Soil studies
    — Technical Feasibility studies
    — Traffic studies
9. Are the studies available to the public?

Figure 8-1 (continued)

10. Is there reason to distrust or dispute any of the findings of these studies? Have the citizens been misinformed (i.e. an incorrect calculation of a tax impact)?

11. Has the application been properly filed to the appropriate board?

12. What are the critical dates for notification, challenges and appeals?

13. Which citizens and groups have a stake in opposing the project (i.e. neighborhoods, Sierra Club, taxpayers, labor unions, etc.)? Do the affected citizens agree on the issues? Will some people suffer personal hardship for the benefit of others? Have you organized a "grass-roots" group to sponsor the opposition? Have you named the grass-roots group?

14. What types of jobs will the new project create? How many jobs? What salaries? Is there a local labor market to meet the project requirements?

15. Is there any hard evidence that would lead the proponents to feel that the project won't be successful when implemented, i.e., a store won't have the patronage due to neighborhood change?

16. Can opposition interest be protected by an alternative course of action?

17. Is the project a power play that might lose support if exploited by the media?

18. Is there evidence that citizen concerns have been addressed by the proponents? Decision-makers?

19. Can an individual who intends to run for public office and will use an issue to gain media exposure be identfed? Will stopping, delaying, or changing this project, constitute an appropriate issue?

20. What are the broad issues involved (neighborhood integrity, community character, growth or no-growth, quality of life)?

21. Is there at least one person who can be counted on to lead the opposition?

22. Has the media shown an interest? A bias?

23. Is there an ongoing organization which is willing to take on opposition to the project?

24. If not, can an organization be put together?

Figure 8-1 (continued)

25. Do city, county, etc. staff members support (oppose) the project?

26. How many people can be depended on to testify for the position at the public hearing(s)? Are they persuasive witnesses?

27. Is there a credible former supporter of the proposal who has had a change of heart? Is he willing to testify at a public hearing?

28. Are there legal, moral, political or other bases for compensating those opposed to the project for damages caused by the project?

29. Will a delay in the decision benefit or harm the opposition?

30. If a delay is advantageous, is there a clear basis for requesting a delayed decision?

31. Will a favorable decision adversely impact minorities, women, children, elderly?

32. Does the proponent have an unfavorable record of responsible management?

33. Does the decision-making body have a record of unpopular decisions, or decisions favoring special interests?

34. Has the discussion indicated that the statutes or ordinances requiring the decision do not reflect the lawmaker's intent?

35. Are the applicable rules poorly drafted?

36. Are there other allies who might be expected to oppose, but would be harmed by the decision (i.e., an air quality permit that would consume most of the area's quotas for smoke and dust, prohibiting other industries from obtaining permits)?

37. Is this an issue on which school children or any other citizens who might be "surprise witnesses" could testify?

38. Are confrontation tactics (i.e., boycotting, picketing, placard parades, sit-ins) appropriate before the public hearing?

39. Do the statutes require public hearings on this issue or development? If not, will a request for public hearings be initiated?

40. Do the statutes provide for a public hearing only if requested after a notice of opportunity was published? Was such a notice published? Was it in a newspaper of general circulation?

Opposing Proposed Legislation or Regulations

Opposition to proposed legislation or regulations usually involves a scale more global than opposing local or regional projects. The following account shows how commitment and sensitivity to the methods of influencing people can be used to muster public opposition to proposed legislation.

The story begins in 1921 when New Mexico Senator Holm Olaf Bursum introduced a bill to determine once and for all whether 12,000 white settlers really owned the 60,000 acres they believed they had bought on the Pueblo Indian Reservation in New Mexico. At issue were the Pueblo's water rights and the continuity of their unique form of self-government. The Bursum Bill angered the Pueblos and outraged their friends. The campaign to defeat the Bursum Bill dramatically changed America's attitude toward its native Indians.

The political power behind the Bursum Bill appeared unbeatable. It was backed by President Harding's Secretary of the Interior, Albert B. Fall (better known for his part in the Teapot Dome scandal), the Commissioner of Indian Affairs Charles Burke, and the political might of New Mexico. Challenging this political bastion was a young, unknown New York social worker, John Collier, who had been invited to visit Taos, New Mexico by the wealthy, fabled Mabel Dodge Luhan. Another Luhan guest at the time was the British novelist, D. H. Lawrence.

Collier became the catalyst to orchestrate the defeat of the Bursum Bill; preservation of the Indian way of life became his sacred crusade. Without influence, without funds, his unerring instincts for the principles of social change led him to success in this effort. To gain influence, he persuaded Californian Stella Atwood, who chaired the Indian Welfare Committee of the General Federation of Women's Clubs, that the Bursum Bill threatened the survival of the Indians. Mrs. Atwood tapped funds from Mrs. Kate Vosburg, a philanthropist from Azusa, California.

Collier based his plan on the Fairness Strategy, using the Public Consensus Strategy to gain political support. To demonstrate that the Indians were underdogs, mistreated and deprived, Collier embarked on a campaign of consciousness-raising. He turned out a stream of articles for *Sunset Magazine* and the progressive *Survey*. "The Pueblos Last Stand," "Persecuting the Pueblos," and similar articles raised the consciousness of several intellectual Americans who, in turn wrote articles for *New Republic, Outlook* and other popular magazines. Spurred by Collier, these writers assumed a militant leadership, persuading newspaper editors and influential columnists to write editorials against the Bursum Bill. "Let's Save the Pueblos" became the rallying cry.

While the consciousness of America was being raised, Collier prepared for the Public Consensus Strategy. Volunteer organizations to defend the Pueblos against the Bursum Bill were formed in all sections of the country. Most of the members had never visited New Mexico or an Indian reservation, but so vivid were Collier's and the other articles, readers adopted the Pueblo cause as their own. The Pueblo Indians themselves were organized into the All-Pueblo Council.

Collier was ready to set the stage. Prior to the public hearings on the Bill, Stella Atwood hired an attorney to prepare a blue book (really a White Paper), "Shall the Pueblo Indians of New Mexico Be Destroyed?" Distributed to every member of Congress and all over the country, the blue book served as the focus of the lobbying activity by the two million members of the General Federation.

The combined tactics worked. Senator William Borah led the House of Representatives to unanimously recall the Bursum Bill. Meanwhile, the Pueblos, under Collier's tutelage drafted "An Appeal by the Pueblo Indians of New Mexico to the People of the United States," which stated that the Bursum Bill would destroy "their common life and rob us of everything we hold dear. . . ." Using this appeal, the Pueblos raised $3,500 to send a delegation of Indians to the hearings of the Senate Committee in Washington, D.C.

On the way to the public hearings in Washington, Collier arranged for the Indians, wearing feathered headdresses, to speak before such prestigious groups as the Chicago Urban League and the Explorers' Club in New York City. In a visit to the bankers and businessmen at the New York stock exchange, which temporarily suspended its rule forbidding speeches, the Indians sang native songs and beat their drums. Reports state that the stock exchange went wild and many bankers sent "kill the Bursum Bill" telegrams to their congressmen.

The public hearing before the Senate Committee on Public Lands and Surveys showcased the Indian cause. A model for persuasive testimony, Collier's orchestration included every angle. Stella Atwood, representing two million women, said the Bill would break the Indians' spirit and "annihilate the hope that still burns in their souls." An attorney suggested that the Senators take up the "white man's burden." Pablo Abeyta, a member of the Pueblo delegation, told the senators that the Bill would turn "us into the wild" and pointed out the needs of the Indians. Testimony to make the record was presented by the General Federation of Women's Clubs' attorney, who hammered home the fallacies and inequities of the Bill.

Shortly thereafter Secretary Fall resigned.

The convoluted path of the Bursum Bill, the second Bursum Bill, the additional public hearings in Washington, and John Collier's acquired celebrity status which led to his eventual appointment as the Commissioner of Indian Affairs by President Franklin Delano Roosevelt, are an interesting vignette in influencing public opinion.

John Collier followed a classic path to defeating proposed legislation which, concisely stated, includes:

- Find a committed, articulate leader.
- State the problem in simple, identifiable emotion-laden terms.
- Define the outrage.
- Orchestrate the outrage*.
- Enlist the aid of writers and public figures to take the issue to the people.
- Undertake a broad-based consciousness-raising campaign.
- Develop and execute a strategy.
- Locate and use influential support, preferably support that has an existing network.
- Organize special interest groups; organize a coalition of the special interest groups; use the coalition as a network.
- Dramatize the issue.
- Carry the message to the largest, most diverse audience.
- Help the public carry the message to the decision-makers.
- Use the public hearing as the focal point of the strategy.
- Follow up.

---

*From prize-winning reporter Gaylord Shaw, whose articles on the collapse of the Teton Dam in Idaho recount how he found that it was necessary to "orchestrate the outrage" as well as report it.

9
Business and Industry Presentations

Public hearings offer the public an opportunity to influence business decisions such as the construction of a facility, how products are manufactured, what products are produced and sold, and relations with employees.

This treading on what used to be solely business turf causes businessmen to approach public hearings with trepidation, especially when opponents of business are planning to utilize the opportunities to manipulate decisions. Failing to master the public hearing process, businessmen tend to take "pot luck" at the hearings, finding out too late that their adversaries control the ingredients in the pot. Only recently have businessmen recognized that the traditional economic trio—labor, capital, and materials—has been joined by a modern fourth component—the stakeholders of business. Although industry is the prime mechanism for long range social change (e.g. products to mechanize home tasks), it handles public hearings, particularly at the local level, ineffectively, compared to the stakeholder's superior public hearing gamesmanship.

WHY BUSINESS FINDS THE PUBLIC HEARING PROCESS FRUSTRATING

From small Mom and Pop businesses asking for permission to locate a neighborhood grocery, to heads of multi-national concerns attempting to secure a permit to operate a mine, businessmen find the public hearing process difficult and often demeaning. The difficulties stem from the nature of business activities and businessmen.

•Industrial processes provide a fertile field for conflict. Mining

minerals from the earth, converting the forests into lumber, and producing chemicals all utilize natural resources in a noisy, smelly, dusty,
and sometimes hazardous manner. Arrayed against almost any action
involving conversion of natural resources are environmental protection
advocates, conservation advocates, recreation special interests, and
a broad spectrum of concerned citizens. Proposals to site new manufacturing facilities almost always generate some opposition, no matter
how hungry the area is for jobs. Business finds itself caught in a conflict
between its role of providing needed products and the national effort
to protect the public in a risk-free society. The conflict is staged in
the public hearing.

•*Business assumes the defensive.* As a consequence, business often
finds itself on the defensive. In a public hearing, business interests
stand alone confronted by citizen "interests," including the League
of Women Voters, social service agencies, taxpayer groups, senior citizens, racial groups, homeowners, and neighborhoods.

Murray L. Weidenbaum points out in *The Future of Business
Regulation*[1] that until the 1950's the interest groups advocating changes
in business-government relations were the producer groups concerned
with some aspect of economic activity. "In contrast," he writes "a
newer type of interest group has tended to be the most prominent factor
in public policy discussions in more recent years. The newer interest
groups have concerns that are essentially social, and . . . they are usually oblivious to the economic aspects of their proposals. They range
from ecological associations to civil rights organizations to consumer
groups. Many . . . have appropriated the very term 'public interest
group' and their views tend to be reported as representative of the
views of the citizenry as a whole."

The public hearing is viewed as one of the increasingly burden-
some regulations under which industry must function. Industry feels
that it suffers from lack of understanding of its problems, not only
from the public but from the regulatory agencies. Implementation of
The Federal Water Pollution Control Act Amendments of 1972
(familiarly known as PL 92-500) was an instance of societal objectives confronting the realities of technology. The Environmental
Protection Agency attempted to set a compliance requirement of one

---

[1]Excerpted, by permission of the publisher, from *The Future of Business Regulation* by Murray L. Weidenbaum, pp. 141–142. Copyright © 1979 by AMACOM,
a division of American Management Associations, New York. All rights reserved.

standard manufacturing process for all industries. As business struggles to keep its products affordable and to satisfy customers in an aggressively competitive world market, it finds complying with regulatory
agencies a distracting burden.

•*Business resents outsiders usurping its functions.* A business
manager's responsibility includes evaluation of entrepreneurial risk
and the cost/benefits of assuming that risk. A restaurateur planning
to expand his seating capacity requests permission to use parking spaces
in a neighboring business some 200 feet from his building. The
restaurateur has made a management decision that a 200-foot walk
will not discourage customers. At the public hearing, a citizen comments that 200 feet is too far for him to walk. The city's zoning hearings board rejects the restaurateur's request, on the basis that 200 feet
was too far for customers to walk.

•*Business prefers a low-key approach to avoid media attention.*
"Let's not raise that issue; perhaps it won't come up." "Let's not
rock the boat."—are two often-heard management policies on the
public hearing process. Business fears negative media treatment.
Donald MacNaughton, former chairman of the Prudential Life Insurance Company, is quoted as saying: "Sixty seconds on the evening
news tonight is all that is required to ruin a reputation . . . or impair
a company's profitability. The power of the press with today's methods
of mass communication has become . . . the power to destroy."[2]

•*Businessmen fear public hearings that function as kangaroo
courts.* Public hearings sometimes function as kangaroo courts in which
authorities judge business guilty without a trial. This is particularly
distressing when the business has made every effort to comply with
the rules, only to find unwritten "street" rules barring the way.
Hewlett-Packard, the respected high technology giant, felt the sting
of individual citizen action that was aided by a law that makes it possible for any state resident to shut a project down at any time, in its
long struggle to develop property in Lake Stevens, Washington. The
project had been approved by every authorized state agency.

•*Business training and practices are incompatible with the public
hearing process.* Business takes seriously the adage, "The business of
business is business," although businesses' business now encompasses
a wider range of community concerns than its leaders have been trained
to anticipate. Business has not developed sensitive methods for hear-

---

Weidenbaum, *The Future of Business Regulation*, p. 158.

ing and interacting with its numerous and diverse stakeholders. Centrally managed companies are out of contact with the special interest groups in local communities and are poorly equipped to keep pace with rapid social change. As a result, the public hearing becomes the first notification that some profound social change has occurred.

Businessmen are rarely schooled in the techniques of testifying at public hearings. Moreover, they find the interminable evening meetings incompatible with the necessity of arising early the next morning and putting in a day's work. "The power in this community belongs to those who can sit through the meetings," one executive complained. "We relinquish the power because we don't have the time to sit."

•*Public hearings are incompatible with business responsibilities.* Responsibility to stockholders may overweigh responsibility to other stakeholders. Businessmen fear that their remarks may encourage retaliatory legislative action and possible accusations of anti-trust violations. Quiet compliance appears to offer the safest course.

As a result, the public hearing has become a fighting arena in which business is not sure of the rules of the game, not convinced it ought to play the game, and resentful that it is forced to fight.

MAKING BUSINESS AND INDUSTRY PRESENTATIONS WORK

Modern businessmen perceive that these public hearing problems must be solved if business is to be equitably represented in public hearings. By deliberately placing itself into the public hearing process, business can exert some control of the menu instead of reluctant acceptance of the pot luck furnished by the public.

Business presentations at public hearings can be designed to improve the acceptance of proposals and policies. Prerequisite to a successful design is a commitment to planning for public hearings as a management function. Implementation of this commitment follows.

A Proactive Approach to Public Hearings

A proactive approach includes preparing for the public hearing process as part of project and policy planning. Controversial issues should be examined prior to the public hearing. The "let's not raise the issue" practice renders business vulnerable to any citizen who wants to and will raise an issue. The time to explore the problems is before a pencil touches the drawing board, or an application filed, or a plan announced.

Discovering Emerging Issues

Methods for discovering emerging issues range from making a simple Public Acceptance Assessment to establishing long-range advisory committees.

- 1) The *Public Acceptance Assessment*. The Public Acceptance Assessment is a useful tool for evaluating the probability of the acceptance or rejection by the public of any specific project, proposal, or proposed action. It predicts quantitatively the possibility that any segment of the public may attempt to restrain or stop a proposed action. It goes a step further to predict the success of such opposition. (Figure 4–4 in Chapter 4 lists the ten steps in making a Public Acceptance Assessment. Preprinted forms for making the Assessment are available.[3])

- 2) The *Social Impact Analysis*. A ten-step process developed by the USDA Forest Service helps predict social changes resulting from resource developments. The Social Impact Analysis depends on narratives and sociological relationships and does not include checklists. The first four steps describe the culture of the area, statistical data, forest uses, and the effect of the "resource development force." Steps five, six and seven predict the future of the resource development, changes in economic indicators, and changes in cultural descriptors. The last three steps are interpretive and relate public issues to management goals, developing alternatives for management action.

The Social Impact Analysis can be applied to other resource developments. A familiarity with sociological terms is helpful in making this analysis. Techniques for conducting a Social Impact Analysis are described in *An Approach to Social Resources Management*"[4].

- 3) *A Community Survey*. A more generalized assessment, not related to specific projects or impacts, is an ongoing computer-modeled survey. This is used to help companies keep informed of local issues crucial to maintaining a profitable operating climate. The Community Survey is conducted by a management or marketing consultant, or

---

[3]Jean Mater, *Citizen's Involved: Handle With Care! Public Acceptance Assessment Checklist* (Forest Grove, Oregon: Timber Press, 1977).

[4]James A. Kent and others, *An Approach to Social Resources Management* (Denver, Colorado: Foundation for Urban and Neighborhood Development, Inc. and the John Ryan Co., 1979).

sometimes in-house by the marketing or public relations department.

• 4) *An Emergency Information Network.* An Emergency Information Network is a tool for crisis-prone industries—nuclear energy plants, chemical facilities, herbicide sprayers, any industry that might impact the "psychological health" of a community. Social behaviorists attribute the emotional reaction to the Three Mile Island Nuclear accident in 1979 to the failure of communication between officials and the public. The accident released small, abnormal levels of radioactivity into the atmosphere. Studies have identified no immediate or expected long-term physical health effects from the accident, but the social and psychological effects have been profound.

Emergency Information Networks are used in nuclear plant operation. However, in the Three Mile Island nuclear accident the existing mechanisms for information exchange among government officials were inadequate to the task. Barbara Gricar and Anthony Barratta of Pennsylvania State University record that "the normal public information process did not address the depth of public concern over the proposed purge [of the radioactive Krypton from the disabled reactor] and did not facilitate public understanding or acceptance of the proposed plans. Instead the project was hampered by substantial public resistance . . . there was a serious deficiency in the information exchange process. . ." The Citizen Radiation Monitoring Program initiated after the Three Mile Island accident was designed to remedy this deficiency.[5]

"Turf" problems and inadequate attention to the emotional context of the emergency impede the effectiveness of the Emergency Information Network. Rarely does government or industry request the views of those affected by the plans. Nor is the public involved in generating the technical approaches to solving the problem created by the emergency. Gricar and Barratta attribute the success of the Citizen Radiation Monitoring Program at Three Mile Island to the involvement of the public in the process. The Citizen Monitoring Program reduced, rather than enlarged, the information gap and gave credence to citizen monitors as a legitimate source of information.

• 5) *A citizen advisory committee.* Businessmen say: "We don't want outsiders telling us how to run our business." A citizen advisory committee can improve the relationship between neighbors and any

---

[5]Barbara G. Gricar and Anthony J. Barratta, "Bridging the Information Gap at TMI: Radiation Monitoring by Citizens." *Journal of Applied Behavioral Science,* February 1983.

business or industry that is a dominant force in its community. Citizen committees, consisting of volunteers, have willingly addressed and solved innumerable community problems in cities of all sizes and in rural communities across America. They can also help solve industry problems by advising on goals, policy development, specific programs, reviewing performance, and carrying out special objectives.

Participative management, hailed by many organization theorists as a method for improving employee satisfaction and motivation, has been successfully applied to community relations. By co-opting community members the company can, through a citizen advisory committee, mitigate the tension created when industry actions conflict with community aspirations. These committees serve business and industry by:

— Expanding interest in and understanding of the problems of business.
— Providing feedback from the community to prevent confrontations.
— Serving as a conduit of information and education to the community.
— Improving citizen insight into the difficulties of the business decision-making process.
— Encouraging citizens who participate to become advocates of the programs or policies which they have adopted as their agenda.
— Opening communication with the public.
— Increasing businesses' accountability for its actions.
— Increasing the responsiveness of business to citizens' perceptions.
— Encouraging new ideas and innovative solutions to old problems.
— Providing opportunities for communication with people of different backgrounds who would not usually share their concerns with the business community, except to object to some particular action.
— Serving as a forum for testing ideas and concepts and resolving legitimate differences of opinion.
— Providing an effective link between the business community and the public sector.
— Enhancing the legitimacy and credibility of business efforts.

Additionally, the citizen advisory committee may serve to bring together disparate parts of a business organization in a neutral, objective setting. Management, labor representatives, technical personnel, and office workers broaden their perspective on business by listening to outsiders' views.

Citizen committees may also invite problems:

— They may not represent diverse interests of the community. Deliberate selection of members who represent the same social and economic status as the company executives to avoid "troublemakers" sterilizes the entire advisory process.

— If business does not commit itself to working with the committee, token participation may disenchant otherwise effective members.

— Vested interest groups may control or dominate a committee, shielding the business from realistic public perceptions.

— The committee may absorb a considerable amount of executive time.

— The committee may screen the company from public sector professional staff opinions.

— The committee requires a leader skilled in participative techniques.

• 6) *A task force* to solve particular problems. Limiting the task force to a specific task with a specific time frame within which to propose solutions eliminates some of the disadvantages of advisory committees. A task force could use: the Charette—an intensive, interactive problem-solving process with meetings convened around a specific project; the Delphi method—a method of solving problems by synthesizing solutions suggested separately by knowledgeable persons; or other citizen participation techniques.

Preparing for Public Hearings in the Engineering Phase

A manufacturing facility may receive permits to construct and operate a plant, but public opposition may jeopardize the use of that permission. A facility operates only with public consent; complaints about pollution, perceived hazardous operation, or other adverse effects put any facility at risk. The problem does not have to be legitimate to receive public scrutiny. In most localities, any citizen can bring a perceived infraction to public notice; immediately the company must defend its operation.

Anticipation of this risk is an engineering function. Noise, odors, traffic congestion, aesthetic offenses, despoiling a hunting or fishing area, dust, air or water pollution—these are but some of the red flags that can lead a community to battle against an industry. Some mitigating actions are relatively inexpensive when incorporated in the original engineering design—locating a noisy air compressor as far away from a residential area as possible, although it may be more efficient to locate it closer to the plant; routing traffic on back roads away from the busy intersections; using a screen of trees to shield the plant from public view and to assist in noise and odor absorption. Design the plant to meet the demands of an irritated community. Engineers are trained to maximize cost effectiveness in design and operation; the hidden costs of repeated public hearings and litigation are rarely considered in the cost/benefit analysis.

Some of the regulations that require government approval also provide for public hearings in which the public indicates its acceptance or opposition to the construction or expansion of a plant:

1. Requirements of the Clean Air Act Amendments of 1977 to implement the Prevention of Significant Deterioration (PSD) and non-attainment programs.

2. The permit program for disposal of hazardous wastes under the 1976 Resource Conservation and Recovery Act (RCRA).

3. Numerous state plans under the Coastal Zone Management Act of 1972.

4. Restrictions against new discharges into water bodies and filling of wetlands.

5. Numerous energy-related restrictions.

By requiring Environmental Impact Statements, these regulations involve the public hearing process. This represents, says John Quarles, ". . .confronting a vastly expanded group of large industrial projects with a totally new and difficult regulatory obstacle course." To cope with this obstacle course Quarles advises: "Most companies must learn to deal more creatively with local officials and local public opinion. Companies should apply thoughtfulness and skill to the timing and conduct of public hearings."[6]

Quarles' advice inserts engineers and engineering into the public hearing process, despite the preference of most engineers to "stay out of politics." The burden of public hearings should be lightened for many engineers by recognition that sensitivity to public concern augments acceptance of technological innovation. John Naisbitt believes

---

[6]John Quarles, "Federal Regulation of New Industrial Plants" (Washington, D.C., 1979), pp. 209, 214.

that technological advances won't be accepted by the public unless there are "counterbalancing human responses." "High Tech," he states, needs "high touch."[7] A public hearing is a felicitous event for demonstrating "high touch."

Preparing for Public Hearings in the Public Relations Program

A public relations program designed to carry out the strategy is an adjunct to the public hearing process. The public relations program outlined here is targeted especially to citizen stakeholders. The public relations program provides the company an opportunity to:

— Inform citizens about the nature of a proposed project.
— Dispel fears, quell rumors, correct misconceptions.
— Create a perception.
— Cultivate advocates for the company position.
— Network for the public hearing.
— Prepare advocates to testify at the public hearing.
— "Set the stage" for the public hearing.
— Target specific audiences such as opinion leaders, Congressmen, students, educators, social workers, and others.
— Initiate a public participation campaign.

Business considers tactics outside the accepted social norms imprudent and inappropriate. Although adversaries may be enthusiastic to the point of fanaticism, business believes in responsible tactics. But when business is provoked to a response, opponents are in control. To regain control, businesses can intensify proactivity within the spectrum of acceptability by using communication techniques.

Business communication techniques for the public hearing process include:

•Contacting *schools*—participating in assemblies, career days, intern days, Junior Achievement programs, after-school clubs, competitive games, visiting teacher programs.

•Using *civic group* meetings—to inform community opinion leaders, the persons to whom other persons listen.

•Holding a *public meeting*—another government practice that industry can adopt. Though the private sector has no authority to "call" a meeting, it can hold one. A public meeting provides the opportunity to inform citizens about the nature of a project and affords them the opportunity to voice their concerns. Unveiling a model of

---

[7]John Naisbitt, *Megatrends* (New York: Warner Books, Inc., 1982), p. 39.

a controversial facility, pictures, movies, dramatic skits and other tools to show rather than say, clarifies perceptions. A meeting serves the same functions for industry as it does for government: allowing citizens to complain and let off steam. Listening to fears and comments sensitizes the industry to public concerns. Occasionally a remark made at a meeting suggests a possible solution to a conflict. Relating information presented at the meeting to the concerns perceived by the public helps the company understand local value choices in addition to narrow technological options. A critical study of the former U.S. Joint Committee on Atomic Energy suggests that the Committee consistently prevented fair and reasoned consideration of the controversies on nuclear power "by failing to give critics of the nuclear program a forum and a hearing. . ."[8]

A public meeting merits the same careful planning as a media conference. The Checklist for Planning a Public Hearing, Figure 5–4, serves as a guide for business sponsored public meetings. Two types of public meetings accomplish the purpose: (1) a standard meeting format with speakers facing the audience and with opportunities for the audience to ask questions; and (2) a workshop in which experienced facilitators lead small groups in discussing problems and reaching consensus conclusions.

Including Labor in Public Hearing Planning

The narrow scope of business communications with labor perpetuates the adversarial relationship established in grievance procedures and collective bargaining. One method for broadening the dialogue is to include labor in the public hearing process. Burying the adversarial relationship for public hearings benefits both business and labor. In some communities, employees and management are often the persons with a direct stake in creating or preserving jobs and, therefore, the only supporters of siting or expanding a plant. Without employee participation in the hearing, management finds itself in a lonely position.

This was the plight of the management of a chemical processing company proposing a plant expansion, which was opposed by the neighbors surrounding the plant. The neighborhood opposition frightened off expected supporters: town businessmen were reluctant to testify for the company and risk antagonizing customers. Townspeo-

---

[8]As reported in *Technology on Trial* (Paris: Organization for Economic Co-operation and Development, 1979), p. 59.

ple shied away from the controversy. It appeared that the only advocates would be plant management. Persuaded to take its dilemma to the union, the company reluctantly made the Fact Sheet available to union officials. The union quickly spotted its role in the controversy: jobs were at stake. The union representatives recruited members to testify at the public hearing, using the company consultant to assist members—most of whom had never attended a public hearing—to prepare testimony. The public hearings ran for three long evenings. The employees and their wives proved more persuasive advocates than the company executives or the four attorneys engaged to fight for the permit. As an added bonus, the next round of labor negotiations was conducted in a much more cooperative atmosphere: labor and management had shared the experience of facing a common enemy.

Training Management for Public Hearings

Many managers regard public hearings as a nuisance, an interruption of normal routine, an add-on function outside the scope of management duties. Governments have learned the importance of training executives in citizen participation techniques. This is another practice industry can borrow. Executives trained in the principles of the public hearing process are better equipped to use the process as an opportunity instead of a burden. For the prepared executive, the public hearing is a forum for explaining company ideas, motivation, practices and plans. Coordinated with product marketing strategy, hearings are another avenue for exposing the benefits of the company's products. A planned public hearing complements all company activities from complying with government regulations to winning consumer acceptance. Executives trained in the public hearing process learn how to obtain maximum public relations mileage from testimony.

Elevating Preparation for Public Hearings to a Top Management Function

The fate of a plant, program or product may rest on company performance at public hearings. If top management does not understand the issues, the concerns and the opportunities for mitigation of these concerns, it is not likely to make an adequate or relevant response. A public hearing that unveils surprises signals that top management has failed to use the public hearing process. Many a local strategy has been scuttled by a personal statement from the president of the company a thousand miles distant, or a financial statement reporting increased profits published the day before the public hearing.

Only top management has the authority to commit the necessary resources, planning, and personnel to influence the outcome of public hearings. Innovative companies have added *issues managers* to provide a broader qualitative approach to predicting emerging issues, such as the Arab oil embargo or the environmental revolution. Issues managers are in an advantageous position to predict issues in public hearings. One method for assuring coordination of the elements for public hearings is the designation of an inter-departmental task force. The task force may consist of some key members for continuity and experience, adding expertise as required for each hearing. For example, engineering personnel may be called upon for some hearings, facility or transportation managers for others, and appropriate experts for still others.

Cultivating Allies for Public Hearings

One businessman complained, "I had to make 112 telephone calls to get nine people to speak for us. Friends I had counted on were too busy, too preoccupied, or reluctant to get involved in the controversy." It is at public hearings that grass-roots groups—individuals and organizations who share industry concerns and are willing to enter the fray on behalf of their convictions—prove their value. When farmers' wives learned that farmers were being outlobbied and outmaneuvered in public hearings at state capitols and Washington, they organized Women for Agriculture. Citizens for Food and Fiber, Women in Timber, Outdoors Unlimited, "Rational Approach" (to pesticides, energy, and other concerns) are typical of the groups whose livelihood depends on industry and who have determined that industry alone does not adequately represent them. These groups are privately supported—some reject financial support from industry; others depend on it. All share the belief that they have an obligation to speak out on their own behalf and do so with skill to match their adversaries.

Grass-roots groups are a source of strength for industry. Some executives have expressed hesitancy about these groups. "I don't like anything I can't control," one executive declared. The grass-roots groups argue that independence is the source of their credibility. This argument will be resolved as the informational, coalitional and personal support networks gain stature as forces for social action, particularly in communities where industry objectives have been poorly expressed.

Ron and Janet Arnold's *Directory of Pro-Industry Citizen*

Organizations (12605 N.E. Second Street, Bellevue, Washington 98005) helps "pro-industry people find each other." The Arnolds state: ". . . there are many factions that continually mount campaigns to shackle and limit private enterprise . . . Part of the reason industry's foes have succeeded is their grass-roots citizen action . . . If industry defends itself vigorously, opponents can easily claim it is merely greedy and has no feelings at all for the public interest. . ." The Arnolds conclude that if the citizens do not come to industry aid in grass-roots action they'll be leaving the field to others with opposing ideas.

SECTION FOUR

For Elected and Appointed Local Public Officials

10

Managing Public Hearings

Most elected and appointed officials of nearly 83,000 local jurisdictions, the 50 states and the federal government conduct public hearings, a responsibility for which few are trained. Many find the hearings a time consuming nuisance; others enjoy the sense of power the hearings process grants them over the lives and fortunes of fellow citizens. Most officials struggle to make fair decisions, despite the confusion of testimony, multiple citizen pressures, and frequent inability to sort out facts from allegations. Some public hearings do perfunctory obeisance to regulations; others last three or four hours. Some test endurance; others provide interesting listening.

Whatever the topic, however long, the official must remain glued to his chair; he is expected to listen attentively and to stay for the duration of the hearing, no matter how pressing other business. The official who departs before the conclusion of the hearing is criticized in the press. Asking many questions also invites media criticism for "interruption by argumentative, pin-the-witness-down type questioning" and "irrelevant musings from board members." [Both remarks quoted from media stories.]

Expectations that public hearings can solve public problems run from high to none. When the State Department of Veteran's Affairs fouled up a new mortgage payment policy, one editor wrote: "The foul-up proves the value of allowing the public to participate in government decisions—or at least letting people know when a government decision is likely to affect them."[1] An editorial in another newspaper complained that the public hearing "democratic process is only for the hardiest."

---

[1] *Corvallis Gazette Times,* Editorial.

TRAINING OFFICIALS FOR THE PUBLIC
HEARING PROCESS

Herbert H. Smith, veteran of more than 30 years of city planning, says: ". . . the conduct of both public meetings and public hearings is one of the most vital and important aspects of local government and of planning, and one to which too little attention has been paid. The manner in which these are conducted often determines the success or failure of a proposal or plan. A tremendous responsibility thus rests on the commission or agency, and in particular the chairperson, for the conduct of each meeting or hearing."[2]

The National Conference of State Legislatures advises committee chairmen to aggressively pursue citizen involvement for "a profound and positive effect on the legislature's image. . .Greater citizen involvement helps increase public understanding of the process, thereby bolstering the institution's image."[3]

Few officials receive formal training in conducting public hearings. A nationwide survey of 4000 planning commissioners conducted by the American Planning Association reveals that over 61 percent received no training in their functions and that relatively few of those who did receive initial training also received follow-up instruction.[4]

THE ACCOUNTABILITY OF PUBLIC
OFFICIALS

Trained or otherwise, public officials are accountable to their constituents. To pass the test of accountability, most public officials agree any official holding a public hearing owes citizens:

1. Familiarity with the problem under consideration. This is a major chore for the volunteer inundated with volumes of material to study before the hearing.

2. Courteous attention to public testimony, continuing the hearing if it spans a time period too long for concentration.

3. Consideration of the public as a whole, weighing whether

---

[2]Reprinted with permission from *The Citizen's Guide to Planning* by Herbert H. Smith, p. 135. Copyright © 1979 by the American Planning Association, 1313 E. 60th St., Chicago, IL 60637.

[3]Janice L. Petty, *A Chairman's Guide to Effective Committee Management* (Denver, Colo.: National Conference of State Legislatures, 1981), p. 50.

[4]Carolyn Browne, *The Planning Commission: Its Composition and Function* (Chicago: The American Planning Association, 1979), p.12.

speakers truly represent the public or are speaking solely in their own interest.

4. Treatment of all participants fairly and objectively. In the words of the Supreme Court of the State of Washington: ". . .Members of commissions with the role of conducting fair and impartial fact-finding hearings must, as far as practicable, be open-minded, objective, free of entangling influences and capable of hearing the weak voices as well as the strong. . . ." (*Buell vs. City of Bremerton,* 1972.) Another Washington Court decision emphasized further: ". . .the hearing must be conducted as to be free from bias and prejudice; it must not only be open-minded and fair, but *must have the appearance of being so."* (*Smith vs. Skaget County,* 1969.)

5. Exercise of best judgment. The public official has a moral obligation to exercise his best judgment, based on information tempered with his experience.

6. A timely decision. An applicant's option to purchase property may expire while a commission delays decisions. Inflation increases costs while decision-makers dawdle; the future of jobs and businesses may be at risk. Public officials who get so bogged down in details, distractions of procedure, or requests for additional data cannot resolve important matters in a timely manner. An instance of indecision was reported by the media on the fate of a condominium project which remained unresolved after a three-hour debate: "The developers and opponents agreed on one thing—the project is very controversial." The city council hearing the discussion agreed that it was controversial, but couldn't agree to a solution.

7. Compliance with the hearing's goals and objectives, assuring that the hearing delivers its promise to hear citizens.

8. Intelligible discussion. Sometimes public officials adopt government jargon as a sign that they have familiarized themselves with program details. Governmentese may impress a citizen that he is not as smart as an official, but it also obfuscates discussion. "Prioritizing so that you can zero fund a program that benefits behavioral and life-style modifications within individual control in the HUD program that interfaces with the MSD of the PDC" intimidates the most hardy citizen.

IMPLEMENTING ACCOUNTABILITY

A fair hearings board implements its accountability for public hearings by following this procedure:

•*Electing or appointing a skillful chairperson.* The chairperson explains how the meeting will be conducted, what the meeting intends to accomplish, how the hearing will proceed, and the ground rules for decorum. The chairman calls on speakers, instructs speakers to give full names and addresses, thanks each speaker politely, maintains order, and attempts to keep individuals or groups from manipulating the hearing for their own purposes.

The chairperson is responsible for controlling the meeting, rationing speaking time so that all may be heard, or continuing the hearing to another time. The chair disciplines interruptions, controls cheering or booing, limits harangues and filibusters, cuts off insulting exchanges from the audience or from fellow board members and tries not to waste time. By these actions, the chairperson signals to the watching public that the hearing is being conducted fairly. A perception of unfairness destroys credibility.

The chairperson moves the discussion towards a vote. It is the chair's conduct of the meeting and the ability to summarize the feelings and opinions of the hearings board that prods the group into producing a motion. The chair shelters the decision-making process from amateur judgments on complex technical matters and knows when to turn to experts for assistance. The chairperson guards the integrity and legitimacy of the decision by calling upon counsel for legal advice.

The chairperson of a public hearing is too important to the process to risk appointing an unskilled person to the position. The public is entitled to a chairperson who guides the board to define the issues, skims off the rhetoric to get at the facts, and leads the board to a decision based on evidence and sound reasoning.

•*Provide a reliable record of the hearing.* The decision is based on the record, which may consist of tape recordings, published minutes, informal notes, or verbatim transcripts of a court reporter. Reliable records may cost more than smaller jurisdictions can afford but citizens are entitled to maximum reliability.

•*Make adequate preparations* including:

— Appropriate notice: legal notice, adequate notice to attract proponents and opponents.
— An agenda: rules on the sequence and procedure to be followed, timing of hearings, adjournment.
— A convenient, comfortable place to meet with working microphones and adequate seating.

LEGAL ASPECTS OF PUBLIC HEARINGS

Few actions impair a board's credibility as quickly as overlooking some legal requirement of a hearing. When several hundred property owners are informed that the three-hour public hearing they attended did not comply with legal notice requirements and that they will need to repeat their testimony on another evening, they are justifiably irritated.

Notices for hearings require announcement in a newspaper in general circulation in the area. Citizens complain that these notices get buried in very small print in the classified section and ask for more conspicuous notification. The more controversial the issue, the more the hearing should be advertised including posting notices in public places, mailing notices to interested groups, and releasing news stories.

Planner Albert Solnit advises planning commissioners to clarify the issues being considered: ''In cases of public confusion over what's being decided, the citizens will often exhibit an 'off with their heads' attitude toward the applicant, the commission, the staff, and anyone else connected with the proposal. As one irate homeowner told the commission . . . 'I don't care if this hearing is only zoning or not, a man who thinks of bringing buildings like the ones in the paper to our town ought to get turned down and turned out!' '' [5]

Regulations specify the type and extent of advertising for state and federal public hearings. States use the legislative calendar and the federal government uses the Federal Register. Most agencies maintain mailing lists of citizens and organizations interested in the scope of their hearings.

Some regulations specify quasi-judicial proceedings, with witnesses sworn in, opportunity for cross-examination, and the prohibition of *ex parte* contact between officials and the public. Other procedures permit the public to appear in the official record only if they have filed as intervenors in a contested case hearing. Some attorneys advocate total courtroom practice including requiring a list of witnesses and a summary of testimony. Advance disclosure permits the opposing attorney to round up a list of comparable witnesses

---

[5]From *The Job of the Planning Commissioner,* Third Edition, by Albert Solnit, pp. 96–97. Copyright © 1982 by Wadsworth, Inc. Reprinted by permission of Wadsworth Publishing Company, Belmont, California 94002.

and to better prepare for the hearing. Under these procedures the public hearing becomes a battle of attorneys rather than an opportunity for citizens to be heard.

In quasi-judicial hearings, attorneys sometimes forget that a public hearing is not a murder trial where almost any tactics to establish guilt may be used. Intimidating witnesses, pressure tactics to impair credibility, bullying by interruptions, objections, and threats are inappropriate at public hearings. The chairperson protects citizens by controlling the behavior of attorneys, remembering that the commissioners are not sitting as judges in a court of law.

Attention to *full disclosure* requirements saves possible reversals on appeal of the decision. Although due process laws differ from state to state and from city to city, most provide participants an opportunity to see, hear and study all staff reports, plans, drawings, surveys, statements and evidence. Solnit notes three rules to protect due process:[6]

> "1. If a citizen or applicant calls your home or office to discuss a matter before the commission, refuse firmly and invite this testimony to be given at the hearing so it can be heard out in the open. This includes calls from elected officials.
>
> 2. Never go on ad hoc field trips with an applicant or opponents alone or even in pairs. It is best to announce the time and place of such field trips at a commission meeting where they are recorded in the minutes. The press and other interested parties should be invited to come. It is best if the whole commission can make these field trips with staff as a body but, failing this, at least three members should go as a subcommittee designated by the chairperson.
>
> 3. All travel costs and food should be at public expense. Trips and entertainment for commissioners paid for by people who would like a favorable decision look like payola and should be prohibited by the commission's own bylaws or rules of procedure."

FACILITATING PUBLIC HEARINGS

Inadequate physical facilities plague public hearings. A hearing on a controversial issue often lands in the high school auditorium,

---

[6]From *The Job of the Planning Commissioner,* Third Edition, by Albert Solnit, p. 99. © 1982 by Wadsworth, Inc. Reprinted by permission of Wadsworth Publishing Company, Belmont, California 94002.

a school cafeteria, a fairgrounds, or a library selected for its ability to hold, rather than accommodate, a crowd. The board is seated at a table at the same level as the audience. Citizens testify in the front of the room, facing the hearings board, backs to the audience. Poor acoustics and out-of-order microphones add to the discomfort of a room usually either too warm or too cold. Hard chairs and over-crowded or "out of order" lavatories add to the irritation of partici-pants. By 11:00 p.m. participants begin to drift away. As the Chairman calls names on the sign-up sheet, he compiles a longer list of no-shows. Only the hardy, committed citizens remain to attempt to influence the weary board. As a result, the board hears only those who can sit the longest.

Public officials can facilitate public hearings by arranging:

• 1. *The appropriate Hearing Date:* The public hearing sched-uled the evening of a major football game effectively eliminates fami-lies and sports fans. Schedule the hearing on union meeting night and labor representation is diminished. A fair hearing date does not force citizens to choose between the hearing and other activities including popular TV programs.

• 2. *The appropriate Hearing Time:* A morning or afternoon hearing precludes most working persons, leaving only housewives, small business owners, or applicants. In a town with evening shifts, split hearings accommodate a variety of working schedules.

• 3. *The appropriate Hearing Location:* An accessible location with ample seating room, comfortable ventilation, and adequate lights sometimes must yield to the necessity of holding the large crowds in-terested in controversial issues. "I knew I was in for trouble," one chairman remarked, "when I showed up at 7:15 for a 7:30 p.m. hear-ing and the room was already overflowing. It was obvious that the opponents had jammed the room and the proponents were storming that they weren't being given a fair chance." Disappointed partici-pants booed when the Chair announced that the hearing would be post-poned to the next week. The local press commented, "The board should have known that the hearing room would not be large enough."

Three quantitative "Indexes" can supplement gut feelings in pre-dicting the turn out at a hearing.

a. The *Letters-to-the-Editor Index.* Count the number of letters to the editor in the local or regional newspapers. A rough rule of thumb is 20 participants in the hearing for each letter to the editor. Using this ratio, 20 letters predict about 400 partici-pants. Index reliability increases if letters have been both pro and con the issue. A lopsided distribution indicates that only one side has orchestrated support.

b. The *Editorial Index*. Each editorial on the issue may be expected to draw the interest of about 50 people, independent of letters to the editor. An editorial plus 20 letters to the editor strengthens the 400 attendance forecast.

c. The *Interested Parties Index*. If many citizens contact the public officials by mail, person, or phone, the hearing should plan for a sizable turn-out. Each contact may represent attendance of 10 people: if 50 citizens contact the officials, the attendance may reach 500.

Temper these indexes with evaluation of the population, area affected, and type of issue. (A neighborhood issue may draw fewer attendees than a city-wide or statewide issue; any discussion affecting nuclear energy or hazardous waste or similar issues may promote a larger attendance.)

• 4. *Appropriate Seating Arrangements:* Seating arrangements influence the participative opportunities in the hearing. Seating arrangements for a public hearing should provide opportunities for citizens to:

1) view displays
2) complete comment forms
3) obtain general information
4) see and hear the speakers and the decision-makers

Participative activities may take place before or after the formal public hearing with models, maps, information displays, and resource specialists (usually staff) available to answer questions.

• 5. *Audio-Visual Arrangements:* Citizens presenting testimony bear the responsibility for making their audio-visuals effective. Public officials arrange the physical environment for using audio-visuals. Audio-visuals at public hearings can be improved if the hearings board provides:

a. A raised screen visible to the audience and officials.
b. A method of dimming the room.
c. A platform or stand for the projector.
d. A handy electric outlet or extension cord.
e. A wall or easel for hanging posters or maps.
f. A table for literature or models.

Staff members have the responsibility to check audio-visual facilities when selecting a hearing room. The emerging field of telecommunications, computer hook-ups, and videotapes can greatly enhance communications, if the equipment is available. To avoid the 30-minute boring slide show, the chairperson should announce audio-visual rules at the beginning of the hearing. The board can only facilitate. The presenter determines in advance what will or won't work at the hearing.

• 6. *Amenities:* Although amenities are not required, the environment for public hearings is improved by providing:

—Greeters: a staff member or members of a civic club at the door to say "Hello," direct attendees to the sign-up sheets, and answer questions.

—A table for citizen comment with a chair or two, and a pad or notebook, to encourage informal citizen comments.

—Staff or resource specialists strategically placed, with identifying name tags, to answer technical questions.

—Refreshments. A cup of coffee, or lemonade enhances a friendly atmosphere. The chairman accents the friendly tone of the hearing by announcing when, where, and if refreshments are available. Manning a refreshment booth at public hearings qualifies as a service club project.

—Lavatories that work.

—Media. A table for the media and room for cameras, tape recorders and other paraphernalia. The media serves the decision-makers and their public and should be offered the consideration a host would give a guest.

To break or not to break is sometimes the question at public hearings. If a break is not announced, attendees getting up and down and shuffling chairs may disrupt the hearing. On the other hand, some attendees may use a break to leave the hearing.

As television cable systems proliferate throughout the country, *to televise or not to televise* becomes the question. In some areas the cable system regularly televises city council meetings. A public address system that is not in good order compounds the audio problems. Camera work tends to be ragged. One viewer of a televised council meeting noted that the wide shot was something like "watching the Superbowl from a blimp." State and federal hearings do better as meeting rooms are equipped to be friendly to TV presentations.

CONDUCTING A FAIR HEARING

Citizens demand assurance that they are receiving fair treatment and that they have equal access to the hearing. Experienced public officials assure citizens that they are being treated fairly by:

1. Drafting a set of rules and procedures. Delineation of the order in which testimony will be heard, time limits, code of conduct, and decorum during the hearing assures that the same rules apply to all citizens.

2. Announcing the rules of the hearing before and at the beginning of the hearing and maintaining the rules throughout the hearing. One chairman decided to give each side a fair chance by calling a representative from one side first, then one from the other side, and continuing the rotation through the evening. Opponents had packed the room, planning to present testimony early in the evening, while the media was present. The howls of protest at the alteration of the usual rules eventually cost the chairman his position.

Rules address the order of presentations: staff, a representative of the proponents, a representative of the opponents, experts for either side, and then public testimony; the order in which the public will be called; time limits; anticipated time of adjournment; scheduled breaks. Experienced confrontational activists may insert unwritten rules, which they loudly proclaim. The chairman plays fair with all participants by firmly disallowing these unwritten rules.

3. Facilitating citizen access. Solnit emphasizes: "[the opportunity to be heard] is the major and most sensitive element of due process. It is essential that the chairperson have the skill to make everyone feel that they have had their say, while at the same time maintaining control of the meeting and moving it along to a conclusion."[7]

Facilitating citizen access includes:

- *Selecting a fair order of speaking.* Fifty citizens have indicated that they wish to speak. What's the fairest way to handle them? The chairman selects from several methods:

  — Sign up. Citizens are called in the order in which they sign up on the official speakers' sheets. This method rewards those who have made the effort to arrive early.

  — By row. Citizens are called in the order in which they are seated: row one first, row two next and so on. This method also rewards the early birds but sometimes encourages a physical scramble for seats.

  — Alternation of proponents and opponents. This method re-

---

[7]From The Job of the Planning Commissioner, Third Edition, by Albert Solnit, p. 97. Copyright © 1982 by Wadsworth, Inc. Reprinted by permission of Wadsworth Publishing Company, Belmont, California 94002.

quires that citizens must indicate whether they are for or against a proposal. Many persons resent being asked for a commitment prior to the hearing.

(Any of these methods offer opportunities for manipulation by the attendees. Placing participants for maximum effectiveness is part of public hearings gamesmanship.)

- *Setting time limits.* A city councilman confessed that he had been up until 2:00 a.m. the previous morning listening to public testimony. "I can't absorb anything after three hours," he said, "It's all a blur." The Council made an important decision based on the public hearing, despite the blur. When another councilman moved that time limits be placed on the testimony, the blurred councilman voted "No." Setting time limits is a delicate decision, particularly in local hearings. Announcing time limits before the meeting, at the beginning of the meeting and as often during the meeting as practical, requiring all speakers to adhere to the same limit, is the fairest method.
- *Continuance of the Hearing.* A "house count" indicates whether all testimony can be presented in one session. The Chair announces the closing hour and the continuance of the meeting, including how holdovers will be accommodated: Will they be first at the continued hearing? Will persons who did not have the opportunity to testify be required to sign up for a position in line again?

4. Findings of Fact. Fair decisions are based on findings of fact at the public hearing, assuring participants that conclusions were based on a logical not random procedure. An appearance of prejudice or unfairness impugnes a decision. Decisions should be written, including the specific factual findings for support.

5. Controlling the Hearing. Skilled activists know how to manipulate the hearing to capture media space and monopolize the decision-maker's attention. Experienced officials soon recognize the citizen groups and local organizations who become the "regulars" at public hearings. They also recognize the special interest groups—Sierra Club members, Chambers of Commerce, unions, developers—and the anti-special interest groups who regularly attend hearings. Michael Marien's "Handy Guide to Public Policy Proposers and Their Proposals," suggests a number of policy proposers public officials may recognize. The Handy Guide is reprinted in Figure 10–1.

Figure 10-1

Handy Guide to Public Policy Proposers and Their Proposals

General Guidelines for Post-Industrial Citizenship: (1) pick up any position or combination thereof; (2) don't look at other policy proposals—you are right.

Ideological Positions	View of Present and Future	Proposals for Future
1. Horrified Humanist	A slim chance of surviving our chaos and obsolescence	Sweeping reforms, world government, national planning.
2. Languishing Liberal	Troubled times	More money and programs, racial integration
3. Middling Moderate	No thoughts; cross-pressured	Various platitudes to avoid offending other policy proposers
4. Counteracting Conservative	Crime, centralization, and crumbling civilization	Law, order, soap, hair-cuts, Truth and Morality
5. Rabid Rightist	It's getting REDder all the time	Wave flags and stockpile arms (public and private)
6. Primitive Populist	Domination by pointy-headed pseudo-intellectuals	Throw briefcases in Potomac, restore common sense
7. Passionate Pacifist	A garrison state	A peaceable kingdom
8. Radical Romantic	A cancered civilization	Small experimental communities

Role		
9. Rumbling Revolutionary	A repressive, racist, Imperialist, capitalist establishment	Confront and destroy The System (other details worked out later)
10. Apocalyptic Apostle	Armageddon coming to a sinful world	Be saved

Role-Related Positions

1. Urgent Urbanist	Decline and fall of cities	More funds and programs sidestepping states
2. Emphatic Ecologist	Decline and fall of everything else	Control contaminators and restore nature
3. Boiling Blackman	Here a pig, there a pig, everywhere a pig pig	Black everything
4. Status-Seeking Sibling Sender	Crisis in our schools and colleges	More funds and programs, tax deductions
5. Multi-Megamuscled Militarist	Growing Chinese and/or Russian capabilities	More National Security regardless of national security
6. Technocrat-on-the Take	No thoughts; not within scope of specialty	Well-funded studies and use of arcane models
7. Sincerely Sorry Scientist	Profligate technology	Think of alternative futures and their consequences
8. Bullied Budget-Binder	Up-tight	Making this year's budget and getting more for next year
9. Tortured Taxpayer	Growing gaps between income, aspirations, and expenditures	Cut, cut, cut, cut, cut

Figure 10–1 (continued)

10. Stultified Student	Entrapment in *their* world	Inner and interpersonal exploration, and other relevant learning
11. Contracting Conglomerator	Cybernation, diversification, and internationalization	Withering of the state
12. Hi-throttle Highwayman	Paving the nation	Re-paving the nation
13. Frustrated Feminist	Futility, frivolity, and frigidaires	Fun-filled fulfillment
14. Star-Struck Spaceman	Up, up, and away	Science must not be impeded
15. Bonded Bureaucrat	Six years to retirement	Longer coffee breaks

Source: Figure by Michael Marien. Reprinted from *Public Administration Review*, March-April 1970, p. 154. Copyright 1970 by The American Society for Public Administration, 1225 Connecticut Ave. NW, Washington, DC 20035.

The Chairperson can minimize the disruptions of demonstrations, interruptions, applause, emotional outbursts, and other interference with an orderly hearing by:

— Evaluating the possibility of manipulation by discovering the pressure groups and anticipating the type of pressure they may exert. Letters-to-the-editor, news stories, editorials, TV or radio comments, bring the media to the hearing and the advocates center their activities around the media.

— Holding a pre-hearing workshop. The controversy may be defused by holding a pre-hearing workshop in which small groups attempt to reach a collaborative recommendation. Discussing the controversy illuminates the complexity of the problem.

— Announcing the rules of the hearing ahead of the meeting and at the beginning of the meeting and allowing no exceptions. A fair hearing should be mentioned so frequently that there is little doubt that the chairperson is determined to be scrupulously fair.

— Treating all sides equally. If one special interest does break the rules and engages in a demonstration of any sort, timing the demonstration—using the largest, most conspicuous stopwatch available—and announcing that, to be fair, the other side has equal time emphasizes the equality.

— Allowing staff more time for presentation of options, structuring their reports to present background material early in the meeting. TV crews may not stay for the later public presentations. On the other hand, if TV coverage is desired allow the more newsworthy presentations to come as early as scrupulously fair treatment permits.

— Borrowing from the Interaction Method of holding meetings and displaying a "group memory." The major points made during the hearing are recorded on a large easel manned by a volunteer. In an intense controversy, two easels may be used to record the arguments on each side of the issue. The chairperson uses the "group memory" to remind the audience that a point has already been stated. By displaying the pro and con arguments equally, the "group memory" reinforces fairness.

— Maintaining strict discipline. If individuals are particularly disruptive, call a recess until order is restored.

6. Board Decorum. The Dallas, Texas City Council worries about council members showing up late and talking too much: ". . .We don't ever do anything on time because we are all talking so much."[8] The City Council of the isolated town of Rajneeshpuram, Oregon requires jokes to be told at the beginning and end of each Council meeting in order to avoid "dull, boring, and conducive to unconsciousness (meetings); . . .seriousness leads to indigestion, ulcers, cardiac conditions, mental rigidity and exaggerated self-importance. . ." The Rajneeshpuram Council also advises that during public commentary "any citizen who wishes to tell a joke may do so."[9] Public officials recognize that their decorum is public business.

Public hearing decorum demands that officials provide respectful consideration, refraining from bullying witnesses or asking questions for the purpose of demonstrating cleverness, sarcasm, or wit. Officials owe the public productive hearings that result in a decision based on the answers to the intelligent technical questions they are expected to ask on complex projects. Five key questions have been identified for public officials to ask about any proposed technical project. The five questions are listed in the Checklist, Figure 10-2.

Figure 10-2

**Five Questions for Public Officials to
Ask About Technical Projects**

Question #1: Is there an identified need for the project?
                The answer should include:
                — How was the need determined and by whom?
                  (Special interest group; public initiative; mandatory requirements—EPA, DEQ?)
                — Is the proposed project needed *now*? (wants vs actual needs)

Question #2: What will the cost of the project be?

---

[8] *The Dallas Morning News*
[9] *The Oregonian*

Figure 10-2 (continued)

The answer should include:
— What is the initial cost of the project?
— What will the periodic operation and maintenance costs be?
— Is the project designed to encourage less costly projected future expansions?
— Can the project be accomplished through private enterprise, versus the use of public funds? If so, what are the cost comparisons?
— Will the project pay for itself? If not, how much tax money will be used?
— What is the source(s) of funds to pay for the project? Are the funds secured?
— Are the people paying for the project receiving the direct benefits of the project?

Question #3: What are the capabilities/capacities of the project?
— How many people, households, etc. will be serviced?
— Does the project accommodate only an existing need without examining future needs?
— Does the project comply with the comprehensive plan and applicable local, state and/or federal regulations?
— Is there adequate land available for future expansion of the project, if needed?

Question #4: How will the project impact the community? The answer should include:
— Who will benefit?
— Who will be adversely impacted by the project?
— What has the track record been for public support of similar types of projects?
— What are the environmental impacts of the project?
— Is the project planned to generate community revenue?
— What are the spinoff impacts? (Example: The development of a new water storage and transmission system may encourage expansion of existing industries or bring new industry into the area.)

Figure 10-2 (continued)

Question #5:   Is there another way to satisfy the need?
The answer should include:
— Can a nearby facility be shared rather than develop a new facility? (Example: Is it necessary for a city to build its own sewage treatment plant, or is there a possibility of sharing an existing sewage treatment facility with a nearby municipality?)
— Have all the alternatives and associated alternative costs been presented? (Example: What are the aesthetic alternatives and their costs? What are the structural alternatives and their costs? What are functional (practical use) alternatives and their costs?)

Reprinted by permission of Mater Engineering, Ltd. 101 SW Western Blvd., Corvallis, Oregon 97333.

PUBLIC OFFICIAL'S RESPONSIBILITIES TO THE MEDIA

Some public officials feel that they have satisfied their obligations to communicate with the public by inserting the required legal notice in the paper or splurging on a paid advertisement. Others recognize the value of providing the media access to information and assisting the media by:

1. Providing adequate facilities. A table, a stand for cameras, attention to requirements of tape recorders, electric outlets, extension cords and chairs for the media close to the action are minimum amenities.

2. Alerting the media to future hearings; apprising the media of the decision.

3. Providing a Fact Sheet containing analyses, background information, handouts, agenda and names of key players.

4. Preparing a news release on the hearing.

5. Establishing a working relationship with media personnel to become a credible, reliable news source.

PUBLIC TESTIMONY AS A DECISION COMPONENT

Decision-makers sift through staff reports, voluminous data, legal advice, implementing legislation, media stories, and hours of public hearing testimony before arriving at a decision, attempting to determine the public interest while recognizing that the public's interests are as many and disparate as there are people. A survey conducted by Cambridge Reports, Inc. for the Union Carbide Corporation reveals scant agreement on the credible spokespersons who represent the views of the "Average American."

The decision-maker finds little to help him determine which of the conflicting interests best represents the public as a whole. Many officials object to any formalized process for evaluating testimony, although some find it helpful to organize thinking by subjecting testimony to two tests:

- 1. The test of relevancy. How relevant is the testimony to the decision? A typical example is a request for a variance of a zoning ordinance to permit construction of a church. Testimony may range from discussion on the equity of the state tax exemption of churches to America's foreign policy—issues that are not relevant to the decision. The mental notes relegate that testimony to the irrelevant column for the variance decision.

- 2. The test of credibility. Decisions are confused by "facts" that appear to refute other "facts." How does the official determine which is the more credible information? The Test of Credibility may assist him in determining which data are credible. The Credibility Test, Figure 10-3, evaluates the source of information as a basis for accepting data.

Figure 10-3

The Test of Credibility

Topic: _____

Speaker: _____
        (Name)

Opinion: _____

        _____

Speaking as: Expert ____ Interested citizen ____ Public or quasi-
    public official ____

Apparent objective of statements: Challenge accuracy of prior
    information ____ (1); generate emotion ____ (−1); make
    available accepted scientific and technical data ____ (3).

Education related to topic: extensive ____ (3) some ____ (2)
    none ____ (0)

Experience related to topic: extensive ____ (3) some ____ (2)
    none ____ (0)

Why testifying on topic: paid expert ____ (1) interested
                        citizen ____ (1) directly affected by
                        decision ____ (1) not directly
                        affected by decision ____ (2) history
                        of advocacy or opposition ____ (−3)

Occupation relation to topic: none ____ (2); affected by
                        decision ____ (0); representing
                        organization or organized
                        group ____ (3); official
                        duty ____ (1)

Opinion based on: factual presentation ____ (3); circumstantial
                        evidence ____ (1); fear ____ (0); basic
                        attitude ____ (0); social
                        preferences ____ (0); authoritative
                        report ____ (3); special report ____ (2);
                        comment by group ____ (−1)

Figure 10-3 (continued)

Conclusion based on: documented statistical evidence ____ (4);
                      presumptive linkage ____ (1); extensive
                      research ____ (3); limited
                      research ____ (1); experts'
                      opinions ____ (3); general
                      opinion ____ (0); hearsay ____ (– 1)
Credibility Index: Not credible ____ Credible ____
                   Authoritative ____

How to use the CREDIBILITY INDEX: Check the description that
applies in each category. Add the numbers in parentheses ( ) to
the right of each description checked. Numbers preceded by
minus should be subtracted from the total. If the numbers add
up to 27, the testimony is authoritative. Between 20 and 27, the
testimony is credible; below 20, credibility might be questioned.

Index

257